1 MONTH OF
FREE
READING

at

www.ForgottenBooks.com

By purchasing this book you are eligible for one month membership to ForgottenBooks.com, giving you unlimited access to our entire collection of over 1,000,000 titles via our web site and mobile apps.

To claim your free month visit:

www.forgottenbooks.com/free493368

ISBN 978-0-484-61085-8
PIBN 10493368

For support please visit www.forgottenbooks.com

MEMORIES

OF

RUFUS CHOATE

WITH SOME CONSIDERATION OF

HIS STUDIES, METHODS, AND OPINIONS, AND OF
HIS STYLE AS A SPEAKER AND WRITER

BY

JOSEPH NEILSON

BOSTON
HOUGHTON, MIFFLIN AND COMPANY
New York: 11 East Seventeenth Street
The Riverside Press, Cambridge .
1884

The Riverside Press, Cambridge:
Electrotyped and Printed by H. O. Houghton & Co.

To

CONTRIBUTORS.

JOSHUA M. VAN COTT.

ALFRED P. PUTNAM, D. D.

WILLIAM STRONG.

RICHARD S. STORRS, D. D.

MATT. H. CARPENTER.

JAMES T. FIELDS.

HENRY K. OLIVER.

W. C. BOYDEN.

PROFESSOR WASHBURN.

ENOCH L. FANCHER.

GEORGE H. NESMITH.

PROFESSOR SANBORN.

EDWARD B. GILLETT.

NATHAN CROSBY.

ROSWELL D. HITCHCOCK, D. D.

EDWARD E. PRATT.

OTIS P. LORD.

WILLIAM W. STORY.

GEORGE P. MARSH.

JOHN WINSLOW.

AND OTHERS.

PREFACE.

In this series of articles, I have sought to revive somewhat the love and reverence due to the memory of Rufus Choate. There was, indeed, little hope of doing justice to his learning and genius. That had been attempted by abler hands. But I was led to believe that, with the aid of others, his gifts and services, the devotion, dignity, simplicity, and usefulness of his life might be so recalled and illustrated as to be useful to my professional brethren, and interesting to the general reader. It was also believed that facts and incidents, resting in the silent memories of his friends, might be called out and preserved; and herein lay the motive for taking up the subject.

With these views, I sought the coöperation of gentlemen known to have been intimate with him. The kindness with which my applications were treated left me no reason to regret the office which I had assumed. I received many letters approving of my purpose. But some of my correspondents, advanced in years and feeble in health, were not equal to the labor proposed. Their letters, written with tremulous hands, cannot be read without emotion. They refer to Mr. Choate in affectionate terms, and some of them express the hope — now known to be delusive — that returning strength might enable them to comply with my request.

The writers whose contributions are now published held various relations to Mr. Choate, — his associates in the college, his students in the law office, his professional brethren, his friends, — those friends who were with him in hours of joy and of sorrow, and those who saw and heard him occasionally, and knew him in the supreme felicity and attraction of his genius and character.

In respect to almost any other memory, those writers might not have been inclined to turn aside from their favorite studies or official labors to take part in a commemoration. But, in this instance, a loving spirit moved them, and presided over their work. With the loyalty of disciples, and the faithfulness due to a trust, they give delineations of Mr. Choate. The poetical, the practical, the earnest, the loyal, the serious, the reverential traits of his character, as revealed at home and abroad, are set forth with freedom and fidelity.

Mr. Edwin P. Whipple, who had written of Mr. Choate as early as 1847, was requested to take up the subject again. After some time and preparation, he wrote me that — the materials having accumulated on his hands to an extent not adapted to my use — he had concluded to send his paper to the Harpers, and was pleased to say, "I have taken great delight in your series of articles and communications." His recollections were published in the "Half-Hour Series."

Mr. Augustus Russ, of the Boston bar, had the kindness to send me a list of all the cases — the titles, books, and pages — given in the law reports, in which Mr. Choate had appeared as counsel. I was much impressed by his courtesy, as the clerical force in his office must have been severely taxed in making that collection.

I take special pleasure in expressing my grateful sense of the kindness of Mr. Brown, President of Hamilton College. In the Preface to the last edition of his "Life of Rufus Choate," he makes favorable mention of the papers which I furnished to the "Law Journal" in 1877 and 1878, and expresses the hope that they "will be published in a form easily accessible to the many who would delight to read them."

I am indebted to Mr. Edward Ellerton Pratt, Mr. Choate's son-in-law, for special and valuable information.

My thanks are due to Messrs. Little, Brown and

Company for allowing me to use, in my Appendix, Mr. Choate's Remarks at the meeting of the bar on the occasion of Mr. Webster's death.

Some of my articles were submitted to the late Emory Washburn. In a letter received from him, written a few days before his death, he said, " I am glad that Mr. Choate is taking his true position as the scholar, the orator, and the jurist, among the men of genius and learning of our country. I am glad that you have told the public, in coolness, candor, and discrimination, just what sort of a man he was, and his true claims upon their admiration and respect."

It was gratifying to receive like suggestions from gentlemen of distinction, residing in different States, to whom I had not applied for help. I am induced to make an extract from one of these letters, as readers will be desirous of knowing the opinion which the late William Cullen Bryant entertained of Mr. Choate. He says, " The lives of distinguished lawyers and great orators are peculiarly interesting; and in the subject of your memoir you have a most remarkable man of that class, endowed with the gift of persuasion to a degree of which there are very few instances on record."

An application to the late William Adams, D. D., LL. D., President of the Union Theological

Seminary, for his recollections of Mr. Choate, was made at a time when the burden of work and duty on his hands was too great for his strength. His letter in reply contained the first information I had of his declining health. To the sorrow which the fact of his illness gave me was added the regret that I had troubled him with such an application. But his letter was so genial and kind, the tone and spirit of it so cheerful — as if present troubles were chastened by hope and trust — that I almost ceased to regret my untimely interference. As I valued highly the few words he was able to write about Mr. Choate, I was grateful for permission to use them as I might see fit. In the last clause of his letter, he says : —

"I feel a profound interest in everything pertaining to Mr. Choate, and sincerely regret my inability to add anything to your own valuable recollections. It was not my good fortune to hear Mr. Choate in public assemblies, or at the bar, very often. My acquaintance with him was personal and domestic, and my admiration for him unbounded. I heard his New England Society oration in New York (December, 1843), being the chaplain on that occasion, and remember well his turning to me for an explanation of the extraordinary bursts of applause which prevented his advance three several times, after he had uttered what may have seemed to him very simple sentences. You will readily admit, my dear sir, the reasonableness of what I have stated as excusing me from a service which otherwise would have been a pleasure and an honor. Thanking you again for the enjoyment I have had, in hours of illness, in reperusing the brilliant oratory of Mr. Choate in the books you have so kindly sent me, and in reading your contributions to his fame in the ' Journal,' I remain," etc.

When some of my articles, and of the letters received, were sent to the "Law Journal," this form of publication had not been contemplated. I have since rewritten parts of those articles, omitted parts, and have taken up some additional topics. As it was not my purpose to dwell upon subjects which my correspondents had considered, I have had no occasion to speak of Mr. Choate's studies at Dartmouth College or at the Law School in Cambridge, little occasion to speak of his genius as an orator and advocate, of his learning as a jurist, of the wit and wisdom which characterized his conversation, or of the qualities which drew others to him in love and sympathy. Even his birthplace has been so described by one who made a loving pilgrimage to it that the "Hill by the Sea" seems as if visibly present.

The reader will also find — it may be contrary

to expectation — that, owing to the nature and variety of Mr. Choate's gifts and peculiarities, more than twenty correspondents have found material for their narrations without repeating each other.

Mr. Choate's use of language has excited so much remark that I have deemed it proper to give that subject special consideration. I have caused his entire vocabulary, as found in print, to be collected, and so classified as to show its constituents. With a view especially to the relative proportions of Anglo-Saxon and of classical terms used, I have also taken twenty notable papers, — arguments, orations, essays, — by minds of the first order within the last hundred years, in England and America, and have had them subjected to the same analysis.

The illustrations — a likeness of Mr. Choate, and views of his birthplace and of his grave — have been approved by friends of the family.

J. N.

BROOKLYN, N. Y.

CONTENTS.

———◆———

CHAPTER I.

CHAPTER II.

CHAPTER III.

LETTERS.

APPENDIX.

Eng'd by Geo. E. Perine, from Photo.

BIRTHPLACE OF RUFUS CHOATE.

CHAPTER I.

came of Puritan ancestry.
rst of the lineage who came
, ttled at Ipswich, now Essex,
of his descendants in
we have interesting
for several years a mem-
Colonial Legislature, and died in 1695
bate, born in 1671, uphold his pastor,
John Wise, in opposing the tyranny of
Andros, and was devoted to public
he was commonly called " Governor
Francis Choate, born in 1701, was a jus-
peace for about thirty years, and was a

Fig. 5. Sample Farm Front

MEMORIES OF RUFUS CHOATE.

CHAPTER I.

Ancestry and Birth. — Home Influence. — Early Promise. — Admission to the Bar.— Practice at Danvers and at Salem.— Choate and Webster. — Criminal Cases. — Popular *Fallacy*. — Erskine. — Counsel in Criminal Cases necessary ; *Familiar* Instances. — Opinions of Professors Washburn and Parsons. — The Case of Professor Webster. — Statements of Mr. Pratt and Judge Lord. — Duty and Privilege of an Advocate.

RUFUS CHOATE came of Puritan ancestry. John Choate, the first of the lineage who came over from England, settled at Ipswich, now Essex, in Massachusetts. Of some of his descendants in the next four generations we have interesting particulars. His son was for several years a member of the Colonial Legislature, and died in 1695. Thomas Choate, born in 1671, upheld his pastor, the Rev. John Wise, in opposing the tyranny of Governor Andros, and was so devoted to public affairs that he was commonly called " Governor Choate." Francis Choate, born in 1701, was a justice of the peace for about thirty years, and was a writer and a speaker of some repute. William Choate, born in 1730, followed the sea for several years, and later in life was a teacher in the public schools. One of his sons, David, was born on the 29th day of November, 1757. At the age of nineteen, he went into the army under General Gates, and afterward served in a Continental regiment under Lafayette. After peace had been declared, he made voyages to Southern ports and to Spain. On the 15th of October, 1791, he married Miriam, a daughter of Aaron Foster; and from that time until his death, in 1808, he resided at Ipswich, his native place. To them were born six children, — Mary, Hannah, David, Rufus, Washington, and Job.

Rufus Choate was born at Ipswich, on the first day of October, 1799.[1] Until fifteen years of age, when he went for some months to the Academy in Hampton, N. H., he remained at home. In this he was fortunate. His father and mother were persons of rare endowments. Intelligence, principle, cheerfulness, sound common sense, in each of them, were wrought together in the integrity of a complete character. The family training gave the proper bias to his sentiments. In his youth he was full of promise; in a marked degree, aspiring and intellectual. At an age when boys

---

[1] See Dr. Putnam's description of his birthplace.

are expected to care for none of these things, he had a thirst for knowledge, a fondness for reading, and a fine sense of the use of words. It appears that when he was six years old he had " devoured the Pilgrim's Progress," and used to surprise his playmates by recitations from it; and that, before his tenth year, he had read most of the books in the village library. Beneficent influences, acting on a delicate, docile, susceptible, emotional nature, — á nature easily chilled, if not perverted, by contact with the world, — had been at work in advance of the schools. Thus it was that, in due time, the boy went out to those schools mature in moral and intellectual strength, prepared to exercise the manly patience given to his riper studies. He carried with him the devotion, the genial spirit of his home life; and the early love never faded from his heart.

In his sixteenth year he entered Dartmouth College, and, after his graduation there, remained a year as tutor. He then went to the Law School at Cambridge, and, after the usual course of study, became a student in the offiee of Mr. Wirt, Attorney-General of the United States. Still later he was a student in the law offices of Mr. Andrews at Ipswich, and of Judge Cummins at Salem. He was admitted to practice by the Court of Common Pleas in 1823, and by the Supreme Court in 1825.

He began practice at Danvers. The building
in which he had his office has been taken down.
While living there, he married Helen Olcott, an
alliance which gave grace and dignity to his social
life. He was chosen a member of the Legislature
and of the State Senate, and was thus brought
into near relations with the leading men of the
Commonwealth, some of whom became his life-
long friends. In 1828 he moved to Salem. There
further political honors came to him. He was
elected to Congress, and, having served one term,
was reëlected; but, at the close of the first session,
he resigned, and soon after settled in Boston.
He had then acquired great repute as an advocate. But, although his knowledge of the law
and his command of all that gave power and
beauty to illustrations of it had been severely
tested at Salem, where there was a strong bar, he
may have had some misgivings as to the competition that awaited him in his future labors. The
field chosen was occupied by lawyers who, in learning, eloquence, experience, judgment, and dignity
of character, compared favorably with the members of the profession in any city of the world.
Among such men, by the studies and contentions
of a few years, he won his way to the highest
and best assured professional renown. The gifts
and acquisitions, the zeal, energy, and persever-

ance necessary to secure that distinction must have been very great. The highest proofs of merit are found in that achievement, and in the fact that the members of the bar loved him; as is shown by brotherly attentions while he lived, and by the eloquence of sorrow when he died.

From their first appearance at the bar, as opposing counsel, comparisons were made between Daniel Webster and Rufus Choate, as if their relative merits as lawyers and advocates could be thus determined. But these men were so unlike in genius and in style that the comparison was futile; it was unjust. When Mr. Choate came to Boston, Mr. Webster stood on vantage ground. It was not merely that he had had great experience, and was enjoying the fame of his triumph in the Dartmouth College case before Mr. Choate took up the study of law, but that, by a series of signal and impressive services, ministering to the interests, the pride, and the honor of the people, he had won their love and confidence, and had become invested with a degree of weight and authority which no member of the bar, as such, could have secured. The glamour of his greatness would impress, if not mislead, the average juryman. In the forensic tournament he was thus doubly armed, whether his quarrel were just or not. Mr. Choate had no such special claim to attention, had no armor but such as industry, learning, and eloquence could supply. He led no one to regard him as the rival of Mr. Webster; his taste would have been offended at the suggestion of such rivalry. His estimate of Mr. Webster's powers was too generous to admit of such qualification. In the like spirit, Mr. Webster often expressed his admiration of Mr. Choate's learning and eloquence. Indeed, it may be doubted whether he ever went into a trial or an argument in opposition to Mr. Choate without being conscious that he was meeting an athlete whose dexterity and strength were equal to his own. Enough is known of their causes to justify the belief that none of them was lost or won because either counsel had failed to make a proper presentation of the facts to the jury, or of the law to the Court, in whatever form or domain of jurisprudence that law might have been discoverable.

Most young lawyers of shining parts have had occasion to undertake the defense of criminal cases as a source of income, or as the most direct approach to popular notice and favor. As Mr. Choate's relation to such cases has been freely and, at times, unfavorably mentioned, some observations on that subject may be proper.

While in practice at Danvers and at Salem, he had often acted as counsel for persons accused of crime. It has been said that no one defended by him was convicted. The like fortune, to a great extent, attended his subsequent efforts. In important cases, where the indications of guilt were thought to be strong, his clients were acquitted. Such instances gave rise to the popular notion that his powers of persuasion could lead jurymen to sympathize with and shield the guilty. Some laymen were shocked on learning that shades of mental disorder, with new names, had been discovered. Others — as if one who, while walking in his sleep, kills another, should be punished — objected to the defense of somnambulism interposed for the benefit of Tirrell. There were, I may say in passing, two indictments against Tirrell; one for murder, the other for arson; both depending on circumstantial evidence. The verdicts were not obtained against the rulings or the instructions of the Court. Indeed, in one of the cases, Chief Justice Shaw, in his charge to the jury, strongly discredited some of the witnesses for the prosecution. These cases excited as much effeminate criticism as any in which Mr. Choate was supposed to have had undue influence with the jury, but the general sense of the profession was satisfied with the acquittal of Tirrell.

Mr. Choate was not less sought for, nor less successful, in civil cases. But his brilliant de-

fenses in the other department of the law had
excited more attention, and led to the imposition
of a title which represented the least important
part of his labors: that of "The Great Criminal Lawyer." To those familiar with legal and
forensic history this title implied no disparagement; none, certainly, not equally deserved by
advocates of historic renown, ever to be held in
reverence, who, after counsel could be heard for
the accused in State Trials in England, devoted
their skill and influence to the protection of life
and liberty.

There came a time, perhaps about midway in
his professional career, when the pressure of criminal cases was especially distasteful to Mr. Choate.
He may have been conscious that his sympathies
were not always under his control, and that in the
fervor of discussion he was liable to be carried beyond the line of logical argument which his deliberate judgment would have approved. It may
be believed, however, that he had no other or further cause for regret. No one has suggested that
he ever practiced any artifice or evasion to enable
the guilty to escape. It would seem, therefore,
that the eulogist of that other great criminal lawyer, Daniel O'Connell, could have had the assent
of few sensible persons when he referred to Rufus
Choate as the man " who made it safe to murder;

and of whose health thieves asked before they began to steal."

Mr. Wendell Phillips may have known little of the matter implied in that aspersion, of the merits of the cases in which Mr. Choate had been engaged, or of the spirit which led him to defend the rights of persons charged with crimes of which they may have been innocent. To no one was the pure, inflexible, benign administration of the law more dear than to Mr. Choate. His letters and speeches prove that devotion. But to no one could the feeble presentation of a case, half giving it away, have been more offensive. This is shown by his example. From first to last, he did his work with all his might. It is further proved by an entry in his Journal as to a trial which he had witnessed at the Old Bailey : that of Pate, charged with striking the Queen. Mr. Choate says, " The prisoner's counsel, in my judgment, gave up his case by conceding, ' he feared he should fail.' I thought and believed he might have saved him." It is apparent that he should have saved him, as " All seemed to admit that the prisoner was so far insane as to make whipping improper, yet that he was not so insane as not to be guilty." No counsel could thus neglect the rights of the accused without being guilty of a moral offense deserving the severest reprobation. In such a case, it would be more just and humane to err, if at all, by excess of zeal than by want of it.

The fact that, as occasion required, Mr. Choate did defend criminal cases, is to be regarded with grateful pride. It illustrates not merely a spirit of self-sacrifice, the sympathy which led him to consider those who were in sore, perhaps undeserved, distress, but also the sense he had of his duty as an advocate. Still he does not seem to have adopted the opinion of Cicero : that, where life was at stake, it was more honorable to defend than to prosecute. He had respect for the wants of the State as well as for those of the citizen. In one of the few cases in which Mr. Webster acted for the people, that of Knapp, charged with aiding and abetting in the murder of White, Mr. Choate, then too young at the bar to take a prominent part, was with him as associate counsel; and, twenty-three years later, when he could select the work best suited to his taste, he accepted office as Attorney-General of Massachusetts.

The popular fallacy which imputes want of moral tone to lawyers who are willing to defend those apparently guilty of crime has been exposed by Dr. Johnson and other moralists.[1] Sydney Smith's article on " Counsel for Prisoners "[2] bris-

---

[1] Boswell's *Life of Johnson*, vol. iii., ch. ii. ; ib., ch. ix.; vol. iv., ch. i.
[2] *Edinburgh Review*, 1826.

tles with facts and arguments in favor of the
rights of the accused. Erskine, in terms and by
example, denies the right of counsel to withhold
their services. In his defense of Thomas Paine,
the author of the " Rights of Man," in which he
utterly failed, Erskine went further in asserting
the duty of the advocate than, under like circumstances, Choate might have done. But, in
resisting the importunity of his friends who
sought to prevent his undertaking that defense,
the question with Erskine became one of right or
privilege, rather than of duty. He was asserting
his independence as a member of the bar. Yet, in
a later case, one in every sense more inviting and
respectable, he speaks as though he had the right
to withdraw. Except in the case of Paine, he was
fortunate in the character of his professional work.
His name is dear to us, and will be to future generations, because, in defending those who were
charged with offenses against the State, he had
occasion to expose the fallacy of constructive trea-
son, and to assert the independence of the jury
and the liberty of the press. Therein lies his
claim to remembrance.

That the services of counsel are necessary in
criminal cases has been proved by bitter experience. In England, able lawyers were called in to
represent the Crown, even when the accused was

denied such aid. Thus Coke and Bacon served, and in some cases to their lasting discredit. This course largely contributed to the "judicial murders" which darken the pages of history prior to the reign of William and Mary, and which eminent English authors — Hume, Mackintosh, Campbell, Macaulay — have deplored.

Mr. Scarlett, afterwards Lord Abinger, whose experience at the bar had been great, was of opinion that, unless the prisoner had the benefit of counsel, justice could not be safely administered. He declared that he had often seen persons, whom he thought innocent, convicted for want of acute and intelligent counsel. Expressions of like import abound in debates in Parliament and in legal biography.

In illustration of this view it may be well to refer to a few familiar cases at home.

In 1770 some British soldiers were to be tried in Boston for murder. The circumstances were such as to excite popular indignation and horror. Josiah Quincy, Jr., then a young lawyer, came forward to defend them. For a time he suffered great reproach. But a letter of remonstrance from his venerable father, evidently written in great distress, must have given him deeper concern. He answered the letter in becoming terms, stating the principle by which he was governed;

and acting with John Adams and Sampson S. Blowers, he went on in the discharge of his duty. Some of the accused were acquitted; others were found guilty of manslaughter; not one of them was convicted of murder.

In a lecture on the "Study and Practice of the Law," delivered in the Law School of Harvard University, the late Professor Washburn refers, with exultation, to the fact that the case was thus defended, and says that it secured to the State one of its "noblest moral triumphs." That distinguished jurist, Theophilus Parsons, in an address to the students of that Law School, in 1859, upon the "Character and Services of Rufus Choate," said, "There never was a case nor a criminal that a lawyer should not defend, with the profound conviction that, while he keeps the law with him, he is safe in his reputation, safe in his standing in the community and among his fellows." He refers with pride and satisfaction to the defense of the British soldiers by Adams and Quincy. He also refers with shame and sorrow to "the dark and bloody page upon which are recorded the trials of the witches in 1692," and says, "that none of the protective forms or rules of justice shielded those unfortunates, and that no lawyer was permitted to act as their counsel." He adds, "If a lawyer had defended them, and had applied the test of cross-examination to the wild and frantic stories of the witnesses, and a judge had been there who could tell the jury what the law was, and a jury had been there willing to learn the law and to obey it, this black and ineffaceable spot had not fallen upon the childhood of Massachusetts."

In 1741, what has been known as the "Negro Plot," a supposed conspiracy to burn the city of New York and to massacre its inhabitants, threw the people into great excitement and alarm. The accused, put on trial, had no counsel. The Attorney-General, assisted by several counsel, conducted the prosecution. Of the persons arrested and tried, some were hanged, some burned, and others transported. In his "Criminal Trials," Chandler refers to the testimony as contradictory, and insufficient to prove the crime charged; and agrees with Bancroft that the pretended plot "grew out of a mere delusion." That view has been generally accepted.

In 1735, John Peter Zenger, against whom the Attorney-General had filed an information charging him with having published a malicious and seditious libel, was tried before the Supreme Court in the city of New York. The counsel, who first appeared for him, raised a question of jurisdiction, and were excluded from the bar. Zenger's friends brought Andrew Hamilton, then about eighty years of age, from Philadelphia, and he conducted the defense. He admitted the publication, but sought to show the truth of the paper, and claimed that the jury were to pass on the motive and intent of the defendant, and so determine the question of guilt or innocence. The jury found the defendant not guilty, " in the teeth," it is said, " of the instructions of the Court."

These instances may suffice. Is it not reasonable to infer that some of the British soldiers might have been found guilty of murder, and that Zenger would have been condemned, if the aid of counsel had been denied them, and that, with such aid, the victims of the supposed " Negro Plot " could have been saved ?

When Professor Webster was charged with the murder of Dr. Parkman, it came to be generally understood in Boston that Mr. Choate was unwilling to act as his counsel. That he refused to undertake the defense was known only to his family and to those who had a special interest in the fate of the prisoner. Indeed, so reticent was Mr. Choate that all his friend, Professor Brown, could say, long afterwards, was that, for reasons which he judged satisfactory, he had declined. This statement excited, rather than satisfied, curiosity.

But, now that the occasion for such silence has passed away, it seems proper, as due to Mr.

Choate's memory, that all doubt should be removed. Entertaining this view, Mr. Edward Ellerton Pratt and the Hon. Otis P. Lord, Judge of the Supreme Court of Massachusetts, an intimate personal and professional friend of Mr. Choate, have kindly made to me the following statements.

Mr. Pratt says, "Mr. Franklin Dexter, one of the leaders of the bar in New England, was greatly interested in Professor Webster's case, believed that he was innocent, and was persistently earnest that Mr. Choate should defend him on that ground. The Hon. Charles Sumner, also holding that view, urged Mr. Choate to undertake the defense, as he expressed it, in the interest of humanity, and was quite angry with him for refusing. At that time the testimony taken before the coroner was known; that taken by the grand jury, by whom the indictment had been found, was not publicly known. The question of the Professor's guilt or innocence was the absorbing topic, and the excitement in all classes of society was intense.

"Mr. Dexter was determined to secure Mr. Choate's services, and, after much study of the case, called, by appointment, one evening to lay before him what he called its merits. Mr. Choate listened to him, as a juror might have done, for nearly three hours; and, as he afterwards told me, it was one of the most vigorous and persuasive arguments he ever heard. That estimate may well be accepted, when we remember Mr. Dexter's ability, his friendship for Professor Webster, and his belief that, if Mr. Choate could be secured as counsel, the accused might be saved.

"The argument having closed, Mr. Choate walked up and down his library several times, and then, pausing before Mr. Dexter, who was keenly observing him, said, 'Brother Dexter, how do you answer this question, and this?' I cannot now state the points thus presented, but my general recollection of the account given me by Mrs. Choate and Mr. Dexter is, that those questions presented insuperable difficulties underlying the defense. Mr. Dexter, as if transfixed, sat musing deeply, his head bent upon his hand, for several minutes, and, finally, as if hopeless of finding an answer, and seeking relief, he arose suddenly, and said, 'Brother Choate, have you read ——'s book? If not, do so, and you will find it charming.' Mr. Choate accepted this changed mood, parted from him soon after with kindly expressions of interest, and the subject was never again alluded to between them."

Judge Lord says, "I had a conversation with Mr. Choate on this subject. It was more than

twenty years ago, and, of course, it is impossible
to reproduce precisely his language, but the interview was substantially this. I said to Mr. Choate,
'Is it true that you refused to defend Professor
Webster?' to which he replied, — not in direct
terms, but by implication, — that he did not absolutely refuse, but that they did not want *him.*
Pausing for a while, he added, 'There was but
one way to try that case. When the Attorney-
General was opening his case to the jury, and
came to the discussion of the identity of the
remains found in the furnace with those of Dr.
Parkman, the prisoner's counsel should have risen
and said, substantially, that, in a case of this importance, of course counsel had no right to con-
cede any point, or make any admission, or fail to
require proof, and then have added, 'But we
desire the Attorney-General to understand, upon
the question of these remains, that *the struggle
will not be there.* But, assuming that Dr. Parkman came to his death within the laboratory on
that day, we desire the Government to show
whether it was by visitation of God, or whether,
in an attack made by the deceased upon the
prisoner, the act was done in self-defense, or
whether it was the result of a violent altercation. Possibly the idea of murder may be suggested, but not with more reason than apoplexy,

or other form of sudden death. As the prisoner himself cannot speak, the real controversy will probably be narrowed to the alternative of justifiable homicide in self-defense, or of manslaughter by reason of sudden altercation." '

" Having said this, he added, ' But Professor Webster would not listen to any such defense as that,' accompanying that statement with language tending to show that the proposed defense was rejected, not only by the accused but by his friends and advisers.

" He then said, ' The difficulty in that defense was to explain the subsequent conduct of Professor Webster,' and he proceeded with a remarkable and subtle analysis of the motives of men, and the influences that govern their conduct, to show that the whole course of the accused, after the death, could be explained by a single mistake as to the expediency of instantly disclosing what had happened; that hesitation or irresolution or the decision, ' I will not disclose this,' adhered to for a brief half-hour, might, by the closing in of circumstances around him, have led to all that followed. Having concealed the occurrence, he was obliged to dispose of the remains, and would do so in the manner suggested, and with the facilities afforded by his professional position. He concluded, ' It would have been impossible to convict

Professor Webster of murder with that admission.'

"I suggested that the possession of the note by Professor Webster, as paid, was an awkward fact. He said, 'Yes, but it might seem to become a necessity after his first, false step of concealment.' He added, 'Dr. Parkman was known to have been at the hospital. When, and under what circumstances, and to explain what statements made by him, the Professor thought it expedient to say he had paid the note, or to obtain possession of it, would probably never appear. It was simply an incident whose force could be parried, if he could obtain credit for the position that the concealment was a sudden and impulsive after-thought, which took possession of and controlled him in his subsequent conduct.'"

We have, in these statements, the desired testimony as to Mr. Choate's relation to that case. We have also an illustration of his view of the duty and privilege of an advocate. It is apparent that, while accepting the theory that, in a criminal case, a lawyer is not at liberty to withhold his services absolutely, Mr. Choate did not think him bound to go into court, contrary to his own convictions, and assert what he did not believe to be true, or take a line of defense which he considered untenable. Thus, for instance, as he was satisfied that, at the time and place alleged, Dr. Parkman had died in Professor Webster's presence, Mr. Choate was not willing to act on the theory that Dr. Parkman was alive after that time, and to call and examine witnesses to testify, as they finally did, under a mistake as to identity, that they had seen him day after day in the streets of the city. That theory was set up on the trial and failed, as Mr. Choate had foreseen that it would fail.

In taking leave of this subject, and recalling the fact that, in England, the right of the accused to speak by counsel in State trials was secured, as a national reform, long desired by the people and by the best and wisest men in Parliament, we may well be grateful that our system of criminal practice was, at an early day, framed on just and humane principles. With us, the right of the accused to be defended by counsel has been respected, indeed secured, by the Constitution; and, if need be, counsel is appointed for that purpose by the Court. It is to be confessed, however, that, even with our improved methods of discovering the truth and our humane administration of the law, mistakes have been committed. Instances have occurred where skill and learning could not unravel complicated circumstances, and the innocent have been condemned to die. So also, in the light of newly discovered evidence, it has been seen that men have been unjustly consigned to the state prison; and after they may have suffered the bitterness of death for years, we open the doors with a humiliation scarcely less than that inflicted on them. We are thus admonished to improve our methods, to give the accused every reasonable means of defense, and to accept cordially whatever aid can be properly rendered in determining the guilt or innocence of those who are tried as criminals.

CHAPTER II.

ALTHOUGH endowed with great intellectual powers, Mr. Choate was as careful, methodical, and solicitous in regard to mental helps as any student who might have been less conscious of innate strength. He seems to have been mindful that excellence was attainable not only by those who could pass on swiftly and easily, but by those who, less favored of nature, were superior in diligence. Thus, regarding genius as the mere capacity to acquire knowledge and to use it, he gave himself up to habitual study.

Some perils attend students who possess great intellectual gifts. From the time when such a one perceives how receptive he is to suggestions of truth and beauty, and how readily the barriers which impede others yield to his touch, he may become the victim of a delusive self-confidence,

and be led to accept the notion that the fruitful-
ness of his life will be of spontaneous growth. As
he seems to apprehend intuitively the less occult
relations of things, he regards close and prolonged
study as unnecessary. So, content with some appearance of culture, he falls into easy ways, and
goes through life as the lounger saunters through
the streets. He is like the slothful miner who
gathers up the bits of precious metal exposed to
view, without acting on the hint nature gives of
the wealth hidden beneath the surface. Another
student, of like gifts, moves on earnestly, acquires
knowledge, does some good work. Having found
that what he should learn is easily acquired, he
assumes that there need be no limit to his attainments. Like the student in " Faust," he confers
with the evil spirit and is encouraged to inquire
into mysteries too subtile for his comprehension.
He takes to such studies, and thenceforth swims
not with the current but against it. He is vain
and unstable in proportion as he evades the influence of natural laws, the checks and hindrances
designed to hold him in restraint, and which are
as necessary for his safety as the wall built at the
side of the road by the river is for the protection
of travelers. He undertakes to inform the school-
men in their specialties, and his speculations on
science and on the nature and relations of man

partake of the artificial texture of his life. As he has done some good work in certain departments, his speculations secure respect and confidence. Thus his best efforts may have an evil influence.

Rufus Choate escaped the perils which thus beset students. He knew the need and the use of study; he knew also the limitations that were to be respected. A conservative spirit held him in restraint, and repressed longings to slake his thirst at fountains beyond his reach. In early life he refused to follow a friend into the labyrinths of German mysticism, or to explore the region which Swedenborg had made his own. This reserve became him, not simply because he did not wish to be "shocked, waked, or stunned" out of settled convictions, but because the duties before him, with the studies they involved, would consume his time and strength. So he put aside as improvident whatever was remote from the purposes of his life. He never lost his balance by reaching out too far, nor, like one of old, walked into the water while gazing at the stars.

The special and seemingly alien qualities of Mr. Choate's nature were strongly marked. He was gentle, yet exigent; simple, yet subtile; natural, yet artistic; poetic in conception and tone, yet acute and logical. But his studies were so consonant to his wants, and his work so wisely chosen, that those qualities of mind, acting in harmony, were moulded into perfect unity of character. In the record he has left, we can clearly discern his love of nature, and of all that is good and true and beautiful; the loyalty, sagacity, and prudence that guided him in his public services, and the tenderness and cheerfulness that made his home-life as a perpetual summer. But, however we may indulge in speculations as to his peculiar genius, he should finally be accepted as his own interpreter.

We owe a debt of gratitude to Professor Brown for having collected the fragments that could be found of Mr. Choate's Journal. A part of it, written when he was traveling abroad, he no doubt intended for his family and friends. The other part, especially that which relates to his studies, may have been for the benefit of his son, then a student. But the Journal having, as we may assume, served its purpose, shared the fate of much else that he had written. How much of it was lost is not known. The parts of it which we have are rich in suggestion and instruction, the style exquisite in its unstudied grace and beauty.

Mr. Choate's study of the law was extraordinary. I find in legal biography no instance of equal devotion. In speaking of his early course, he told Mr. Parker, the author of the " Reminiscences," that in studying law he gave his mind wholly to it; that his habit was to read until two o'clock in the morning. After that early experience, his legal studies became less exclusive, as he was seeking a broader and more generous culture than the law could give. But, even in his latest years, he sought inspiration from Coke on Littleton, lest his legal taste should decline. That he might be in full communion with the spirit and philosophy of our language and institutions, and of our legal science, — the law of the law, — he studied, almost daily, other languages and other systems of jurisprudence and of government.

He was wont to accept judicial determinations of important questions with jealous scrutiny. His modes of inquiry, adhered to long after he had attained great fame for his learning in the law, were peculiar and characteristic. He was in the habit of collecting the facts stated in cases reported in the books, and of preparing arguments for or against the decisions; of criticising the authorities cited, and finding others to confirm or to qualify them; and of seeking to discover how far a doctrine, underlying a series of adjudications, might be made to appear more or less just in the light of history, of reason, and of scientific principles.

Equally special and exhaustive was his study of the cases in which he was to appear as counsel.

Each case was tested and tortured until every conceivable phase of strength and of weakness was revealed. His son-in-law and partner, the late Mr. Bell; his student, the late Senator Matt. H. Carpenter; and Judge Fancher, who was concerned in a case with Mr. Choate, agree as to the thoroughness of his preparation. He studied pen in hand. The facts and qualifying circumstances were entered in a little book. Books of this kind, with notes of decisions, were used by Erskine. Mr. Espinasse says that, after great experience at the bar, Erskine used to bring his little book into court and read cases from it. On one occasion his opponent, affecting to ridicule the habit, said that he wished Erskine would lend him his book. Lord Mansfield said, " It would do you no harm, Mr. Baldwin, to take a leaf from that book, as you seem to want it." Erskine thus used his book when he sought to show that the impeachment of Warren Hastings was at an end, owing to mere suspension on the dissolution of Parliament. Edmund Burke, easily excited by opposition of any kind in regard to that impeachment, had a fling at " ideas that never traveled beyond a *nisi prius* case," and a sneer for the book.[1] Mr. Choate had little need

---

[1] In this relation it is grateful to recall the fact that, a short time before his death, Burke called on Erskine, and, holding out his hand, said, " Come, Erskine, forget all. I shall soon quit this stage, and wish to die at peace with everybody, especially with you."

of his book in court, as what he had written was deeply, if not indelibly, impressed upon his memory. But the book of facts, thus useful in preparation, would be further useful to be revised and extended, should the case be put over to another term. So, too, in the multitude of cases, it might prevent confusion. It is said that Sugden once got hold of the wrong brief and argued in support of his opponent's side of the case, and that Dunning made a like blunder. No such mistake has been reported of Erskine or of Choate.

In his Journal, Mr. Choate describes his studies; tells how the early hour was employed. He had a few minutes with favorite authors, English, Greek, Latin, French, often a lesson from each, and then the genius of the law beckoned him away. Thus, for instance, he is in London, and after saying, " Mr. Bates called and made some provision for our amusement," he adds that he read the Bible, the Prayer Book, a half dozen lines in Homer and Virgil, and a page of Williams's " Law of Real Property." It was a rule with him to read at least one page of some law book daily. All this to keep the simple elements of the law fresh in mind; a purpose from which not even the delights of travel, of new scenes and associations could wholly divert him. Thus trained and strengthened, his vision could take in, as from a tower of observation, the domain of the law. It lay before him as a familiar and inviting landscape. Hence it was that when, on a trial or an argument, principles apparently adverse or decisions not anticipated were cited against him, the countervailing doctrine, if there was any, was in his mind ready for use. The study of law, thus pursued, leads to logic, to ethics, to metaphysics; in a word, to the whole range of special sciences. Mr. Choate may have accepted the Justinian definition, " Jurisprudence is the knowledge of things divine and human; the science of what is just and unjust." If so, that may suggest some of the reasons which led him to adopt more liberal studies than are usually thought necessary to professional success.

We all know that many men less studious and learned than Mr. Choate become distinguished and useful lawyers, and have great weight and influence in public affairs. But it may be safely said that only those who are endowed with special gifts, as if set apart and consecrated to the service, can become great advocates. How some of these special gifts waited upon Mr. Choate and served him may be readily recalled.

His power of memory was so marvelous and so useful that some further reference to it may be proper. The " Law Reporter,"[1] in describing the

_____
[1] Vol. vi., p. 385.

trial of the Phœnix Bank cases (1844), in which Mr. Webster and Mr. Choate were counsel for different defendants, has the following note : —

"In the course of the trial, and in a most exciting passage, when all the counsel *appeared* to be intent upon the case and nothing else, Mr. Webster wrote on a slip of paper the favorite couplet of Pope, and passed it to Mr. Choate : —

> ' Lo, where Mæotis sleeps, and softly flows
> The freezing Tanais through a waste of snows.'

Mr. Choate wrote at the bottom ' wrong ' —

> ' Lo, where Mæotis sleeps, and *hardly* flows
> The freezing Tanais through a waste of snows.'

Mr. Webster rejoined ' right,' and offered a wager. A messenger was dispatched for Pope, when it appeared that the present Senator (Choate) had the advantage of his predecessor (Webster), and was right. Mr. Webster gravely wrote on the copy of Pope, ' Spurious edition ! ' and the subject was dropped. All this while the spectators were in the full belief that the learned counsel were in earnest consultation on some difficult point of law."

In his " Reminiscences of Daniel Webster " (p. 358), Mr. Peter Harvey gives what would seem to be the same incident, though referring to another author. The title of the case on trial is not stated, nor are the lines of the poet. But it is said, " Mr. Webster sent an extract from Cowper, which Mr.

Choate corrected and returned, intimating that there had been a misquotation. Mr. Webster repeated his first version and claimed that he was right. A messenger was sent for Cowper's ' Task ; ' the place was found, and Mr. Webster saw that the sentiment was as Mr. Choate had corrected it. He smiled, and wrote with a pencil upon the margin of the page containing the disputed passage, ' A spurious edition.' "

Mr. Parker, in the "Reminiscences of Rufus Choate" (p. 183), relates how, at a special gathering in Washington, in the winter of 1850, the conversation having turned upon "Young America," Mr. Webster referred to the lad in severe terms, but Mr. Choate, claiming that he was no new thing in the world's history, cited the following passage, as proof of the antiquity of the character : " *Statim sapiunt, statim sciunt omnia; neminem verentur, imitantur neminem, atque ipsi sibi exempla sunt.*" Which may be translated, less liberally than by Mr. Parker, At once they are wise, at once they know all things ; they reverence no one, they imitate no one, and follow only their own example. Mr. Benton thought that the quotation was too happy to be genuine ; and Mr. Choate referred him to the younger Pliny, where it was found in the twenty-third letter of the eighth book.[1]

[1] As felicitous as Swift's quotation from Virgil upon the injury of

It is obvious that, with such power of memory, Mr. Choate could readily recall the proofs peculiar to a case on trial and apply them to instant use. In special cases, he might not know, often could not know, upon what proofs his adversaries relied. But he could, by an intellectual and reflective process, infer much that belonged to the other side of a case. This power of reasoning from the known to the unknown, of judging how men would act, was possessed by him in a remarkable degree. Of this an esteemed correspondent gives an illustration. He says, " In my early experience I had a complicated case of some importance, in which Mr. Choate was retained as counsel. There had been no consultation, and I was to prepare a full statement of the facts. With the aid of my client, I arranged the points, more than thirty in number, with the proofs as to each, in their apparent order and relation. I then went to Mr. Choate and read the paper to him. He said, ' Please repeat numbers 26 and 27.' I did so. He said, ' There is something wanting; the human mind does not work in that way. The case drifts on naturally enough down to 26, but there a peculiar complication comes up, and your statement does not meet it. At that juncture, the par-

a violin by fire communicated from a lady's garment hanging next it: " *Mantua, væ! miseræ nimium vicina Cremonæ.*"

ties, influenced by business habits, by interest, or by desire to overreach each other, had several courses open to them ; ' and he proceeded to indicate each in his peculiar way. I resumed the study of the case, had conferences with witnesses; my client found additional correspondence ; and it finally appeared that Mr. Choate was right. The new matter under 26 presented a more full and connected view of the case on its merits, quite in harmony with one of Mr. Choate's illustrations, and on the trial of the action had controlling influence."

Mr. Choate was almost always able to fix upon the theory on which his cases should be tried. This called for the exercise of great judgment. He seldom disclosed his theory until it was seen that the proofs at large were consistent with it. But, when the current of testimony set in against it too strongly and baffled expectation, his theory was abandoned and a new one devised. The transition was made so adroitly that few could perceive that he had been disappointed.

A correspondent, long a leader of the Boston bar, in referring to Mr. Choate's perception and sagacity as exceptional, says, " He could read the mind and infer the character of a juryman or of a witness with wonderful readiness and certainty. I have sat by him in court when jurors were selected, and when witnesses, strangers to him, were called, and been told what he thought of each of them in turn, and I cannot remember an instance in which he was mistaken. Nearly allied to that was his ability to judge of circumstances in their relation and bearing. I have been with him in the trial of cases when the party and the attorney for whom he acted had little conception of the difficulties to be encountered, and have often witnessed the ease and readiness with which he met and unraveled complications which threatened defeat. In this relation, an action I had brought to recover the price of a cargo of goods which my client had sold on credit may be worthy of notice. The defense set up was fraud. The defendant claimed that my client had represented the goods to be sound and merchantable when he knew that they were not; that, relying on that representation, he had purchased and shipped the goods to a foreign market and had suffered great damage. My client denounced the defense as a scheme to put off the payment of an honest claim, and was too indignant to confer about it. Accepting his views, I assumed that there would be no attempt to prove the defense, and on the day of trial attended with him and a witness to prove the account. Brooks, the broker who had acted with us in making the sale, had recently died. (I pause a moment to state some facts of which we were then ignorant. In the same month and before my client's sale, the defendant had purchased of another person and shipped to the same market a like cargo of goods, and had, it seems, been defrauded as in his plea alleged. Brooks, the broker, had also acted with that person in making the sale.) At court, the defendant and his counsel met us ready for trial; my client still had his 'Pshaw! pshaw!' as to the defense. But I got nervous, and sent for Choate to help me, and happily he came.

" Our formal proofs were put in. The defendant's counsel then opened the defense, and proceeded to prove it. My client was in great wrath. Choate said to me, 'He is honest,' and we shall find our way out of the scrape.' The last and principal witness for the defense appeared to be a sensible, substantial sort of person. He spoke to the whole case, and explained how he knew that the goods were made of bad materials, not fit for use. He was employed on the ship that had taken the goods, and was the only witness to prove the false representations alleged. I said to Mr. Choate, 'He is inventing that.' He replied, 'No, he is truthful, but mistaken;' and went on to cross-examine. He and the witness were soon on the most friendly terms. I never saw Mr. Choate appear so simple and slow of apprehension. The witness, not thinking that he was much of a lawyer, took to him kindly, and was anxious to have him understand the whole matter. Mr. Choate, seeming to admit that the representations had been made and were false, was very solicitous about the party making them. The witness was quite clear that the name was that of the plaintiff, and was disposed to argue the question on the ground that Brooks, whom he had known, was with us, as we had admitted. He described the seller of the goods; his size, complexion, whiskers, dress. When all that had been fixed beyond recall, and my client had come forward to be identified, Mr. Choate, turning to the witness, with changed manner and terrible emphasis, said, ' Can you, on your oath, say that this is the man ? ' The likeness which had been given was so unlike, so *flagrant*, as to excite roars of laughter, in which the jury joined. The witness answered, ' You know that 's not the man ; what do you want to make fun of me for ? ' Mr. Choate assured him that he was not responsible for the blunder of charging fraud on the wrong person, and said he would like to have him repeat the name of the ship in which the goods had been taken and state positively the time of sailing. These facts having been given, Mr. Choate said to the Court that he would prove more fully that our goods were sold two weeks later, and were sent by a different vessel. On that having been shown, the defendant's counsel abandoned the defense.

"Without assuming to judge of the defendant's integrity, I am satisfied that his counsel was no party to the trick; had not dreamed of the mistake. But I can say that Mr. Choate was the first to suspect that there had been some real transaction as to which the witness was speaking truly. He discovered the blunder when we were blind to it, and dealt with the witness accordingly. My client was very grateful. Mr. Choate made light of his services, and accepted only half of the fee I brought him. My client refused to take the other half back, and it was sent as a gift to Dr. Adams's church."

Another correspondent says, "I went into court to see Mr. Choate, and found him addressing a jury. The proceedings having been suspended for a few minutes, I said to him, 'We want an interview in B.'s case; how long will you be in closing your argument?' He said, 'I don't know. That red-headed juror on the back seat does not seem to understand the case yet, and I must feel of him, and put some points in a new light.' I went back to my seat, and he remained looking at the jury, without apparent concern. When the Chief Justice came on the bench again, Mr. Choate, rising, said, ' If your Honor please, I detain you no longer. Gentlemen of the jury, that is our case.' He had a verdict. As we walked to his office, I told him how amazed I had been, and asked why he had changed his plan. He said, ' When you mentioned B.'s case, I was conferring with my red-headed juryman, and, after some further conference, I saw I had him.' "

In his address before the Law School of Harvard University, to which I have already referred, Professor Parsons, after speaking of his long-continued intimacy with Mr. Choate and of a trial in which they had been opposing counsel twenty-four years before, says, " I have the more right to make this use of his memory, because he was one of us. It was in this school that he laid the foundations upon which he afterward built up his great knowledge of the law. And we have the right to say that they were ample, deep, and strong, when we remember the vast and beautiful structure which rested upon them." He also says, " I have, indeed, no hesitation in saying that he was one of the most learned lawyers I have ever met with. And his learning was excellent in its kind and quality."

The proceedings of the Suffolk bar, on the occasion of Mr. Choate's death, fitly illustrate the estimation in which he was held as a scholar, as an advocate, and as a citizen. It would be difficult to find in modern biography anything more touching and impressive.

In presenting the resolutions at the meeting of the bar, as instructed by the committee, Mr. Charles G. Loring, among other things, said, " Having been, for more than twenty years after Mr. Choate came to this bar, his antagonist in forensic struggles, at the least, I believe, as frequently as any other member of it, I may well be competent to bear witness to his peculiar abilities, resources, and manners in professional services. And having, in the varied experiences of nearly forty years, not infrequently encountered some of the giants of the law, whose lives and memories have contributed to render this bar illustrious throughout the land, — among whom I may include the honored names of Prescott, Mason, Hubbard, Webster, Dexter, and others among the dead, and those of others yet with us to share in the sorrows of this hour, — I do no injustice to the living or the dead in saying that, for the peculiar powers desirable for a lawyer and advocate, for combination of accurate memory, logical acumen, vivid imagination, profound learning in the law, exuberance of literary knowledge, and command of language, united with strategic skill, I should place him at the head of all whom I have ever seen in the management of a cause at the bar."

Mr. Richard H. Dana, Jr., other parts of whose address have been often quoted, said, " The world knows how he electrified vast audiences in his more popular addresses; but, sir, the world has not known, though it knows better now than it did, — and the testimony of those better competent than I am will teach it, — that his power here rested not merely nor chiefly upon his eloquence, but rested principally upon his philosophic and dialectic power. He was the greatest master of logic we had among us. No man detected a fallacy so quickly, or exposed it so felicitously as he, whether in scientific terms to the bench, or popularly to a jury; and who could play with a fallacy as he could ? Ask those venerated men who compose our highest tribunal, with whom all mere rhetoric is worse than wasted when their minds are bent to the single purpose of arriving at the true results of their science, — ask them wherein lay the greatest power of Rufus Choate, and they will tell you it lay in his philosophy, his logic, and his learning."

When the resolutions were presented at the District Court of the United States, Mr. Justice Sprague made some interesting remarks from which I quote a few words. " Others have spoken fully and eloquently of his eminence and excellence in various departments. We may here at least appropriately say something of him as a lawyer and an advocate. His life was mainly devoted to the practice of his profession, and this court was the scene of many of his greatest efforts and highest achievements. I believe him to have been the most accomplished advocate that this country has produced."

Mr. Choate was, year by year, engaged in the trial and argument of cases more continuously than any other member of the bar whose name I can recall. But the extent of his work cannot, at this late day, be stated. Of the causes in which he was counsel and argued questions of law and equity, in the State and Federal Courts, three hundred and thirty-three have appeared in the regular Reports, and are familiar to the profession. Many of them were of grave importance, and called for the application of principles in special and novel relations. But, as other counsel were often concerned with Mr. Choate, it cannot be said how much of the work should be ascribed to him.

The number of his trials before juries is not known. Many of them were described in the public prints, and parts of some of his arguments were given. But, as the reporters had not the skill men of that class now have, the reports were imperfect. Owing to the same or a like deficiency, I cannot find a fair report of his cross-examination of witnesses. A correct report would be worth preserving as a model. His fairness in the treatment of witnesses often secured their favor and the good-will of the jury. If the witness was timid, he was encouraged; if nervous, soothed; if eager, repressed; if honest, protected; if crafty and adverse, exposed. Witnesses who wished to tell the truth found him patient, courteous, helpful, considerate. He knew that they often err from want of memory, perhaps from inability to distinguish what they know from what they have heard. So, having the sanctity of an oath in mind, he cared for the witness as he cared for himself. Such witnesses often remembered him with gratitude, while dishonest witnesses learned to fear him. Herein Mr. Choate was the friend of the Court. Judge Sprague must have thought so when he said of him, " His skill in the examination of witnesses was consummate. I have never seen it equaled." What Mr. Choate said of this kind of Daniel Webster's work may be fitly applied. " His efforts in trials by jury compose a more traditional and evanescent part of his professional reputation than his arguments at law; but I almost think they were his mightiest professional displays, or displays of any kind, after all."

CHAPTER III.

THE power of making good jokes and telling
good stories, if exercised in public by a man of
eminence, may detract from the proper estimate
of his character. Sydney Smith has won lasting
reputation as a wit; and his wit was often used
in the interest of truth and right, but it stood
squarely in the way of his ecclesiastical prefer-
ment. President Lincoln had a quaint humor that
relieved the terrible gloom of his darkest hours,
but he is credited with jokes and stories that never
fell from his lips. It was somewhat thus with Mr.
Choate. Those who had no personal intercourse
with him, and who formed hasty judgments from
his peculiarities, adopted erroneous views. To that
error he may have casually contributed. In legal
contentions, he was so happy in his retorts that an
adversary seldom gained anything by interrupting
his arguments. But the reports of those retorts

(and they were sure to be reported) wanted the spirit and grace that had charmed his opponents. I can recall but one instance in which his retort gave offense. In answering a lawyer who had addressed the Court in a loud tone, Mr. Choate playfully referred to his "stentorian powers." To his surprise, his opponent rose, and hotly replied that nothing in his mode of address would justify such a stricture. As he went on thus, his voice rose again to a high key, and rang through the court-house; Mr. Choate half rose, and said, in the blandest tones, " One word, may it please the Court; only one word, if my brother will allow. *I see my mistake. I beg leave to retract what I said.*" The effect was irresistible; the court was convulsed with laughter.

Mr. Choate's witticisms in court had their inception and growth at the moment, had strict relation to the exciting cause, and were generally helpful and for practical purposes. But he used occasionally an expression so whimsical as to create great amusement. It was caught up and passed from one person to another, as current coin. The more grotesque the utterance, the better for the gossips; but the more certain was it to give the public a wrong conception of his method and style. Yet it was well to expose a fallacy by some incisive word, some epithet or epigram. Time was thus saved, and the error made more apparent. Thus, when a State line to which he objected was of unstable character, it was pertinent to say, " The Commissioners might as well have defined it as starting at a bush, thence to a blue-jay, thence to a hive of bees in swarming time, and thence to five hundred foxes with fire-brands tied to their tails."   But the people remember that, and repeat it still in various forms; while of the argument made by him on that occasion, however valuable or characteristic, they remember nothing.

It would seem that a knowledge of Mr. Choate's quaint use of words has been treasured up in gentle minds.   I give extracts from the letters of two correspondents, women of culture, who took an interest in his peculiarities.   One extract is called " A Bit of Persiflage."

" When Mr. Choate was in Washington, the ladies were anxious that Mrs. Choate should be there, and often beset him about it.   On one occasion, when they asked if he thought Mrs. Choate would come, he answered, ' Yes, I now think she may; I have written her to come, and have offered to pay half the expenses.' "

The other extract is entitled " A Rebuke," and relates to the cross-examination of a new-light preacher.

" *Mr. Choate.*   What are you, sir ?

"*Witness.* A candle of the Lord.

"*Chief Justice.* A what, sir?

"*Mr. Choate.* A dipped candle of the Lord, if your Honor please."

My correspondent reminds me that "*a dipped candle* is of the cheapest sort; one that gives next to no light at all," and says that " therein lies the sarcasm."

In a letter from the late Professor Washburn, he objected to " the blazing, comet-like creation of fact and fancy in which several writers had been disposed to picture Mr. Choate." He may have had in mind writers whose infelicitous inventions had been taxed to fasten upon Mr. Choate jests and gibes which he never uttered; or those who, not content with treating Mr. Choate as a man, had sought to depict him as a magician. The work of such a writer is before me. I turn the leaves of the volume, and collect some interesting reminiscences of Mr. Choate's special powers and methods. Thus we have, as to his active brain, " his head expanding with a thousand thoughts; " as to his rapid study and apprehension, that " he grasped the thoughts of a book like lightning; " as to the impression he made upon a jury, that he " dashed his view into their minds with all the illuminating and exaggerating lightnings of his portentous passion; " as to his exhaustive argumentation, that he " advanced with a diversified but long array, which covered the heavens; thunder-bolts volleying, auroras playing, and sunlight, starlight, and gaslight shooting across the scene in meteoric radiance ; " and as to his power to excite an audience, that " It was literally almost as if a vast wave of the united feeling of the whole multitude surged up under every one's armpits."

These quotations may suffice ; and yet I am strongly tempted to refer to other statements equally worthy of respect; and especially to notice how Mr. Choate would " hurl his argument home in solid, intense mass that crushed upon the ear ; " how he would " launch a fiery storm of logical thunderbolts ; " and how, " If a witness lay athwart his verdict, he was crushed down and crushed up and marched over."

But that author is not always so complaisant. He says that in 1855 Mr. Choate was injured by a fall ; and that "After the consequent illness, his oratory underwent a marked revolution ; he no longer tore a passion to tatters."

Somewhat akin to this, and equally unjust, is a statement which the author quotes with approbation. " The jury advocate must, to a certain extent, be a mountebank, if not a juggler and a trickster." A more miserable conceit was never uttered. Was Mr. Webster, while before a jury, a mountebank, a juggler, or a trickster? Was Erskine, or Dexter, Pinkney, Parsons, or Curtis, William Kent, Daniel Lord, or Marshall S. Bidwell?

Uncharitable things have been said of many great advocates; but, as an illustration, one of the worst things ever said of Mr. Choate was, that he could play the *artful dodger* in reading a deposition. This is a rude description of fine, forcible, and effective reading; reading which gives significance and character to vital passages, discloses their latent sense and spirit, aids the apprehension, and insures a certain and, it may be, a favorable interpretation. Such a reader, natural, yet artistic, " tells the great greatly, the small subordinately ; " and thus we have heard Macready play the artful dodger; thus Fanny Kemble Butler; thus the gentle Melancthon may have read; thus every pulpit orator, from Whitefield down.

A merely clever man, with no high aims or love of truth; a wordy, sharp, false man, however adroit and plausible; the artful dodger, the mountebank, juggler, trickster, he who tears a passion to tatters, can never be a jury advocate. With all his gifts and acquisitions, the advocate must be a high-toned, moral man, not a harlequin; a vital utterance, not a mere sham. Jurors are representative men and are practical, sensible, and often sagacious men, as fond of fair dealing in

counsel as in suitors.   Hence, in cases involving
life, liberty, or character, an able advocate goes to
the jury in a spirit akin to that with which Esther
went in before the king to plead for her people.
At such an hour, he indulges in no mere fancies,
his style becomes a reflex of his own mind and
heart; if, as in Mr. Choate's or in Mr. Pinkney's
efforts, a flash of poetic thought or beauty gleams
forth, it is merely because the vision is in his
spirit, and reveals itself as naturally as the simplest
conception.   He is not the less dealing with realities after his fashion.

He would be adventurous indeed who should
attempt to correct or reconcile much that has been
written about Mr. Choate.   Failing in such a purpose, he might be driven to adopt the plea of the
poor fellow under constraint, "I am not mad, but
numbers have prevailed against me."   Yet I venture upon some corrections.   In the first place, it
may be said that attention has been diverted
from Mr. Choate's real character by some not
unfriendly writers.   For this there was neither
necessity nor excuse.   His views and principles,
his habits and manners, his daily life, were well
known; in effect he had lived as one with all
doors and windows open; no disguise, no concealment, no reservation.

But Mr. Choate was a genius, as they all declare, and that fact was sufficient to mislead, and stimulate the invention of some critics.

They discovered that he was a man of words, whereas he was a man of ideas fitly represented by his words; that his style is florid, whereas his style is clear and unconstrained, effective in its simplicity. Those who think that prose should have no alliance with poetry, forget that a poetic spirit enters into the growth of language, into the prattle of children, and into the eloquence of savage tribes; forget that the beauty which sparkles and flashes over the natural world was intended to give tone and color to the world of thought, the outer glory to become an inner experience; forget that he who, uniting the wisdom of the past with the sagacity of the present, absorbs the power and grace of other languages into his own, gives to old theories a modern aspect, and to later discoveries their best application, making the truth appear more truthful, the beautiful more beautiful, becomes a benefactor to his age and people. Those who doubt this, who do not perceive that a spirit of poetry, of wit and humor, may be helpful to culture in thought, language, and style, and may be held in such subjection and mellow use that we recognize the poet, though he build no rhyme, the wit though he excites tears rather than laughter, will consign Edmund Burke, Syd-

ney Smith, and Rufus Choate to the upper shelf.
Such spirits, though in a different guise, are, in
effect, near of kin to the Gradgrind school. In
inquiry and argument, they always profess to go
down to what they call the hard-pan. For aught
we know, the mole does that, and without being
the wiser for it. They insist upon the facts; will
be content with nothing less. I commend Mr.
Choate to them, a very high-priest of their order,
a most relentless inquisitor after facts. He would
know the facts in history, what in fact had been
the rulings in the Year Books, and by judges of
later times; the facts as to the policy, dates, and
modifications of statutes; the facts stated in the
pleadings in a cause; and, in a trial, he was so
pertinacious in his quest for the facts that witnesses who began to testify with certain mental
reservations were led, as by gentle compulsion, to
make full and circumstantial disclosures. It must
be confessed, however, that the facts as discovered
by the Gradgrinds may have been dry, inert, and
wanting in relation; the facts as used by Mr.
Choate may have been essential to an exposition
of vital force, instinct with demonstration.

We have been told by one entitled to great
respect, that Mr. Choate created a taste for his
peculiar style. Was the impression made on his
first appearance before Chief Justice Shaw excep-

tional? We learn from Professor Brown that the Chief Justice said, " I had an opportunity to see Mr. Choate and witness his powers as an advocate, very early, when he first opened his office in Danvers; and when I had scarcely heard his name mentioned." " As he was previously unknown to us by reputation, and regarding him, as we did, as a young lawyer just commencing practice in a country town, we were much and very agreeably surprised at the display of his powers. It appeared to me that he then manifested much of that keen legal discrimination; of the acuteness, skill, and comprehensive view of the requirements of his case, in the examination of witnesses; and that clearness and force in presenting questions, both of fact and of law, by which he was so much distinguished in his subsequent brilliant professional career."

It further appears that the taste, which it is said Mr. Choate created for his peculiar style, must have been of sudden growth. His first juries understood him, his early trials, triumphs; and the people, when he appeared before great assemblies, a stranger, hung upon his lips with breathless interest. He was master of the pathetic in oral discourse, and by that power the world has been moved. He always adapted himself to the occasion, and went to the marrow of the business in hand. Professor Brown mentions the favor with which his first speech in Congress was received. Thus, Benjamin Hardin, member of Congress from Kentucky, indisposed to hear others upon the side of a question he intended to advocate, was about to leave as Mr. Choate rose to speak, but having lingered a moment, and noticed the tone of his voice, was constrained to stay, and said, " I was captivated by the power of his eloquence, and found myself wholly unable to move until the last word of his beautiful speech had been uttered." So, as Mr. Everett has it, a Western member said, " He was the most persuasive speaker I ever heard." After hearing Mr. Choate in the Senate, James Buchanan, replying to him, said, " It is the first appearance of the Senator in debate here, and, judging of others by myself, I must say that those who have listened to him once will be anxious to hear him again."

He was heard quite early before the Supreme Court at Washington: Mr. Webster was with him; Randolph and Whipple opposed. Mr. Choate's argument is said to have made a strong impression upon all the judges. Judge Catron said, " I have heard the most eminent advocates, but he surpasses them all." A member of the New York bar, speaking of the address of which Mr. Van Cott and Dr. Adams have written, said, " The people could not keep their seats, but kept clapping and applauding without being conscious of it."

Under date of March 1, 1852, Mr. Webster, writing from New York to Mr. Havens, said, " Mr. Choate must be here Friday evening. The idea of hearing him is universally received with the greatest enthusiasm. He must come; do not fail to persuade him to do so. If he should not, there will be a disappointment not to be appeased."

Mr. Webster knew that Mr. Choate could speak without special preparation; that the people would understand him; and that no one could fill the place which had been assigned to him.

Before attempting to correct an error which confronts us in book form, touching Mr. Choate's natural gifts for oratory, as compared with the gifts of some others, I cite the opinion of a competent critic, Hon. Alexander H. Stephens.

In 1843, when Mr. Stephens was a member of Congress, he heard Mr. Choate in the Senate for the first time. He was speaking on the question of terminating the joint occupancy of Oregon. Mr. Stephens says, " Every one was enraptured with his eloquence." He adds, " Ever after this speech I never let an opportunity go by to hear Mr. Choate. I consider him the most interesting man for impassioned oratory I ever heard. He had a faculty which few men possess, of never tir-

ing his hearers.   Several years after, I heard him
in the Supreme Court argue the case of the boun-
dary line between Rhode Island and Massachusetts.   It was as dull a case as any ordinary land-
ejectment suit.   I was at a loss to understand how
Mr. Choate could interest an audience under such
circumstances.   The court had been occupied five
days by some of the ablest lawyers.   The room
was thronged to hear Mr. Choate's reply.   From
the moment he commenced, he enchained the audience and enlivened the dull subject by apt historical allusions and pleasing illustrations.   The
logical connection of his argument was excellent,
and so well-arranged that in two hours he had
finished a thorough argument which was interspersed throughout with sublime imagery.   Every
paragraph was as the turning of a kaleidoscope,
where new and brilliant images are presented at
every turn.   At the conclusion of that speech, I
was confirmed in the opinion that he was the
greatest orator I ever heard, — in this respect
greater than Calhoun, Clay, or Webster."

A correspondent, long intimate with Mr. Choate,
and having the best means of forming opinions as
to his natural gifts, calls my attention to a work
with an auriferous title which I had overlooked.[1]

---

[1] In his letter, Professor Sanborn says, " Colonel Parker, in his
Golden Age of American Orators, a work much read by students,

On taking up the book, I learn that Mr. Choate was " the first and foremost of made orators," but " was not a natural orator — a born orator," — though " Chatham and Patrick Henry were natural orators of superior order, and Henry Clay was of the same school."

The statement that Choate was not a natural orator would disturb no one who could accept the suggestion that Dr. Johnson was not a natural critic, or Faraday a born chemist. The inference would be that each of them had to " toil terribly " attempts to prove that Mr. Choate was not ' a natural orator,' like Henry and Clay. I think that Mr. Choate's early history refutes that theory. I learned from Professor Shurtleff, his teacher, something of his eloquence in college. He then gives an extract from Choate's Valedictory Address, which, so far as I can judge, indicates the freedom and range of thought and the felicity of expression that might distinguish an orator ' to the manner born,' and adds, ' In this brief paragraph are the key-notes of his life — attachment to friends, love of learning, and admiration of nature. The Professor also mentions two circumstances which illustrate the character of the address and the effect of its delivery, from which it might be inferred that, if nature ever "tried her prentice hand " in fashioning a complete orator, she did so with young Choate. He says that when Choate spoke, " His pathos drew tears from many who were not used to the melting mood." Also that " One rustic maiden was there from Norwich, Vt. She was all ears, eyes, and heart ; she gazed and wept. On the following Monday, while bending over the wash-tub, she said, ' Mother, you can't think how pretty that young man who had the valedictory, spoke. He was so interesting that I cried; and, law ! ' she added, holding up her checkered apron to her eyes, ' I can't help crying now, only thinking on 't.' "

in climbing up to the eminence attained. The idea is as simple as that the tillage of the soil makes possible the harvest. But we are disturbed when told that some men — Chatham, Henry, and Clay — were, as distinguished from Choate, natural, or born orators.

English authors have paid due attention to the preparatory studies of Lord Chatham and of his son. Nature, prodigal in gifts, left to each the common legacy of toil as the condition of his becoming an orator. We are told that " The best clew to Pitt's (Chatham's) own mental tasks, more especially in the field of oratory, is afforded by those which he enjoined to this favorite son." We are also told, on the authority of Stanhope, that " The son ascribed his lucid order of reasoning to his early study of the Aristotelian logic, and his ready choice of words to his father's practice in making him every day, after reading over to himself some paper on the classics, translate it aloud and continuously into English prose." As to Patrick Henry, I would abate none of the praise that can be bestowed upon him consistently with nature and with experience. But it may be observed that, like many fluent speakers, he had acquired great experience by talking " an infinite deal of nothing " up to the hour when the vision of our independence, to be achieved by war, opened before him as an apocalypse, transformed his spirit, and gave a prophetic tone to his utterances. As to Henry Clay, I need only recall his efforts in the debating society to cultivate a habit of speaking, and his confession, made long after, to a class of students, that he owed his " success in life to the habit, early formed and for some years continued, of reading daily in a book of history or science, and declaiming the substance of what he had read in some solitary place." In this, Mr. Clay was not peculiar. Wheaton, in his life of William Pinkney, says that "He always continued to declaim in private."

But in the chapter " On the Study of Forensic Eloquence," which Mr. Isaac Grant Thompson has inserted in his edition of " Warren's Law Studies " — perfecting the work by the scholarly treatment of an important topic which Warren had neglected — illustrative instances are given. He regards " the opinion that excellence in speaking is a gift of nature, and not the result of patient and persistent labor and study," as mischievous; and happily enforces that view by referring to the studious efforts of Cicero, Chatham, and Fox, Curran, Choate, and others. Of Choate, he says, " Forensic rhetoric was the great study of his life, and he pursued it with a patience, a steadiness, a zeal, equal to that of Chatham and Curran." He reminds us that Murray, afterwards Lord Mansfield, carried on the study of oratory with the utmost zeal, and that a friend had caught him in " the act of practicing before a glass, while Pope (the poet) sat by to aid him, in the character of an instructor," and adds, " Such are the arts by which are produced those results that the uninitiated ascribe to genius."

This matter is of present interest, as I would not have the student adopt the notion that Mr. Choate was goaded on in his studies by a sense of want of which other great orators had not been conscious. Nor should he regard the statement that Chatham and others were natural orators as signifying anything more than that they possessed gifts favorable to the cultivation of eloquence. A good memory and ready command of language, fine and quick perception, delicate wit and fancy, a fervid imagination, an exquisite sense of the beautiful, a voice sweetly tormenting the hearer, even in the remembrance of it, a graceful and impressive manner, — all of which Mr. Choate had, — however important as prerequisites, do not qualify the orator. It is his office to instruct, persuade, and convince; but without study there can be no knowledge, without knowledge no argument, without argument no real influence in the discussion and disposition of public affairs. In the courts and in legislative and popular assemblies, the question certain to arise is, whether the speaker is master of his subject in its substance, details, and relations. The persons addressed may distinguish immature from ripe thought; information from knowledge; mere impressions from experience. They know that, while the voice may be trained for oral discourse, as it may be for music, the mind should have a corresponding culture. Many of them, pitiless as critics, would accept the statement of Cicero that the orator must possess a knowledge of many sciences, without which a mere flow of words is vain; and would agree with Dr. Johnson, when he checked the praise bestowed on a fine speaker, not often heard, as having great resources, " You cannot know as yet; the pump works well, but how are we to know whether it is supplied by a spring or a reservoir?" Mr. Choate's view of the studies proper to the orator was most exacting. His ideal of excellence in oratory, considering it as one of the fine arts, may have been so high that he never could have fully satisfied his own aspirations. But, in his lectures and addresses, his sentiments are given in the spirit of an unfaltering disciple; his precepts have an electric touch — glow like stars in the firmament of thought. He knew what he taught, in large measure, and in minute details. He fortified himself by appeals to history, to experience, and to natural laws. The moral element in his topics, however obscure, never eludes his grasp; the most rugged event or feature he touches palpitates as with a spirit of life and beauty. The philosophy of history is taught suggestively, not by a tedious process, but flashes upon the page as a revelation. His illustrations have a logical flavor; his inferences the certainty of mathematical deductions; and his language, when rising to the utmost fervor, is tempered by earnest and constant attention to practical affairs. The student may, therefore, follow him with assured steps. Indeed, no student should fail to study addresses like those on "The Colonial Age of New England," on "The Power of a State Developed by Mental Culture," on "The Conservative Force of the American Bar," and on "The Eloquence of Revolutionary Periods."

He who has given his days and nights to Demosthenes and Cicero, Thucydides and Tacitus, will find his apprehensions quickened, and the wealth he has garnered up in his mind enriched by the spirit of Mr. Choate's expositions.

CHAPTER IV.

IT has been considered strange that, with all his work, Mr. Choate could find time for classical study. The explanation may be found in his intellectual methods, and in his mental activity and economy of time.

In his address at the dedication of the Peabody Institute, he gave advice to those who were in pursuit of knowledge under difficulties and restraints, in which he seems to have drawn upon his own experience. He reminded them that vacations for the still air of delightful studies were fragments of time, — half-hours before the morning or midday meal was ready, a rainy afternoon, the priceless evening, — and that such were the chances they could borrow or create for the luxury of reading. Mr. Choate himself gave to study the time he might well have given, the time others gave, to repose. He could read some verses in the Greek Testament, a few lines in Virgil, in Bacon, or in Burke, and go out to his walk repeating these lessons in their order and turns. I do not know that he ever advised others to adopt this method, but it was wisely chosen for himself. He could thus lessen the burden of study by so changing its forms as to combine intellectual and physical exercise, and, in passing from one form of study to another, find relaxation.

Such may have been his habits when he was young, and in practice at Salem. A correspondent of Mr. Parker says that, in Mr. Choate's long, solitary walks in the pastures, his " full and melodious voice was sometimes heard by other strollers in those solitudes." In his " Recollections of Mr. Choate," Mr. E. P. Whipple refers to this habit of out-door study, and says that, when he met Mr. Choate in one of his contemplative moods, he made it a point of honor not to interrupt his meditations.

In the last conversation I had with the late Matt. H. Carpenter, Mr. Choate's special studies with his books and without them were mentioned. Among other things, Mr. Carpenter said, " It was one of the efforts of Mr. Choate's professional life to extend and perfect what he called a lawyer-like memory. In his view, a mere every-day memory, left to take care of itself, would not enable an advocate so to hold in mind as instantly to recall, for use, the facts disclosed in a long trial before a jury, and the name, appearance, and manner, the speech, too ready or too reluctant, of each witness examined." He also said, " Mr. Choate had found that special kind of memory improved by reading fragments of authors on divers disconnected subjects, and recalling and repeating them after his books had been laid aside."

As Mr. Choate's faith in study was unqualified, we can well believe that, to one who spoke of a fine, intellectual performance as the result of accident or inspiration, he said, " Nonsense! you might as well drop the Greek alphabet on the ground and expect to pick up the ' Iliad.' "

I am indebted to Mr. Edward Ellerton Pratt for some interesting particulars. He says, " Mr. Choate was the most untiring worker I ever met. He was up by five o'clock in the morning, as a rule, made a cup of tea for himself, worked a while over his books, went out for a walk, came home to breakfast, went to business at nine, worked all day, and perhaps was before some legislative committee for an argument in the evening; and I have known him to be all that time without taking any food. Indeed, I have seen a check for half a dollar which he had given at the close of such a day, when, having no money with him,

5

he had become conscious of the need of refreshment.

"When the late James T. Fields was collecting and editing Thomas De Quincey's works, he showed Mr. Choate an article which had appeared in some magazine, with no external evidence as to the author. On looking over it, Mr. Choate said it was written by De Quincey. Mr. Fields then wrote to De Quincey, who answered that he had not written the paper, had never thought of the subject-matter of it. With some exultation, Mr. Fields showed that letter to Mr. Choate, who said, ' Never you mind ; let me have the article again, and I will go over it more carefully.' He did so, and the next day Mr. Choate wrote him, ' De Quincey did write it, De Quincey to the contrary, notwithstanding.' After a time, De Quincey sent to Mr. Fields the original manuscript of the article, with a letter stating that he had found it among old papers ; and, as it was the work of his pen, he must confess the authorship, though all recollection of it had passed away.

" In his studies, Mr. Choate kept pace with the colleges, and with modern thought as there illustrated. He used to buy the text-books of Harvard and Yale, beginning with the Freshman year, and, in effect, graduating with the students. I once asked him why he did this. He said, ' I don't like to have those young fellows come out of college crowing over me; they fresh and bright, I dull and rusty; we must habitually go back to the elements, first principles, and note new applications of them by those whose special business it is to teach."

In his zealous striving after higher culture, Mr. Choate had a steadfast belief in the value of translation as an intellectual discipline, and as a means of testing the power and spirit of our words as equivalents for the words of other languages. Speaking of Mr. Choate's method in translating, Professor Parsons says, "He would return day after day to the same passage, until he had exhansted the resources of the language in giving to the sentence exactness, strength, and elegance."

In the "Reminiscences," Mr. Parker reports Mr. Choate as saying, "Translation should be pursued to bring to mind, and to employ, all the words you already own, and to tax and torment invention and discovery, and the very deepest memory for additional, rich, and admirably expressive words. In translating, the student should not put down a word until he has thought of at least six synonyms, or varieties of expression, for the idea. I would have him fastidious and eager enough to go, not unfrequently, half round his library pulling down books to hunt up a word — *the* word."

By this kind of work, Mr. Choate sought to perfect his knowledge of things as well as of words.
Thus, he says, that, in translating Cicero's "Cati-
line Orations," he had in view the matter and the
manner of a great master of speech, and a remarkable portion of history. So, also, he translated
Thucydides for the purpose of deducing lessons of
history and applying them to America.

In his Journal, Mr. Choate recalls with fidelity,
as if for his own encouragement or admonition,
his studies in various departments. At times he
seems hopeful, almost glad in view of what he
perceives he may attain; at other times, he appears sad, as if his studies had been partial and
inadequate. As an instance, after he had garnered up in his mind and heart such wealth of
learning as only one so devoted and receptive
could acquire, we find him saying: —

"I have written only this translation of Quintilian since Saturday; professional engagements
have hindered me. But I have carefully read a
page or two in Johnson's Dryden and a scene or
two of 'Antony and Cleopatra' every morning —
marking any felicity or available peculiarity of
phrase — have launched Ulysses from the Isle of
Calypso, and brought him in sight of Phæacia,
kept along in Tacitus, and am reading a pretty
paper in the 'Memoirs' on the old men of Ho-

mer. I read Homer more easily and with more appreciation, though with no helps but Cowper and Donnegan's Lexicon. Fox and Canning's speeches are a more professional study, not useless, not negligently pursued. Alas, alas! there is no time to realize the dilating and burning idea of excellence and eloquence inspired by the great gallery of the immortals in which I walk!"

Again, he says, "How difficult it is to arrest these moments, to aggregate them, to till them, as it were, to make them day by day extend our knowledge, refine our tastes, accomplish our whole culture!"

His solicitude as to the improvement of his taste is freely confessed. Thus he says:—

"I have been long in the practice of reading daily some first-class English writer, chiefly for the *copia verborum,* to avoid sinking into cheap and bald fluency, to give elevation, energy, sonorousness, and refinement to my vocabulary. Yet with this object I would unite other and higher objects,— the acquisition of things, — taste, criticism, facts of biography, images, sentiments."

In the same spirit, as to a contemplated course of study, he says:—

"The investigations it will exact; the collections of authorities; the constant use of the pen, the translations, the speculations, ought to constitute an admirable exercise in reasoning, in taste, in rhetoric, as well as in history."

Again, noting some classical works he must have and use on a journey, he says, "This, lest taste should sleep and die, for which no compensations shall pay."

Referring to a course of reading considered too desultory, he states the benefits thus : —

" No doubt taste has been improved, sentiments enlarged, language heightened, and many of the effects, inevitable, insensible, and abiding, of liberal culture, impressed on the spirit."

Mr. Choate's taste was exacting and severe in a sense not perhaps to the fancy of some sentimental scholars; of this a few words from Chief Justice Chapman may be illustrative. He says of Mr. Choate, "He was talking of Burke's speeches, of which he was known to be a great admirer, and remarked to a friend of mine who was extolling Burke above all other men, that he thought on the whole that the most eloquent and mellifluous talk that was ever put together in the English language was the speech of Mr. Standfast in the river. I went home and read the speech soon afterwards, and I confess I appreciated John Bunyan's eloquence as I never had done before."

In a plea for mental culture Mr. Choate refers to John Quincy Adams, " the old man eloquent," and finds him using " the happiest word, the aptest literary illustration, the exact detail, the precise rhetorical instrument, the case demands." Mr. Choate had a clear conception of the means by which such powers of argument might possibly be acquired. His theory of preparatory study was as exacting as that of Hugh Miller, who thought that an anatomical acquaintance with the bones and muscles was necessary for the painter who represents the human figure, and that he who describes natural scenery should know the strata and the science of the rocks.

In a letter of advice to a student, — Richard S. Storrs, Jr., — Mr. Choate says, " As immediately preparatory to the study of the law, I should follow the usual suggestion, to review thoroughly English history, — constitutional history in Hallam particularly, and American constitutional and civil history in Pitkin and Story. Rutherford's Institutes, and the best course of moral philosophy you can find, will be very valuable introductory *consolidating* matter. Aristotle's Politics, and all of Edmund Burke's works, and all of Cicero's works would form an admirable course of reading, ' a library of eloquence and reason,' to form the sentiments and polish the tastes, and fertilize and enlarge the mind of a young man aspiring to be a lawyer and statesman. Cicero and Burke I would know by heart; both superlatively great, — the latter the greatest, living in a later age, belonging to the modern mind and genius, though the former had more power over an audience, — both knew everything.

"I would read every day one page at least, — more if you can, — in some fine English writer, solely for elegant style and expression. William Pinkney said to a friend of mine, 'He never read a fine sentence in any author without committing it to memory.' The result was decidedly the most splendid and most powerful English *spoken* style I ever heard."

A like result may be traced to Mr. Choate himself. Perhaps no great orator ever owed less to borrowed thoughts and forms of speech, or, in a higher and better sense, more to the ministration of other minds. But the benefits were absorbed by a process as natural as that by which trees gather nutriment from the sun, air, rain, and from a generous soil. In reading him, we are reminded of his favorite authors. As, in hearing a preacher full of divine instruction, one may perceive indications of his familiarity with the Scriptures, so Mr. Choate reveals his intimate communion with master minds.

It was perhaps well for him that some degree of poverty fell to his early lot. I believe he would have chosen such a lot, had the choice been left to him. He valued, as few men have valued, the discipline and the strength which came as the fruits of toil and study; the faith and the constancy of those who, having sown the seed, could wait patiently for the harvest. He appears to have had a clear conception of the spiritual meaning which resides in material things, and of the law of compensation that governs men in all their relations, and makes or mars their fortunes.

To illustrate his views as to the formation of character and the elements which may minister to its strength, I quote a few detached passages from one of his lectures.

After having referred to the planting of the Colonies along our coast, in the seventeenth century, and to events which furnished the matter of colonial history, he says, "I regard those events altogether as forming a vast and various series of influences, — a long, austere, effective course of discipline and instruction, — by which the early settlers and their children were slowly and painfully trained to achieve their independence, to form their constitutions of State governments and of Federal government, and to act usefully and greatly their part as a separate political community in the high places of the world.

"It has been said that there was never a great

character, — never a truly strong, masculine, commanding character, — which was not made so by successive struggles with great difficulties. Such is the general rule of the moral world, undoubtedly. All history, all biography, verify and illustrate it, and none more remarkably than our own. It has seemed to me probable that if the Puritans, on their arrival here, had found a home like that they left, and a social system made ready for them, — if they had found the forest felled, roads constructed, rivers bridged, fields sown, houses built, a rich soil, a bright sun, and a balmy air; if England had covered over their infancy with her mighty wing, spared charters, widened trade, and knit child to mother by parental policy, — it is probable that that impulse of high mind, and that unconquerable constancy of the first immigrants, might have subsided before the epoch of the drama of the Revolution. Their children might have grown light, luxurious, vain, and the sacred fire of liberty, cherished by the fathers in the times of the Tudors and Stuarts, might have died away in the hearts of a feeble posterity.

" Ours was a different destiny. I do not mean to say that the whole colonial age was a scene of universal and constant suffering and labor, and that there was no repose. But in its general course, it was a time of suffering and of privation, of poverty or mediocrity of fortune, of sleepless nights, grave duties, serious aims; and I say it was a trial better fitted to train up a nation ' in true wisdom, virtue, magnanimity, and the likeness of God,' — better fitted to form temperate habits, strong character, resolute spirits, and all the radiant train of public and private virtues which stand before the stars of the throne of liberty, — than any similar period in the history of any nation, or of any but one, that ever existed.

" The necessaries of freedom, if I may say so, — its plainer food and homelier garments and humbler habitations, — were theirs. Its luxuries and refinements, its festivals, its lettered and social glory, its loftier port and prouder look and richer graces, were the growth of a later day; these came in with independence. Here was liberty enough to make them love it for itself, and to fill them with those lofty and kindred sentiments which are at once its fruit and its nutriment, and safeguard in the soul of man. But their liberty was still incomplete, and it was constantly in danger from England; and these two circumstances had a powerful effect in increasing that love and confirming those sentiments. It was a condition precisely adapted to keep liberty, as a subject of thought and feeling and desire, every moment in mind. Every moment they were comparing what they had possessed with what they wanted and had a right to; they were restive and impatient and ill at ease; a galling wakefulness possessed their faculties like a spell. Had they been wholly slaves, they had lain still and slept. Had they been wholly free, that eager hope, that fond desire, that longing after a great, distant, yet practical good would have given way to the placidity and luxury and carelessness of complete enjoyment; and that energy and wholesome agitation of mind would have gone down like an ebb-tide. As it was, the whole vast body of waters all over its surface, down to its sunless, utmost depths, was heaved and shaken and purified by the spirit that moved above it and through it, and gave it no rest, though the moon waned and the winds were in their caves; they were like the disciples of the old and bitter philosophy of Paganism, who had been initiated into one stage of the greater mysteries, and who had come to the door, closed and written over with strange characters, which led up to another. They had tasted the truth and they burned for a fuller draught; a partial revelation of that which shall be hereafter had dawned; and their hearts throbbed eager, yet not without apprehension, to look upon the glories of the perfect day. Some of the mysteries of God, of Nature, of Man, of the

Universe, had been unfolded; might they, by prayer, by abstinence, by virtue, by retirement, by contemplation, entitle themselves to read another page in the clasped and awful volume?

" How glorious a triumph of patience, energy, perseverance, intelligence, and faith! And then, how powerfully, and in how many ways, must the fatigues, privations, interruptions, and steady advance, and ultimate completion of that long day's work have reacted on the character and the mind of those who performed it! How could such a people ever again, if ever they had been, be idle or frivolous or giddy or luxurious? With what a resistless accession of momentum must they turn to every new, manly, honest, and worthy labor! How truly must they love the land for which they have done so much! How ardently must they desire to see it covered over with the beauty of holiness and the glory of freedom, as with a garment! With what a just and manly self-approbation must they look back on such labors and such success; and how great will such pride make any people!"

Thus it appears that this man, so delicate, refined, emotional, with a keen sense of what was sweet and beautiful in life, sentiment, and study, was not the less able to deal with stern and sober subjects, to appreciate the trials and struggles of

those who labored in obscurity with no embellish-
ment to their lives, save such as came from the
performance of humble yet important duties. He
loved to dwell upon and illustrate such examples,
and may have found strength and encouragement
in the conviction that the toil and service which
conferred benefits upon others would most surely
enrich himself.

CHAPTER V.

Classical Studies. — Ancient Greece. — The Saxons. — The Latin. — English in India. — Macaulay's Service. — As to Equivalents in Saxon for Some of our Words.

By way of review, and as a solace in weary hours, Mr. Choate's communion with the classics was continued to the end of his life. He found therein some of his chief delights and consolations; and, in final token of his appreciation of them, the "Iliad" and the "Georgics" were among the books selected as companions in his last voyage.

It may be thought that such studies were not wisely chosen or pursued. Such, no doubt, is the popular impression. Indeed, some authors of repute have declared that an acquaintance with what is called the dead languages need not be sought by those who wish to excel in the use of English. In support of this opinion, reference is made to instances of good, exceedingly good, English, written by men without classical training, — Franklin, Erskine, Shakespeare, Bunyan, and some others.

Of these authors, Bunyan alone is well cited. He was, indeed, exceptional. In a divine frenzy, he could look into his heart and write.

It is to be remembered that the style of Franklin was formed by the study of "The Spectator," and that of Erskine by intense devotion to Milton and Burke; and that, in seeking to acquire the spirit and diction of authors whose English was the representative and outgrowth of classical study, these men reaped the benefit at a single remove.

The reference to Shakespeare, as an example, is not fortunate. The saying of Ben Jonson's that Shakespeare possessed " small Latin and less Greek," may be taken as proof that he knew something of those languages. Of his early youth and studies, we know nothing; and, where much is left to conjecture, one supposition is often as good as another. In speaking of "Love's Labour's Lost," Coleridge refers to the strong presumption which the diction and allusions of that play afford of Shakespeare's scholarly habits, and Mr. Charles Knight suggests that his happy employment of ancient mythology lends countenance to the supposition. As to the " Comedy of Errors," Knight says, " The commentators have puzzled themselves, after their usual fashion, with the evidence this play undoubtedly presents of Shakespeare's ability to read Latin, and their dogged resolution to maintain the opinion that, in an age of grammar-schools, our poet never could have attained that common accomplishment."

In a loving and profound estimate of the elements of greatness peculiar to Shakespeare, Emerson notices the fact that, when he came from Stratford to London, "A great body of stage-plays, of all dates and writers, existed in manuscript," and that Shakespeare altered and made them his own. He says, "In 'Henry VIII.,' I think I see plainly the cropping out of the original rock on which his own finer stratum was laid. The first play was written by a superior, thoughtful man, with a vicious ear. I can mark his lines, and know well their cadence." Emerson accepts Malone's laborious computations in regard to the first, second, and third parts of "Henry VI.," in which "out of 6,043 lines, 1,771 were written by some author preceding Shakespeare; 2,373 by him, on the foundation laid by his predecessors; and 1,899 were entirely his own." Thus, in working upon materials, excellent in themselves, the outcome of many other minds, — the minds, it may be, of students in history, in law, in medicine, and in the classics, — Shakespeare adopted parts of the plays which now bear his name. His genius enabled him to make mellow music of what had been discordant. In the mass of preëxisting plays and tales from which he drew, there must have been the work of some minds of classic lore, so that if we were compelled to suppose that he had none of it, yet his works, being eclectic, are not fair specimens of the results attainable without the aid of classical studies.

The theory as to the value of such studies which contrasts the practice of the ancient Greeks in the use of their language with the treatment given to the Saxon and the English need not here receive much attention. It is said that the Greeks studied no language but their own, and, regarding other tongues as barbarous, did not borrow from them. The inference sought to be drawn would seem to be that a like course should have been pursued in the culture and use of the Anglo-Saxon.

It is to be remembered that, when Ancient Greece became known to the modern world, her language had been so perfected that aid from other peoples was not needed; and that the contributions and the culture which, in ante-Homeric times, had given supernal grace and beauty to her speech cannot be stated or defined. It is also to be remembered that after the facts and fables found in Homer had been considered, after such scholars as Porson and Choate, in the spirit of their studies, standing face to face with

the Greek, could make his felicities of speech
their own, an unappeasable curiosity as to the
early progress of the race remained, as it will
remain forever.

Much curious research and ingenious speculation have been displayed in the endeavor to trace
the early history of the Greeks, and to determine
their origin. All the tests afforded by philology,
ethnology, and geography have been applied.
On philological grounds mainly, Mr. Gladstone
ascribes a dual origin to the Greek people like
that of the English. The general belief of historians is, that a race known as Pelasgians, at a
period antecedent to written history, spread from
the south over Greece and Italy. They are described as a dark-eyed, dark-haired, swarthy,
heavily-built race, industrious, patient, excelling
in agriculture and architecture. These characteristics lend force to the supposition that they came
from Egypt; and that those of them who went
to Italy, more remote from the early centres of
population, developed the best capabilities of that
race, and, by their substantial qualities, laid the
foundation for Roman greatness. But, as to
Greece, another race, the Hellenic, was infused
among the Pelasgi, and grafted upon the stock.
They were tall, light-complexioned, light-haired,
blue-eyed, enthusiastic hunters and warriors, and

came probably from a mountainous country, by
northward-lying paths, through Thrace and Mace-
donia, into Northern Greece, forcing themselves
among the Pelasgi, and by their active and aggressive qualities becoming dominant in public affairs.
This infusion of new blood would seem to have
given rise to what, properly speaking, may be
called the Greek people, which thus arose from
the mingling of different tribes on Grecian soil.
To this admixture are to be ascribed the differences which subsist between the Greek and the
Latin tongue, and the wide divergence of the
Greek from that earlier speech, the foundation
of both, of which the Sanskrit is believed to be
the nearest representative. The Greek would appear to be a composite language. In later times,
fixed by custom or pride, it became intolerant of
foreign words. This was a departure from the
principle on which it was formed; — to say otherwise is to beg the question against both evidence
and probability.

Although it is impossible to trace the development of the Greek tongue, it must be assumed
that in its inception and growth it was governed
by universal laws. From a rude state it was carried forward to a more perfect condition by centuries of tasteful culture, and, during all that long
probation, the Greeks, as other aspiring people

have done, profited by external and available means of improvement. As the cultivation and refinement of a people may be known by its language, laws, and works of art, it may be worth noting that the early memorials of the Greek race, as lately brought to light by the researches of Schliemann and others, show a primitive, almost barbarous, condition of the arts, which it is fair to suppose was accompanied by a similar condition of their speech. It is evident that the growth from the rude conception and clumsy execution of early days to the exquisite grace, symmetry, and freedom of later Greek art must have consumed centuries, — time for perfecting and unifying the language, that most enduring token of their civilization.

Mr. Choate had intended to write a history of Greece, and to that end his special studies were for a time directed. But, constrained by professional and other duties, he abandoned that design. How reluctantly he did so may be inferred from the fascination which afterwards held him to the study of the Greek genius and character. In his Journal he makes significant suggestions as to the origin and progress of that people, but he does not seem to think that they had rejected foreign aid until their language had risen to a higher degree of perfection than that of any other nation.

The English-speaking people have not yet reached such supremacy. Their only hope of ever reaching it has been inspired by the use that could be made of wealth derived from alien sources. They have borrowed from almost every other people. The work of verbal adoption might have been easy, if, as has been said, the Anglo-Saxon tongue had had a craving appetite, had been rapacious of words. But it required many years of preparatory training to create that appetite. The influence came from without rather than from within. Indeed, the natural characteristics of the early people of Britain were not favorable to an improvement of their accustomed speech. The Saxons had no conceptions of beauty or grace, of harmony in thought or in expression; and, when they could make their wants and wishes known, had little aptitude to find and use other and better words. As an offshoot of the Teutonic language, the Saxon dialect inherited the rough, hard, inflexible qualities of the parent stock.

Need we wonder that in working upon such materials, in infusing life, variety, and refinement into a semi-barbarous tongue, it was necessary to sift out and cast away many rugged and fruitless forms of speech, and to weave in words more melodious and articulate? Would it have been well if all the uncouth terms that came from

Saxon lips had been retained? What if words expressive of our finer feelings and aspirations, of our sense of grace, beauty, and harmony — words of progress, refinement, and civilization — had not been borrowed! Those who regret that we are largely indebted to the Greek, Latin, and French must be conscious that the improvement of our language has kept pace with the growing intelligence of the people, and that attempts to qualify or dissolve that relation would be unwise and fruitless.

The Latin, spoken of as a dead language, survives in the speech of many nations, with whom we and our mother-country have intimate commercial relations in the Old and in the New World. It has been justly said that in his travels the Latin scholar would find few cities, however strange and remote, where he could not make himself understood by some of the inhabitants. The variety and the fertility of the Latin in forming compounds are important, as this quality the words retain when brought into other languages. An idea of this may be formed by counting the derivatives from a few Latin words. Thus, the terms derived from the verb *nascor*, in various forms, are 17 in number; from *verto* 22, from *teneo* 23, *tendo* 29, *cedo* 21, *duco* 20, *curro* 18, *specio* 19, *video* 14, *lego* 22, *mitto* 22, *venio* 17, *rego* 15, from *capio* more than **27**, and from *sumo*, which has nearly the same meaning, 9 more: — 15 roots yielding 285 distinct terms by the use of prefixes and suffixes. The aid to copiousness of expression thus afforded is self-evident, and justifies Mr. Choate and all others who have the taste, time, and opportunity for the study of that language.

But the Saxon tongue, not thus fruitful, never had, and of itself never could have had, widely extended life and relations. Had it wholly survived, working out its destiny in exclusive use, it would have made England as insular as could the sea itself.

When Macaulay was in the public service in India, he had occasion to consider what system of national education should be adopted. Mr. Trevelyan, in his life of Macaulay, gives the particulars. The Committee of Public Instruction, composed of ten able men, were divided in opinion, and for some time "All educational action had been at a stand." "Half of the members were for maintaining and extending the old scheme of encouraging oriental learning by stipends paid to students in Sanskrit, Persian, and Arabic, and by liberal grants for the publication of works in those languages. The other half were in favor of teaching the elements of knowledge in the vernacular tongues, and the higher branches in English."

The advocates of both systems were heard before the Supreme Council, of which Macaulay was a member. In due time he laid his opinion before the Council, and urged that the people should be taught in the English language. Among other things, he said, " Whoever knows that language has ready access to all the vast intellectual wealth which all the wisest nations of the earth have created and hoarded in the course of ninety generations." " Had our ancestors acted as the Committee of Public Instruction has hitherto acted; had they neglected the language of Cicero and Tacitus; had they confined their attention to the old dialects of our own island; had they printed nothing and taught nothing at the universities but chronicles in Anglo-Saxon and romances in Norman-French, would England have been what she now is? What the Greek and Latin were to the contemporaries of More and Ascham, our tongue is to the people of India." His views prevailed. While in India, Macaulay, in a letter to his father, said, " Our English schools are flourishing wonderfully. We find it difficult — indeed, in some places, impossible — to provide instruction for all who want it. At the single town of Hooghly, fourteen hundred boys are learning English. The effect of this education on the Hindoos is prodigious. No Hindoo who has received an English education ever remains sincerely attached to his religion."

It was fortunate for England and for the people of India that Macaulay could thus secure the adoption of that system of education. It was a more important service than was the preparation of his Code, in which Macaulay took great pride; more important, indeed, than all his other work combined.

To include the study of Greek and Latin in that scheme of national education would have been premature and unwise, yet even that would have been more wise, as tending to make an alliance between the English and the Indian mind possible, than would have been the study of the Sanskrit, the Persian, and the Arabic. Mr. Macaulay knew that the time might never come when those dusky students of the East would wish to study Cicero and Tacitus in the original, and that it would require the culture of English in those schools for centuries before such a question could arise.

It is to be confessed that even with us the study of the ancient languages should be recommended with reserve and discrimination, not simply because the intellectual wealth mentioned by Macaulay is before us in translations, ministering to a great degree of culture, but because, with many students, such a study would be a sacrifice of time and strength. Even some minds of great power have suffered under such studies. It would be hard to find stronger expressions of detestation than Byron used with reference to Horace, or than Gray, as noticed by Moore, applied to the enforced duty of reading Virgil. Lamartine, speaking of his choice of authors, says, " Among the poets the ones that I preferred were not the ancients, whose classic pages had too early been bedewed with my sweat and tears." But we need not seek for examples. It is obviously unjust, it is bad economy, to prescribe such tasks for a student without regard to his taste, or to the course of life he is to pursue. Whatever his calling is to be, he must study his own language closely, critically, profoundly, and be conversant with the best authors in it. Especially must he study the Bible daily, and cultivate a love for its words and style. He may thus become a good English scholar. He must master many subjects of practical importance also, and in the history, life, and contentions of the world be well informed. In all this he will be following Mr. Choate's example.

There is no reason to fear that too much attention will be given to classical study. From lack of taste and inclination, of early training and agreeable association, or by reason of the nature and variety of studies soliciting his choice in the curricula of our higher schools, the student is likely, rather, to undervalue the claims of Latin and Greek.

But he who looks forward to a life of literary leisure, and to the highest intellectual enjoyments attainable, or aspires to one of the learned professions, must take up the ancient classics. Such studies, however, are to be vigorously pursued. In its early stages the work is difficult and full of discouragements. Only after much devotion, after he has passed the region of toil and pain, does the student enter into the spirit of the language, and take delight in the literature. Of that delight he who abandons the study early feels and knows nothing. It is as when two travelers attempt to climb a mountain. In the morning mist they see only the steep and stony path under their feet. After much effort, one becomes weary and turns back. The other pushes on and reaches the top. The rising sun illumines the summit, chases the shadows from the valleys, and gradually takes possession of the earth. He sits bathed in a flood of glory never before conceived, never to be forgotten.

We are reminded of the advice, "Soak your mind with Cicero," — advice often repeated by Mr. Choate, and illustrated in his early life.

Classical study trains the memory, the invention, the imagination, the judgment, taxing them all in a high degree. It furnishes thoughts, which yield themselves up to patient labor and ingenuity. But before they can be expressed in translation they must be grasped and subdued.

The student thus becomes habituated to the thoughts of great minds, in a sense makes them his own, and acquires a power for profound investigations. It cannot be denied that the ancient classics, properly pursued, compel the highest discipline of which the intellect is capable. In the seminaries to which students from other institutions are admitted, some of whom have had classical training, while others have not, it is found, after years of difficult study, that the former show a marked superiority. This has been proved in the German schools, and the statistics are given in the government reports. It has been proved in schools of our own also.

A critical knowledge of Latin, not difficult to attain, is the best preparation for the study of the French and other modern languages. Equipped with this, the acquisition of the other tongues becomes easy. Latin and Greek are also great helps in perfecting a knowledge of the English language. Nowhere else do we find reflected the exquisite grace and beauty of the Greek mind; and, when compared with the works of the great

Greek and Latin authors, those of the French and German appear crude and immature.

It would be lamentable indeed if the study of the ancient classics in our higher schools were unduly discouraged. It would, moreover, be illogical to accept as proof that such studies are no longer necessary, the fact that good English has been written by men ignorant of Latin and Greek, men to whom translations of classical productions have given aid not easily estimated. Such men may not owe much directly to the classic writers, but who can compute their indirect indebtedness, since their ideals have been writers whose style has been formed upon the great models furnished by Athens and by Rome?

The reader may have noticed that some authors, while objecting to the elements of Greek and Latin in our language as excessive, habitually use words of classic derivation, and praise Saxon words for their brevity, simplicity, directness, manly vigor, and moral purity as if these words had been lost; and claim that to relieve our poverty the student should go back to the days of Chaucer to find them. Yet these and other like words, treasured up with a wise economy, are in actual use and have intimate relations with the affairs of every-day life. But they are wanting in scope and variety. It is to be observed that scholars and critics, like Professor

Hunt, who agree with Sharon Turner in extolling the extent and power of the Anglo-Saxon language, have not told us how to find therein equivalents for such familiar words as *religion, line, face, relation, common, animal, nature, page,* and for hundreds of other words. Nor have they shown us why, now that we have such words, we should not use them, rather than search in ancient mounds for roots from which we might possibly cultivate their equivalents.

With a grateful appreciation of our language, we believe that on the grounds of harmony, of expressiveness, of variety, of convenience, the borrowing of terms from classic tongues was wise; and that English reduced to Saxon, if such a decline were possible, would not be a gain or a blessing, but an unspeakable calamity. Standing as the English language does to-day, with its wealth of derived words, its acquisition is made easier to millions of our fellow-men, and its usefulness to ourselves is thereby greatly increased.

CHAPTER VI.

The Study of Words. — The Percentage of Anglo-Saxon,
Latin, and Greek used by Mr. Choate and other Eminent
Scholars. — The Methods of Sharon Turner and George P.
Marsh. — Tables as to Derivatives.

MR. CHOATE'S solicitude as to the choice and
use of words was very great. Professor Parsons
says, " With all his variety and intensity of labor
there was nothing he cultivated with more care
than words." That he was not peculiar in this
branch of study appears from familiar instances.
Cicero had taught that the orator's style must
be formed by the choice of words and the skillful arrangement of them in sentences. That instruction has been repeated by great teachers
from Quintilian down. Dr. Johnson and Dean
Swift refer to a perfect style as proper words
in proper places. When Gibbon wrote, several
times over, the first chapter of his history, and
Brougham the close of his speech in the Queen's
case, they were striving by choice words to improve the style. That Byron found it difficult
to satisfy himself is shown by notes to an ap-

proved edition of his poems. Many changes were made. In one instance which I recall, he erased a word and substituted another; then rejected the substitute and restored the original; still in doubt, he wrote below, " Ask Gifford." Emerson regarded Montaigne's choice with favor, as he says, " Cut these words and they would bleed; they are vascular and alive." Of some of Milton's lines, Macaulay says, " Change the structure of the sentence, substitute one synonym for another, and the whole effect is destroyed." Pitt thought verbal study important when he went twice through Bailey's Dictionary, carefully considering every word. So also did Choate when he formed the habit of reading the dictionary by the page, and when he said to a student, " You want a diction whose every word is full freighted with suggestion and association, with beauty and power."

To acquire such a diction was a work calling for intense and continuous application. But to master the words which Mr. Choate needed was a preparatory study. The question as to their best use remained, and appealed to a large and ripe experience. Writers and speakers differ in that use, as they differ in culture and taste, in perception and judgment; but they would agree that the grace, beauty, and power of the words used depend on the harmony of their relations to each other and to the thoughts expressed.

Mr. Choate valued highly those synonyms which are useful in denoting distinctions, however slight, and in enabling a speaker to avoid a wearisome sameness of expression. His use of adjectives is a noticeable feature of his style. They were chosen with especial reference to the effect desired, and each furnishes a new outline. Used thus, adjectives are important for precision and definiteness. It is by them chiefly (and by their cognates, the adverbs) that qualification, so necessary to exact statement, can be attained. Mr. Choate once said to a friend of mine that the value of adjectives could be learned by studying botany. On taking up this study, one finds that the descriptive language in it is largely composed of adjectives; and that to outline each tint, form, and garniture of leaf and flower is an admirable instance of what can be done by the use of such words.

Mr. Choate was in full communion with the spirit of our language. He knew how strong, yet how flexible, the words are; he knew their lineage and their history. He did not attempt to coin new-words, or to reclaim those rejected because violating the analogies of the language, or to revive those that had become obsolete. Nor did he, when writing or speaking, pause or turn aside to

find or to avoid Saxon words or words of foreign
derivation. In a conservative spirit he accepted
our language as nourished and developed to its
present strength and maturity. Believing that
its wealth is as precious in the realms of thought
as coin and credit in the world of commerce, he
sought to evolve and quicken its power to express
with grace and precision every shade of sentiment
and doctrine, however delicate or abstruse.

No one who has considered the nature of language, or the poverty of which he is conscious
when some of his emotions cannot be described,
and yet believes that the development of language attends the growing refinement of the people, will doubt the wisdom that guided Mr. Choate
in his studies, even when he was seeking a perfection not yet attainable. Much has been said in
vague and general terms as to the quality and
extent of his vocabulary. Some not unfriendly
critics have thought that he gave an undue pref-
erence to words of foreign derivation; and that
his classic studies had perverted his taste and
judgment in respect to our strong, homely, and
simple native words. Such suggestions have had
weight in confirming my wish to ascertain the relative proportions of native and foreign words used
by Mr. Choate and by some other distinguished
scholars.

In his history, Sharon Turner gave some attention to such a question for the avowed purpose of proving " the copiousness and power of the Anglo-Saxon language; " but his method, though suggestive, was partial and inadequate. He quoted a few lines from fourteen authors, and marked the Saxon words, — marked some of them many times. The particulars appear in the table at the end of this chapter.

In his lectures on the English language, Mr. George P. Marsh gave the subject more attention, but his collections and estimates include repeated words. That distinguished philologist, Dr. Weisse, followed a different method.

As the more weighty words, those upon which the sense of an author largely depends, are of classic derivation and not often repeated, and as some of the small words, the Saxon, do recur many times in every sentence, it is obvious that to include the repeated words in an estimate unduly augments the percentage that should be assigned to the Anglo-Saxon. The vocabulary of a speaker or writer cannot thus be determined. When told that Milton used 8,000 words and Shakespeare 15,000, one need not be told that in these estimates repeated words are not counted.

In treating of Mr. Choate's vocabulary, I have caused all his words found in print, found by diligent search, to be written down, and classified according to their derivation, and the percentage of the whole which each class furnishes ascertained. But dates, proper names, and quotations have been omitted, and repeated words avoided; the question really being as to his total vocabulary, and not as to the frequency with which any class of words reappears in his writings. I find that Mr. Choate used 11,693 unrepeated words. Of these, 3,424 are Teutonic; 7,223 are Latin; 736 are Greek; 123 are common or Indo-European; and 187 are scattering. The percentage of the whole number which the Teutonic furnishes is, therefore, .293; the Latin, .618; the Greek, .062; the Indo-European, .011; and the scattering, .016.

A like test has been applied to twenty other authors, ten American and ten British; — the unrepeated words used by each of them in one paper or more, on some subject or occasion of grave importance, have been classified and counted. That these authors differ from each other and from Mr. Choate in the percentage of Anglo-Saxon used may be ascribed in some measure to the varied nature of the subjects discussed by them, and to the number of words considered. The subject discussed in each instance, and the derivations of the words used, are given in the tables at the close of this chapter. These authors, I am persuaded, will be regarded as fit exponents of the English language at its best estate. It is evident that, if they could have expressed their views with equal freedom, fidelity, precision, and force in Anglo-Saxon and had done so, our independence of the classic elements in our language would be generally confessed.

My purpose, at first, was merely to learn the percentage of Anglo-Saxon used by these authors and by Mr. Choate. But, on further consideration, it seemed proper to extend the inquiry to words from other sources. In doing this, the words seemed naturally to fall into these five classes: —

First. The Teutonic. By this I mean principally, and almost exclusively, Anglo-Saxon. But, in all the writings examined, there is a slight sprinkling (1) of Norse, or Scandinavian, words; (2) of old, middle, or modern High - German words; and (3) of Dutch words. These, too few in number to justify separate classification, and not strictly Anglo-Saxon words, though near of kin to them, could properly be classed with such, under the generic heading Teutonic, and so have been.

Secondly. The Latin; including, of course, the words coming into the English through the French, the Italian, the Spanish, and the Portuguese.

Thirdly. The Greek.

Fourthly. The Indo-European. This class embraces words which belong to most or to all of the seven great members of our family of languages. Belonging to most or to all, they could not be classed with any *one* of them.

Fifthly. Scattering. Of the words of this class by far the larger part are purely Celtic. But occasionally there was found a Hebrew or an Arabic word, one distinctly Russian, or Persian, or Indian, or one from some other source, and a separate classification of these in the tables was not called for.

It should be said, further, that what was evidently the most essential part of any compound determined the classification of the word. Where there were prefixes or suffixes, or both, the *root* settled the class to which the word was assigned. Where the parts were still independent words, that part modified in meaning or limited in scope by the other part or the other parts was allowed to determine the class.[1]

In a letter from the late George P. Marsh, to be found in another part of this work, he says that

---

[1] The classification of the words, the determination of the percentages, and the preparation of the tables are, with little of my help, the work of my learned friend, Brainerd Kellogg, Professor of English Language and Literature in the Collegiate and Polytechnic Institute, Brooklyn, N. Y.

he had thought Mr. Choate's vocabulary consisted of more words than I have given. As some of my readers may have a like impression, it is proper to speak of the rigorous excision practiced by the Professor, — an excision by which great numbers of words standing alphabetically in the columns prepared for him were cut out. No word in any one author, occurring as a single part of speech, was counted more than once, though used often by him in the same form, or in different forms. As, for instance, *grow, grows, grew, growing, grown,* found many times in the same author, were regarded as one word; and *taller* or *tallest* was not counted if *tall* had been; nor was the plural of any noun, if the singular had been.

Let me, however, illustrate a *seeming* exception to this guiding rule stated and exemplified above. *Is, was,* and *been* are parts of one verb. But they are from different roots; consequently, when found in an author, they were called three different words. For the same reason, *better* and *worse,* comparatives of the adjective *good* and the adverb *badly,* were counted, though the positives had been. So were the forms, thus differently derived, of all other parts of speech.

The number of Mr. Choate's words as first collected, 15,559, was thus reduced to 11,693.

With these explanations of the principles by

which the learned Professor was governed in the preparation of the tables, the lessons taught may be readily understood.

As a summary of the less obvious teaching of the tables, Professor Kellogg has had the kindness, at my request, to write what follows. He says, "It will be seen by a glance at the tables, that eight of the twenty authors with whom Mr. Choate is compared use a smaller percentage of Teutonic words than he does; that two use the same; that the ten who exceed his percentage of Teutonic exceed it about as much as the others drop below it; and that these relations would not be essentially disturbed if the percentages marked *common* (Indo-European, or Aryan) were added to the Teutonic. It will be seen, also, that thirteen of these twenty authors use a larger percentage of Latin words than Mr. Choate does; and that these thirteen exceed his percentage much more than the remaining seven fall below it. If, with some, we add the Greek words to the Latin, and call the resulting list *classical,* ten of the twenty would exceed Mr. Choate's percentage of classical words; one would have the same; and the remaining nine would fall below his percentage much less than the ten would stand above it."

Mr. Choate's vocabulary, the unrepeated words, is not in any material degree disturbed by the fact that many of his speeches and arguments were not published or preserved. He used in them, no doubt, words not found in the papers before me, but the number of unrepeated additional words would be much less than might be supposed, while the percentage of Anglo-Saxon, of Latin, and of Greek, would be substantially the same.

SOME PARTICULARS OF SHARON TURNER'S WORKS.

Authors.	Number of Words considered.	Of which are Anglo-Saxon.	Of which (Anglo-Saxon) are Repetitions.	Repetition of Words from other Sources.
Shakespeare . . .	81	68	31	–
Milton	89	71	23	–
Cowley	76	68	16	1
Thomson	78	64	22	1
Addison	79	64	20	2
Spenser	72	58	18	6
Locke	95	75	28	3
Pope	84	56	17	1
Young	96	73	18	1
Swift	87	77	26	1
Robertson	114	79	33	1
Hume	101	63	35	2
Gibbon	80	47	23	–
Johnson	87	60	23	3
	1,219	923	333	22

Authors and their Subjects.	Number of Unrepeated Words.	Teutonic.		Latin.		Greek.		Common.		Scattering.	
		Number of Words.	Per Cent.	Number of Words.	Per Cent.	Number of Words.	Per Cent.	Number of Words.	Per Cent.	Number of Words.	Per Cent.
Hon. John Marshall (Chief Justice). Speeches on the Federal Constitution, in the Virginia Convention, June 10, 1788. Argument in the case of Thomas Nash, *alias* Jonathan Robbins, in the House of Representatives, March 4, 1800	1,823	427	.234	1,324	.726	45	.025	18	.01	9	.005
John Quincy Adams. Inaugural Oration at Harvard Uni ry, June 12, 1806. Oration on Life and ler of Lafayette, December 31, 1834. Oration at Plymouth, December 22, 1802. Lecture 1 — General w of Rhetoric and Oratory (Vol. 1); Lecture 2 —Objections against Eloquence Consi ed. Lecture on Proposition and Partition (Vol. 2)	1,751	455	.26	1,126	.643	127	.073	25	.014	18	.01
William Pinkney. Speech on the Bill for the admission of Missouri into the Union, in the United States Senate, February 15, 1820	1,523	446	.293	976	.64	72	.047	16	.011	13	.009
Edward Everett. Eulogy on Lafayette, at Faneuil Hall, Boston, September 6, 1834	1,989	583	.293	1,266	.636	87	.044	42	.021	111	.006

DANIEL WEBSTER. Speech on the Constitution and the Union, in the United States Senate, March 7, 1850.	1,790	568	.317	1,121	.626	49	.028	40	.022	12	.007
CHARLES SUMNER. Oration on the War System of the Commonwealth of Nations, before the American Peace Society, Boston, May 28, 1849.	1,773	534	.301	1,082	.61	114	.064	26	.015	17	.01
REVERDY JOHNSON. Argument in the Methodist Church Property Case, in the Circuit Court of the United States, City of New York, May 28 and 29, 1851.	1,135	346	.305	727	.64	46	.041	14	.012	2	.002
CALEB CUSHING. Speeches in the House of Representatives, on an Independent Treasury, May 21, 1840, and on the Army Appropriation Bill, May 26, 1842.	1,419	446	.314	880	.62	60	.042	21	.015	12	.009
WILLIAM M. EVARTS, LL. D. Closing parts of his argument for President Johnson in the Impeachment Case, April 28 and 29, 1868. Eulogy on Chief Justice Chase, at Dartmouth College, June 24, 1874.	2,299	565	.246	1,570	.683	95	.041	48	.021	21	.009
RICHARD S. STORRS, D. D., LL. D. Oration on John Wycliffe and the First English Bible, before the Board of Managers of the American Bible Society, in the Academy of Music, New York, December 2, 1880.	2,623	787	.30	1,561	.595	208	.079	56	.022	11	.004

Authors and their Subjects.	Number of Unrepeated Words.	Teutonic.		Latin.		Greek.		Common.		Scattering.	
		Number of Words.	Per Cent.	Number of Words.	Per Cent.	Number of Words.	Per Cent.	Number of Words.	Per Cent.	Number of Words.	Per Cent.
James Anthony Froude. Chapter 1, Volume I. of his History of England, and Chapter 3 of his Sketch of Cæsar	1,518	507	.334	876	.577	91	.06	30	.02	14	.009
Arthur Penrhyn Stanley, D. D. (Dean of Westminster). The Study of Greatness. The Hopes of Theology. The Principles of Christianity	1,281	420	.328	722	.564	99	.077	29	.022	11	.009
Rev. Sydney Smith. Speech on the Reform Bill. Sermon on The Lawyer that Tempted Christ. Five of the Plymley Letters	1,675	533	.318	1,002	.598	86	.051	28	.017	26	.016
Thomas Babington Macaulay. Criticism of a Treatise on Christian Doctrine, by John Milton. From the "Edinburgh Review" of August, 1825	3,205	911	.284	2,011	.627	197	.062	45	.014	41	.013
Lord Henry Brougham, F. R. S. Inaugural Discourse on being installed Lord Rector of the University of Glasgow, April 6, 1825	1,550	498	.321	950	.613	60	.039	32	.021	10	.006

Right Hon. W. E. Gladstone. Speech on the Irish Church, in the House of Commons, March 30, 1868	1,403	442	.315	855	.609	64	.046	34	.024	8 .006
Right Hon. Edmund Burke. Speech on his Resolutions for Conciliation with the Colonies of America, in the British Parliament, March 22, 1775 . . .	1,481	422	.285	964	.651	60	.04	20	.014	15 .01
Right Hon. William Pitt. Speeches in the House of Commons: On Mr. Grey's Bill for a Reform in Parliament, May 26, 1797; on His Majesty's Message relative to Mutiny in the Fleet, June 2, 1797; in relation to the late Negotiation at Lisle, November 10, 1797; and on the Bill for the Suspension of the Army Reserve Act, April 25, 1804	1,723	459	.266	1,162	.675	59	.034	27	.016	16 .009
Thomas Erskine. Argument on The Rights of Juries, before the Court of King's Bench, November, 1784	1,142	291	.255	773	.677	43	.038	27	.023	8 .007
Lord John Campbell. Life of Sir John Holt, Chief Justice	1,217	334	.274	800	.657	57	.047	14	.012	12 .01

CHAPTER VII.

THE reader who believes, with Lord Kames,
that to have a specific style is to be poor of
speech, will appreciate Mr. Choate's varied methods. As a speaker he was copious, reiterative,
and much given to illustrations useful in an argument; as a writer he was more simple and
severe.

But, however widely his methods differed, the
same delicate and touching sensibility, the same
vivid and picturesque beauty, the same wealth of
thought and power of expression appeared in what
was spoken and in what was written. In neither
was his brilliant imagery used as a mere embel-
lishment; the visions of beauty in his mind became articulate without effort; the musical flow
and rhythm as inimitable as the melody of the
murmuring brook. He evidently believed that
from the harmony that could exist between a sub-

ject and the tone of its discussion might arise a sense of ideal and emotional beauty, pleasing to the mind; that a brilliant style was consistent with directness of thought and simplicity of speech; and that rhetorical and illustrative imagery, employed with taste and judgment, — pictures to the eye and to the mind, — might add to the spirit and force of an argument.

Mr. Choate wrote with great freedom, and often spoke with vehemence and rapidity; the words waiting instantly and submissively on the thoughts. When the subject moved him strongly and was to be compressed within the limits of a single discourse, he sometimes rushed through one of those long sentences thought to be peculiar to him. However easy it may have been for him, — and it appeared to be easy, — the work in its nature was unique and difficult. To one not having a powerful memory, great command of language, and discrimination in the use of words, the achievement would have been impossible. A long train of thought and the related parts of the discourse were to be held in mind, and the particulars so adjusted as to be in harmony with each other and with the argument. Mr. Choate thus gave, in compact ·form, extended views of the matter in hand, without prolixity, confusion, or ambiguity. The longest sentence he is known to have used was in his eulogy of Webster. In that instance and in other instances of the kind, he was heard with such unbounded delight that no one would have thought of suggesting the common objection that long sentences tend to weary and perplex the hearer and the reader. In reading those sentences, as in reading the sovereign examples of Demosthenes, Cicero, and Milton, the student has a vivid conception of the argument.

In a letter to Mr. Brazer, referring to a work on Logic, Mr. Webster accepts what is said of "argumentative repetition," and of "the effect of particularization," and says, "The skillful, and apparently natural, enumeration of particulars is certainly, in its proper place, one of the best modes of producing impressions. All the standard works are full of instances of this sort of composition." In closing his letter, Mr. Webster adds, "'After all,' says Cobbett, 'he is a man of talent that can make things move;' and after all, say I, he is an orator that can make me think as he thinks, and feel as he feels."

Was not Mr. Choate such an orator? From one of my correspondents I cite a few words relating to an occasion when Choate was speaking upon a familiar topic, "As Choate approached the climax, Webster's emotions became uncontrollable; the great eyes were filled with tears, the great frame shook ; he bowed his head to conceal his face in his hat, and I almost seemed to hear him sob." Was not Mr. Choate's a style that could make Webster think as he thought, and feel as he felt? When, in listening to any other orator, speaking in whatever style, was Webster so moved ? Those tears, that emotion, prove and illustrate his judgment, and blot out forever some of the loose and casual chat about Choate's style which Mr. Harvey reports in his " Reminiscences." If Webster ever did find fault with Choate's style, it would be interesting to know in what mood he was. If he talked of Choate's pile of flowers, and praised his logic rather than his style, Webster must have forgotten the care and patience with which he had cultivated his own flowers of speech, and the interest which they gave to some of his discourses. But he really differed from Choate, in the use of such forms of expression, less than may be commonly supposed. In his popular addresses, Webster employed them more freely than when speaking to legislative bodies or in the courts. He used them, however, in each kind of service, when moved by passion, or when anxious to awaken or quicken the attention of his hearers. Yet, in revising his speeches for publication, he plucked away the flowers whose bloom and fragrance then pleased him less than when they had been adopted.

But Mr. Choate's flowers of speech, of spontaneous growth and use, were left with his other words, in their original relations.

In his essay, introductory to his selections from Mr. Webster's speeches, Mr. Whipple takes special and favorable notice of several figurative expressions which had been retained. They have great merit. I refer to one of them, illustrative somewhat of the deliberation with which such embellishments were sought. Mr. Whipple gives the history. When Webster was once on the heights of Quebec, at an early hour of a summer morning, he heard the drum-beat calling the garrison to duty. It flashed upon him that England's morning drum would go on beating elsewhere to the hour when it would again sound in Quebec. In his speech in the Senate, on the "Presidential Protest," after noticing the fact that our Revolutionary fathers went to war in respect to mere taxation, Webster said, " On this question of principle, while actual suffering was yet afar off, they raised their flag against a power, to which, for the purpose of foreign conquest and subjugation, Rome, in the height of her glory, is not to be compared ; a power which has dotted over the surface of the whole globe with her possessions and military posts; whose morning drum-beat, following the sun, and keeping company with the hours, circles the earth with one continuous and unbroken strain of the martial airs of England."

As indicating the attention which that rhetorical illustration excited, Mr. Whipple notices the report that, at the conclusion of this speech, John Sergeant of Philadelphia came up to the orator, and eagerly asked, "Where, Webster, did you get that idea of the morning drum-beat?"

Mr. Webster evidently believed that the idea of an unbroken circle of power, extending round the globe, originated with him and at Quebec. Mr. Whipple, however, refers to a passage in Goethe's "Faust" for the same idea, but says that Webster never read "Faust." He could also have referred to the "Odyssey," which Webster had read in the original and as translated, for a passage equally suggestive : —

> " Hear me, O Neptune ! thou whose arms are hurled
> From shore to shore and gird the solid world."

The idea was old. Mr. Webster gave it a new form and office.

In respect to the final improvement of their speeches, the difference between the habits of Webster and those of Choate is not less striking and significant. As a consequence, it may be said that he who would know these orators from their printed pages should remember that while one of them appears as in state-dress, every part carefully arranged, the other appears in the unstudied dress of every-day life.

An interesting statement, by the Hon. Enoch L. Fancher, as to Mr. Choate's relation to the Methodist Church case, appears in another part of this work. I am indebted to Judge Fancher for a copy of the report of that case which contains the arguments of counsel. I turn the pages of the book with conflicting emotions, — pleasure, in recalling what interested and impressed me many years ago; sadness, in remembering what the country and the profession have since lost. On that trial, Judges Nelson and Betts presided, and Rufus Choate, Daniel Lord, George Wood, and Reverdy Johnson were of counsel, not one of whom is now living.

The reader will learn, from Judge Fancher's paper, that he sought in vain to have Mr. Choate revise his argument for publication. The refusal was in keeping with Mr. Choate's habit. The work in hand having been performed, he turned to other labors or to his favorite studies, free from the ambition of appearing well in print. He always sought to master his subject before undertaking its discussion. In this he was unsparing. But, in speaking, he could use appropriate terms, and be content to leave his words as they fell from his lips. It would, I think, be admitted by those who have often heard him and have studied him closely, that, owing to the character and extent of his studies and the influence of his natural gifts,—memory, taste, judgment,—the words that would best express and illustrate his views were present to him as they were wanted, even when he was in the free and rapid current of discourse. Professor Parsons was sensible of this when he said that Choate "was never at a loss for *the* word."

In contrast with such command of words and such indisposition to revise what had been said on a trial or in an argument, the reader will find in Mr. Whipple's essay, to which I have referred, a circumstantial account of the manner in which, by changing words, definitions, and illustrations, Mr. Webster " tormented reporters, proof-readers, and the printers who had the misfortune to be engaged in putting one of his performances into type, not because this or that word was or was not Saxon or Latin, but because it was inadequate to convey perfectly his meaning."

Mr. Whipple mentions, also, Mr. Webster's revision of discourses which had been deliberately prepared. Thus he says, " On the morning after he had delivered his Eulogy on Adams and Jefferson, he entered his office with the manuscript in his hand, and threw it down on the desk of a young student at law, whom he greatly esteemed, with the request, 'There, Tom, please take that discourse and weed out all the Latin words.'"

The publication, in pamphlet form, of Mr. Webster's Plymouth oration of 1820 was delayed for about a year. Mr. Whipple says, "It is probable that the Plymouth oration, as we possess it in print, is a better oration, in respect to composition, than that which was heard by the applauding crowd before which it was originally delivered."

Mr. Webster's taste was so exacting and severe that he was not easily satisfied with his own work. In that he was fortunate. He was fortunate also in his close communion with the great masters of speech. In the Eulogy, Mr. Choate refers to several writers from whom Mr. Webster had sought inspiration, and says, " To the study and comparison, but not to the copying, of authors such as these ; to habits of writing and speaking and conversing on the capital theory of always doing his best ; — thus, somewhat, I think, was acquired that remarkable production, 'the last work of combined study and genius,' his rich, clear, correct, harmonious, and weighty style of prose."

Mr. Richard Grant White has like views upon such an acquisition. After suggesting that style cannot be taught, and that the student will derive little benefit from mere rhetoric, he says, " It is general culture — above all, it is the constant submission of a teachable, apprehensive mind to the influence of minds of the highest class, in daily life and in books, that bring out upon language its daintiest bloom and its richest fruitage."

In using picturesque figures of speech and argumentative illustrations, Mr. Webster and Mr. Choate were following the examples of great masters of speech from Cicero down to their own times. But some critics, not able to conform to these standards, commend plainness of style, and object to rhetorical embellishments. Those who condemn what they cannot emulate deserve little attention. But it would seem that views occasionally ascribed to distinguished authors may have given such critics some encouragement. I make special mention of one instance.

Sir James Mackintosh is reported to have said, in a conversation with Alexander H. Everett, " Eloquence is the power of gaining your purpose by words. All the labored definitions of it to be found in the different rhetorical works amount in substance to this. It does not, therefore, require or admit the strained and false ornaments that are taken for it by some. I hate those artificial flowers without fragrance or fitness. Nobody ever succeeded in this way but Burke. Fox used to say, 'I cannot bear this thing in anybody but Burke, and he cannot help it, it is his natural manner.' Mr. Wilberforce's voice is beautiful; his manner mild and perfectly natural. He has no artificial ornament, but an easy, natural image occasionally springs up in the mind that pleases very much." [1]

In some respects, the contrast between Wilberforce and Burke was very great. Yet there is no reason to suppose that images sprang up in the mind of one of them more naturally than in the mind of the other. Mackintosh cites Fox with approbation, and could do so properly, as Fox knew Burke by heart. But when Fox, speaking of the abundant and gorgeous imagery of Burke, says that he could not help it, it was his natural manner, he recognizes Burke's genius, and, in effect, denies that he employed strained and false ornaments or artificial flowers.

In his definition of eloquence, Mackintosh could have said that the speaker who seeks to gain his purpose by words must be true to his nature, and that to check or to stimulate his powers by limiting himself to the use of a plain style, or by striving after ornamentation, would betray great weakness. How far he would have tolerated Choate's and Webster's flowers of speech it would be haz-

[1] *North American Review,* 1832.

ardous to surmise. But he could not think it more feasible or just to apply a law of repression to the luxurious diction of a man of genius than it would be to add " lead and ballast to the understanding " to bring it down to the level of common minds. Either course would be as reasonable as to clip the wings of eagles, formed by nature to cleave the upper air. It is obvious that he who would by words secure the assent of others must be allowed to speak as the spirit moves him, with no other sense of restraint than his culture, taste, and judgment, the character of his hearers, and the nature of his subject may impose. Such freedom is most essential to the advocate.

It has been suggested as the rule for the forensic speaker that he should pass over inferior matters, and concentrate his efforts upon the more material points in a case ; whereas, it was characteristic of Mr. Choate that he did, in some sense, just the opposite. It is to be remembered, however, that with great freedom of suggestion, of illustration, of argument, his discourse was tempered by a keen and steady watchfulness of the effect he was producing. He peered, as it were, into the very souls of the jury to read the stage of conviction to which they had been brought. He knew that the less important points of a case may give the jury trouble, may even prevent their agreeing upon a verdict. Then, too, matters which, as first considered, appear to be of little moment, may in combination, or in their relation to unexpected developments on a trial, become important. It would, indeed, be interesting to know by what prevision, in cases like those of Tirrell, where a life was at stake, and of Dalton, where a woman's honor was in peril, counsel could sift out what might be passed over in silence as immaterial.

It has been suggested, also, that Mr. Choate's arguments before juries were long, with the implication that they were too long. The objection might be reasonable if it had been observed that in any case he did not keep the attention of the jury to the end of the discussion. We can recall no instance of such failure. He often tried questions of fact with the brevity for which Sir James Scarlett and Judge Curtis have been commended. But in desperate cases, the testimony conflicting and doubtful, such economy of time and strength would not have been proper. In his Recollections of Mr. Choate, from which I have permission to quote, Mr. Whipple says, " On one occasion I happened to be a witness in a case where a trader was prosecuted for obtaining goods under false pretenses. Mr. Choate took the ground that the seeming knavery of the accused was due to the circumstance that he had a deficient business intelligence — in short, that he unconsciously rated all his geese as swans. He (Choate) was right in his view. The foreman of the jury, however, was a hard-headed, practical man, a model of business intellect and integrity, but with an incapacity of understanding any intellect or conscience radically differing from his own. Mr. Choate's argument, as far as the facts and the law were concerned, was through in an hour. Still he went on speaking. Hour after hour passed, and yet he continued to speak with constantly increasing eloquence, repeating and recapitulating, without any seeming reason, facts which he had already stated and arguments which he had already urged. The truth was, as I gradually learned, that he was engaged in a hand-to-hand — or rather in a brain-to-brain and a heart-to-heart — contest with the foreman, whose resistance he was determined to break down, but who confronted him for three hours with defiance observable in every rigid line of his honest countenance. ' You fool ! ' was the burden of the advocate's ingenious argument ; ' you rascal ! ' was the phrase legibly printed on the foreman's incredulous face. But at last the features of the foreman began to relax, and at the end the stern lines melted into acquiescence with the opinion of the advocate, who had been storming at the defenses of his mind, his heart, and his conscience for five hours, and had now entered as victor. He compelled the foreman to admit the unpleasant fact that there were existing human beings whose mental and moral constitution differed from his own, and who were yet as honest in intention as he was, but lacked his clear perception and sound judgment. The verdict was, 'Not guilty.' It was a just verdict, but it was mercilessly assailed by merchants who had lost money by the prisoner and who were hounding him down as an enemy to the human race, as another instance of Choate's lack of mental and moral honesty in the defense of persons accused of crime. The fact that the foreman of the jury that returned the verdict belonged to the class that most vehemently attacked Choate was sufficient of itself to disprove such allegations. As I listened to Choate's argument in this case, I felt assured that he would go on speaking until he dropped dead on the floor rather than have relinquished his clutch on the soul of the one man on the jury who he knew would control the opinion of the others."

I may be allowed to say that the stubborn juror could not have been persuaded to adopt Mr. Choate's views by the mere repetition of facts and arguments, or by a determination to break him down. His peculiarities were to be consulted, and his self-respect encouraged by making him feel that he represented the higher intelligence of the jury. To his sense and apprehension there were or should have been no bald and verbal repetitions; these would have offended his pride and been fruitless; would have involved a tautology which Mr. Choate abhorred. In the course of that discussion, no doubt varied relations were recalled, recognized difficulties qualified, points which had been stated put in new lights, and a sense of novelty and interest excited. On the last occasion when I heard Mr. Choate, he dealt with the jury after that fashion. I was reminded of what Stanhope says of Fox's repetitions — that one argument stated in five different forms may be equal to five different arguments.

The critic who thinks that Mr. Choate's arguments were long would do well to recall the success that often crowned his efforts; also that one of Erskine's speeches occupied seven hours; that, with us, counsel, sensible of the value of time, have been known to speak to the purpose in a case and entertain a jury for a week; and that in the Star Route trial the arguments of two of the counsel consumed, each, seven days.

CHAPTER VIII.

MR. CHOATE'S study of the great masters of speech in several languages left him in the use of a style that was best suited to his taste and genius. Hence it is that a wholesome relation appears between the sympathetic power of his early and of his later speeches. Such was the opinion of Chief Justice Perley, who entered college when young Choate was there, and knew him up to the close of his life. In speaking of his early studies, the Chief Justice says, "He was already remarkable for the same brilliant qualities which distinguished him in his subsequent career. To those who knew him then, and watched his onward course, little change was observable in his style of writing or in his manner of speaking, except such as would naturally be required by subjects of a wider range, and by more exacting occasions."

I am indebted to the Rev. Roswell D. Hitchcock, D. D., President of the Union Theological Seminary, New York, for the following : "Between the years 1845 and 1852, when I was living in Exeter, N. H., and was often in Boston, I used to see Mr. Choate in Burnham's antiquarian bookstore, on Cornhill. I had no speaking acquaintance with him, but more than once he gave a sort of gracious half-recognition, which seemed to me the very perfection of courtesy and kindliness. As he moved about among the old books, finding now and then something that pleased him, there was no mistaking the rare quality of the man. That fine face, so deeply furrowed, the keen, but genial, glance of the eye, the whole air so self-respecting and yet so sweetly deferential to others, always thrilled me at the time, and haunted my memory long afterwards."

Of Mr. Choate's style and its effect, Dr. Hitchcock says, " Certainly he seldom failed to carry his point with any jury, or any popular assembly. He caught men up and swept them along, as the wind sweeps leaves and dust. Whoever seeks to know the secret of this will find it preëminently in the innermost, essential character of the man. He was pure, and just, and true, and tender, so that whatever he said commended, and still commends, itself to what is best and highest in our

9

common nature. He was not only thoroughly good, but his goodness was fine and chivalric. The fascination was moral. The heart was captured first, and after that the imagination. His marvelous fertility of invention, wealth of allusion, and swift succession of inimitable felicities of thought and diction never seemed like devices to blind and betray the judgment, but came as naturally as the bloom of fruit-trees, or the foam of crested waves. His voice was one of a thousand, of ten thousand rather, now like a flute for softness, and now like a clarion."

Mr. Choate could say what he would, in whatever style he would, with ease and certainty. He writes and speaks as one thoughtless of mere style, and there seems to be almost no limit to the variety of tone and expression.

I give some extracts, mere fragments, from his Journal,[1] showing briefly some of his impressions in 1850, when he was traveling abroad.

" Monday, August 5, Lucerne. This, then, is Switzerland. It is a sweet, burning midsummer's morning at Lucerne. Under one of my windows is a little garden in which I see currants, cabbages, pear-trees, vines, healthfully growing. Before me, from the other, I see the lake of Lucerne, — beyond it, in farthest east, I see the snowy peaks

[1] *Brown's Memoirs*, vol. i.

of Alps. I count some dozen distinct summits on which the snow is lying, composing a range of many miles. On my extreme right ascends Mount Pilate, — splintered, bare granite, — and, on the other, Righi, high and bold, yet wooded nearly to the top. It is a scene of great beauty and interest, where all 'save the spirit of man' may seem divine. We left Basle at nine on Saturday morning, and got to Zurich that evening at six. This ride opened no remarkable beauty or grandeur, yet possessed great interest. It was performed in a diligence, — the old, continental stage-coach. And the impression made through the whole day, or until we approached Zurich, was exactly that of a ride in the coach from Hanover to the White Hills. I ascribe this to the obvious circumstances that we were already far above the sea, were ascending along the bank of a river, the Rhine, and then a branch which met us, rushing full and fast from its mountain sources — that we were approaching the base of mountains of the first class in a high northern latitude. The agricultural productions (except the exotic vine), the grass, weeds moderate; wheat — clover — whiteweed — the construction of the valley — the occasional bends and intervals — all seem that of New England. There was less beauty than at Newbury and Bath, and, I think, not a richer soil, — certainly a poorer people. They assiduously accumulate manure, and women of all ages were reaping in the fields.

" Zurich is beautiful. The lake extends beautifully to the south before it. Pleasant gardens and orchards and heights lie down to it and adjoining it. And here first we saw the Alps — a vast chain. The glaciers, ranging from east to west, closing the view to the south — their peaks, covered with snow, lay along as battlements, unsupported beneath, of a city of the sky out of sight.

" All things in Zurich announce Protestantism, — activity of mind, the university, the books, the learned men, the new buildings, the prosperity.

" I shall never forget the sweet sensations with which I rode the first five or ten miles from Zurich yesterday. It was Sunday. The bells of Zurich were ringing, — including that honored by the preaching of Zwingle, — and men, women, and children were dressed, and with books were going to meeting. Our way lay for some time along the shores of the lake, through gardens, orchards, and fields, to the water's edge, many of them of the highest beauty. Then it left the lake to ascend the Albis. This is an excellent road, but, to overcome the mountain, its course is zigzag, and is practicable only for a walk of the horses. I got

out, and ascended on foot, crossing from one ter-
race of road to another, by paths through pleasant
woods. As I ascended, the whole valley of Zurich,
— the city, the lake, in its whole length, the
amphitheatre of country inclosing it, the glorious
Alps, and, at last, Righi and Pilate, standing like
the speaker's place in a lyceum, with an audience
of mountains vastly higher, rising into the peculiar
pinnacle of the Alps, covered with snow, ascending before them, — successively evolved itself. I
saw over half of Switzerland. Spread on it all
was the sweet, not oppressive, unclouded, summer's sunlight. A pure, clear air enfolded it, —
the Sunday of the pastoral, sheltered, and happy
world. In some such scenes the foundations of
the Puritan mind and polity were laid, — scenes,
beautiful by the side of Tempe and Arcady, — fit
as they to nurse and shelter all the kinds of
liberty.

" We descended to Zug and its lake, and then
coasted it to Lucerne. Last evening we visited
the emblematical lion and sailed on the lake.
To-day I go to the chapel of Tell. The first view
of the peculiar sharp points of Alps was just from
the very top of Albis, on the southwest brow.
There rose Righi and Pilate, and east — apart
and above — a sort of range, or city, of the tents
of an encampment in the sky. They rested on

nothing, and seemed architecture of heaven — pavilions — the tents of a cavalcade traveling above the earth.

" Berne, Wednesday, 7th.   We left Lucerne at seven, in our own hired voiture, and with one change of horses, treating ourselves to two long pauses, arrived here at eight o'clock — the last two hours through a thunder-shower. The way gave me much of the common and average life of Switzerland, lying through two of its great cantons. What I saw of Lucerne disappointed me. The soil, I should think, cold and ungrateful, and the mind of the laborer not open. Crucifixes everywhere, and all over everything, — weeds in corn and grass. Once in Berne all changes. Man does his duty.   Excellent stone bridges; good fences; fewer weeds; more wheat and grass; more look of labor; better buildings; better, newer, larger houses and barns; no crucifixes; express the change. Throughout I find a smallish, homely race, and pursue the dream of Swiss life in vain. Yet in these valleys, on the sides of these hills, in these farm-houses, scattered far and near, though all is cut off from the great arterial and venous system of the world of trade and influence, — though the great pulse of business and politics beats not — though life might seem to stagnate, — is happiness and goodness too. Sometimes a high Swiss mind emerges, and, speaking a foreign or dead tongue, or migrating, asserts itself. Berne is full of liveliness and recency, as well as eld. I have run over it before breakfast, and shall again before we go.

"I saw at Berne the place of the state bears, and two of the pensioners, the high terraced ground of view, the residence of the patricians, and the Cathedral, containing, among other things, tablets to the memory of those who fell in 1798, enumerating them; and the painted windows of Protestant satire. Our journey to Vevay had little interest, a grim horizon of cloud and a constant fall of rain wholly obscured the Alps. Freiburg is striking, its suspended bridge sublime, and it holds one of the best organs of the world. We arrived here (Vevay) at ten, and I have this morning looked out on the whole beauty of this part of the lake, — from Hauteville, and from a point on the shore above it, and towards the direction of Chillon, — and admitted its supreme interest, and its various physical and associated beauty. The day is clear and warm and still. The slightest breeze stirs the surface of the lake; light clouds curl half-way up the steep shores, float, vanish, and are succeeded by others; a summer's sun bathes a long shore and inland rising from the shore, clad thick with vines; yonder, looking to the southeast upon the water, in that valley, sheltered by the mountain, nestling among those trees, embraced and held still in the arms of universal love, is Clarens, — fit, unpolluted asylum of love and philosophy; before it, on its left, is the castle of Chillon, more directly before it the mouth of the Rhone, here resting a space in his long flight from his glacier-source; far-off, west, stretched the Lake of Geneva, at peace, here and there a white sail, — the home, the worship, the inspiration of Rousseau and De Staël; the shelter of liberty; the cradle of free-thinking; the scene in which the character and fortune of Puritanism were shaped and made possible; the *true* birthplace of the civil and religious order of the northern New World.

" Geneva, 9th August, Friday. The lake was smooth and bright, and our voyage of five hours pleasant and prosperous; and we had the extraordinary fortune to witness what we are assured was the best sunset on Mont Blanc for years. Long after the sun had sunk below our earth, the whole range of the mountain was in a blaze with the descending glory. At first it was a mere reflection, from a long and high surface, of the sun's rays. Gradually this passed into a golden and rosy hue, then all darkened except the supreme summit itself, from which the gold light flashed,

beamed, some time longer; one bright turret of
the building not made with hands, kindled from
within, self-poised, or held by an unseen hand.
Under our feet ran the Rhone, leaping, joyful,
full, blue, to his bed in the Mediterranean. Before us is the city of thought, liberty, power, influence, the beautiful and famous Geneva. More
than all in interest was the house of the father of
Madame de Staël, and the home of the studies of
Gibbon.

"I went on Saturday, August 10, to the nearer
contemplation of Mont Blanc, at Chamouny. Most
of that journey lies through Savoy, of the kingdom
of Sardinia, even as far as St. Martin, and beyond
somewhat, a well-constructed royal road. Within
the first third, I should think, of the day's ride
out from Geneva, and long before Mont Blanc
again reveals himself (for you lose sight of him
wholly in a mile or two out of the city), you enter
a country of much such scenery as the Notch of
the White Mountains. An excellent road ascends
by the side of the Arve, itself a mad, eager stream,
leaping from the *mer de glace*, and running head-
long, of the color of milk mixed with clay, to the
Rhone, below Geneva, on each side of which rise,
one after another, a succession of vast heights,
some a half mile to a mile above you, all steep,
more than even perpendicular, and even hanging

over you, as projecting beyond their base. These are so near, and our view so unobstructed, and they are all of a height so comprehensible and appreciable, so to speak, so little is lost by an unavailing elevation, that they make more impression than a mountain five times as high. It is exactly as in the Notch, where the grandeur, instead of being enthroned remote, dim, and resting in measurement, and demanding comparisons and thoughts, is near, palpable, and exacting. Down many of these streamed rivulets of water, silver threads of hundreds, perhaps of thousands, of feet long from source to base of cliff, often totally floating off from the side of the hill, and the bed in which they had begun to run, in a mere mist, which fell like rain, and farther down, and to the right or left of the original flow, were condensed again into mere streams. These have no character of waterfall as you ride along, but discharge a great deal of water in a very picturesque, holiday, and wanton fashion. This kind of scenery grows bolder and wilder, and at last, and suddenly, at St. Martin, we saw again, above it, and beyond it all, the range of Mont Blanc, covered with snow, and at first, its summit covered too with clouds. Thenceforth this was ever in view, and some hours before sunset the clouds lifted themselves and vanished, and we looked till all was dark upon the unveiled summit itself. Again we had a beautiful evening sky; again, but this time directly at the foot of the mountain, we stood and watched the surviving, diminishing glory, and just as that faded from the loftiest peak, and it was night, I turned and saw the new moon opposite, within an hour of setting in the west. From all this glory, and at this elevation, my heart turned homeward, and I only wished that since dear friends could not share this here, I could be by their side, and Mont Blanc a morning's imagination only."

His impressions as to the contrast between the advantages of living in the Old and in the New World are of special interest.

"The higher charm of Europe is attributable only to her bearing on her bosom here and there some memorials of a civilization about seven or eight hundred years old. Of any visible traces of anything earlier there is nothing. All earlier is of the ancient life, is in books, and may be appropriated by us, as well as by her, under God, and by proper helps. The gathering of that eight hundred years, however, collected and held here, — libraries, art, famous places, educational spectacles of architecture, picture, statue, gardening, fountains, — are rich, rich, and some of them we can never have nor use.

"On how many European minds, in a generation, is felt educationally the influence of that large body of spectacles specifically European, and which can never be transferred? Recollect, first, that all her books we can have among us permanently. All her history we can read and know, therefore, and all things printed. What remains? What that can never be transferred? Picture, statue, building, grounds; beyond and above, *a spirit of the place;* whatsoever and all which comes from living in and visiting memorable places. How many in Europe are influenced, and how, by this last? The recorded history affects us as it does them. In which hemisphere would an imaginative and speculative mind most enjoy itself? In America, land of hope! liberty, — Utopia sobered, realized, to be fitted according to an idea, with occasional visits to this picture-gallery and museum, occasional studies here of the objects we can't have; or here, under an inflexible realization, inequalities of condition, rank, force, property, *tribute* to the Past, — the Past!!!

"Looking to classes: 1st. The *vast mass* is happier and better *in America,* is worth more, rises higher, is freer; its standard of culture and life higher. 2. Property-holders are as scarce. 3. The class of wealth, taste, social refinement, and genius, — how with them?

" Mem. The enjoyment of an American of refined tastes and a spirit of love of man is as high
as that of a European of the same class. He has
all but what visits will give him, and he has what
no visits can give the other.

" What one human being, not of a privileged
class, is better off in Europe than he would be
in America? Possibly a mere scholar, or student
of art, seeking learning or taste for itself, to accomplish himself. But the question is, if in any
case, high and low, the same rate of mind, and
the same kind of mind, may not be as happy in
America as in Europe. It must modify its aims
and sources somewhat, live out of itself, seek to
do good, educate others. It may acquire less,
teach more; suck into its veins less nutriment,
less essence, less perception of beauty, less relish
of it (this I doubt), but diffuse it more.

" What is it worth to live among all that I have
seen? I think access to the books and works of
art is all. There is no natural beauty thus far
beyond ours, — and a storied country, storied of
battles and blood, — is that an educational influence?"

Those who have thought that Mr. Choate had
little taste for music may wish that they had
stood by him in the Cathedral of Strasburg,
" where mass was performing, and a glorious

organ was filling that unbounded interior with the grandest and the sweetest of music, through whose pauses you heard the muttered voice of the priest, and the chanting of a choir wholly out of sight." Or, at St. Denis, where "The organ was played just enough to show what oceans and firmaments full of harmony are there accumulated. Some drops, some rivulets, some grandest peals we heard, identifying it, and creating longings for more."

Mr. Choate had a fervent admiration for Sir Walter Scott. In his lecture on our "Obligations to the British Poets," delivered in 1856, he defends Scott and his novels against one of the detractors. The following will illustrate the moderate tone which was peculiar to Mr. Choate when indulging in controversy. He says, "It has pleased Mr. Thomas Carlyle to record of these novels, — 'The sick heart will find no healing here, the darkly struggling heart no guidance, the heroic that is in all men no divine, awakening voice.' These be sonorous words assuredly. In one sense I am afraid that is true of any and all mere romantic literature. As disparagement of Scott, it is a simple absurdity of injustice. In any adequate sense of these expressions, Homer and Shakespeare must answer, 'These are not mine to give.' To heal that sickness, to pour that light on that gloom, to awaken that sleep of greatness in the soul in the highest sense, far other provision is demanded, and is given. In the old, old time, — Hebrew, Pagan, — some found it in the very voice of God; some in the visits of the angel; some in a pilgrimage to the beautiful Jerusalem; some in the message of the prophet, till that succession had its close; some sought it rather than found it, like Socrates, like Plato, like Cicero, like Cato, in the thoughts of their own and other mighty minds turned to the direct search of truth, in the philosophy of speculation, in the philosophy of duty, in the practice of public life. To us only, and at last, is given the true light. For us only is the great Physician provided. In our ears, in theirs whose testimony we assuredly believe, the divine, awakening voice has been articulately and first spoken. In this sense, what he says would be true of Homer, Shakespeare, Dante, Milton, but no more true of Scott than of Goethe or Schiller. Neither is, or gives, religion to the soul, if it is that of which he speaks. But if this is not his meaning, — and I suppose it is not, if he means to say that by the same general treatment, by the same form of suffering humanity by which Homer, Virgil, Dante, Shakespeare heal the sick heart, give light to the darkened eye, and guidance to blundering feet, and kindle the heroic in man to life, — if he means to say that as they have done it he has not in kind, in supreme degree, — let the millions whose hours of unrest, anguish, and fear he has charmed away, to the darkness of whose desponding he has given light, to whose sentiments of honor, duty, courage, truth, manliness, he has given help, — let *them* gather around the capitol and answer for themselves and him. I am afraid that that Delphic and glorious Madame de Staël knew sickness of the heart in a sense and with a depth too true only ; and she had, with other consolation, the fisherman's funeral, in the ' Antiquary,' read to her on her death-bed ; as Charles Fox had the kindred but unequal sketches of Crabbe's ' Village ' read on his.

" And so of this complaint, that the heroic in man finds here no divine, awakening voice. If by this heroic in man he means what — assuming religious traits out of the question — we who speak the tongue of England and hold the ethics of Plato, of Cicero, of Jeremy Taylor, and Edmund Burke should understand, — religion now out of the question — that sense of obligation, pursuing us ever, omnipresent like the Deity, ever proclaiming that the duties of life are more than life, — that principle of honor that feels a stain like a wound, — that courage that fears God and knows no other fear, that dares do all that may become a man, — truth on the lips and in the inward parts, — that love of our own native land, comprehensive and full love, the absence of which makes even the superb art-world of Goethe dreamy and epicurean, — manliness, equal to all offices of war or peace, above jealousy, above injustice — if this is the heroic, and if by the divine awakening voice he meant that artistic and literary culture fitted to develop and train this quality, that voice is Scott's.

" I will not compare him with Carlyle's Goethe or even Schiller, or any other idol on the Olympus of his worship; that were flippant and indecorous, nor within my competence. But who and where, in any literature, in any walk of genius, has sketched a character, imagined a situation, conceived an austerity of glorified suffering, better adapted to awaken all of the heroic in man or woman that it is fit to awaken, than Rebecca in act to leap from the dizzy verge of the parapet of the castle to escape the Templar, or awaiting the bitterness of death in the list of Templestowe and rejecting the championship of her admirer? — or than Jeanie Deans refusing an untruth to save her innocent sister's life and then walking to London to plead for her before the Queen, — and so pleading? — than Macbriar in that group of Cov-

enanters in " Old Mortality " in presence of the
Privy Council confessing for himself, whom terror,
whom torture could not move to the betrayal of another; accepting sentence of death, after anguish
unimaginable, his face radiant with joy; a trial of
manhood and trust, a sublimity of trial, a manifestation of the heroic to which the self-sacrifice
of a Leonidas and his three hundred was but a
wild and glad revelry, — a march to the ' Dorian
music of flutes and soft recorders,' — a crowning,
after the holiday contention of the games, with
all of glory a Greek could covet or conceive ? "

In an address on the " Intervention of the New
World in the Affairs of the Old," delivered in
1852, Mr. Choate thus speaks of Kossuth. I cite
this passage as illustrative of his style; also because Kossuth's visit to us is of interest as matter
of history, and is nowhere else so fitly given.

" On the fifth day of the last December, there
came to this land a man of alien blood, of foreign
and unfamiliar habit, costume, and accent; yet
the most eloquent of speech according to his
mode, — the most eloquent by his history and
circumstances, — the most eloquent by his mission
and topics, whom the world has, for many ages,
seen; and began, among us a brief sojourn, —
began, say rather, a brief and strange, eventful
pilgrimage, which is just now concluded. Imper-

fect in his mastery of our tongue, — he took his
first lessons in the little room over the barrack-
gate of Buda, a few months before, — his only
practice in it had been a few speeches to quite
uncritical audiences in Southampton, in Birming-
ham, Manchester, and Guildhall; bred in a school
of taste and general culture with which our An-
glo - Saxon training has little affinity and little
sympathy; the representative and impersonation,
though not, I believe, the native child, of a race
from the East, planted some centuries ago in Europe, but Oriental still as ever, in all but its Christianity; the pleader of a cause in which we might
seem to be as little concerned as in the story of
the lone Pelops or that of Troy divine, coming
before us *even such* — that silver voice, that sad,
abstracted eye, before which one image seemed
alone to hover, one procession to be passing, the
fallen Hungary — the ' unnamed demigods,' her
thousands of devoted sons; that earnest and full
soul, laboring with one emotion, has held thousands and thousands of all degrees of suscepti-
bility; the coldness and self-control of the East,
the more spontaneous sympathies of the West,
the masses in numbers without number, women,
scholars, our greatest names in civil places, by the
seashore, in banquet halls, in halls of legislation,
among the memories of Bunker Hill, — every-

where he has held all, with a charm as absolute as that with which the Ancient Mariner kept back the bridal guest after the music of the marriage feast had begun.

"The tribute of tears and applaudings; the tribute of sympathy and of thoughts too deep for applaudings, too deep for tears, have attested his sway. For the first time since the transcendent genius of Demosthenes strove with the downward age of Greece; or since the prophets of Israel announced — each tone of the hymn grander, sadder, than before — the successive footfalls of the approaching Assyrian beneath whose spear the Law should cease and the vision be seen no more; our ears, our hearts, have drunk the sweetest, most mournful, most awful of the words which man may ever utter, or may ever hear — the eloquence of an expiring nation.

"For of all this tide of speech, flowing without ebb, there was one source only. To one note only was the harp of this enchantment strung. It was an appeal not to the interests, not to the reason, not to the prudence, not to the justice, not to the instructed conscience of America and England; but to the mere emotion of sympathy for a single family of man oppressed by another — contending to be free, cloven down on the field, yet again erect; her body dead, her spirit incapable to die;

the victim of treachery; the victim of power; the
victim of intervention; yet breathing, singing,
lingering, dying, hoping, through all the pain, the
bliss of an *agony of glory!* For this perishing·
nation — not one inhabitant of which we ever
saw; on whose territory we had never set a foot;
whose books we had never read; to whose ports
we never traded; not belonging in an exact sense
to the circle of independent states; a province,
rather, of an empire which alone is known to
international law and to our own diplomacy; for
this nation he sought pity, the intervention, the
armed intervention, the material aid of pity; and
if his audiences could have had their will, he
would have obtained it, without mixture or measure, to his heart's content.

"When shall we be quite certain again that the
lyre of Orpheus did not kindle the savage nature to a transient discourse of reason, — did not
suspend the labors and charm the pains of the
damned, — did not lay the keeper of the grave
asleep, and win back Eurydice from the world
beyond the river, to the warm upper air?

"And now that this pilgrimage of romance is
ended, the harp hushed, the minstrel gone, let us
pause a moment and attend to the lessons and
gather up the uses of the unaccustomed performance."

A few pages, taken from Mr. Choate's eulogy of Daniel Webster, happily illustrate the best and most endearing elements of his nature. In no other relation, no other phase or feature of his life and character, however brilliant and imposing, — not even as depicted by Mr. Choate, — does Webster appear more worthy of remembrance. Yet, how clear, simple, compact, with what wealth of thought and economy of words, with what freedom from rhetorical ornament, is the revelation made!

" There must be added next, the element of an impressive character, inspiring regard, trust, and admiration, not unmingled with love. It had, I think, intrinsically a charm such as belongs only to a good, noble, and beautiful nature. In its combination with so much fame, so much force of will, and so much intellect, it filled and fascinated the imagination and heart. It was affectionate in childhood and youth, and it was more than ever so in the few last months of his long life. It is the universal testimony that he gave to his parents, in largest measure, honor, love, obedience; that he eagerly appropriated the first means which he could command to relieve the father from the debts contracted to educate his brother and himself; that he selected his first place of professional practice that he might soothe

the coming on of his old age; that all through life he neglected no occasion — sometimes when leaning on the arm of a friend, alone, with faltering voice, sometimes in the presence of great assemblies, where the tide of general emotion made it graceful — to express his ' affectionate veneration of him who reared and defended the log cabin in which his elder brothers and sisters were born, against savage violence and destruction, cherished all the domestic virtues beneath its roof, and, through the fire and blood of some years of Revolutionary War, shrank from no danger, no toil, no sacrifice, to serve his country, and to raise his children to a condition better than his own.'

" Equally beautiful was his love of all his kindred and of all his friends. When I hear him accused of selfishness, and a cold, bad nature, I recall him lying sleepless all night, not without tears of boyhood, conferring with Ezekiel how the darling desire of both hearts should be compassed, and he, too, admitted to the precious privileges of education; courageously pleading the cause of both brothers in the morning; prevailing by the wise and discerning affection of the mother; suspending his studies of the law, and registering deeds and teaching school to earn the means, for both, of availing themselves of the opportunity which the parental self-sacrifice had placed within their reach ; loving him through life, mourning him when dead, with a love, and a sorrow very wonderful, passing the sorrow of woman ; I recall the husband, the father of the living and of the early departed, the friend, the counselor of many years, and my heart grows too full and liquid for the refutation of words.

" His affectionate nature, craving ever friendship as well as the presence of kindred blood, diffused itself through all his private life, gave sincerity to all his hospitalities, kindness to his eye, warmth to the pressure of his hand ; made his greatness and genius unbend themsevles to the playfulness of childhood, flowed out in graceful memories indulged of the past of the dead, of incidents when life was young and promised to be happy, — gave generous sketches of his rivals, — the high contention now hidden by the handful of earth, — hours passed fifty years ago with great authors, recalled for the vernal emotions which then they made to live and revel in the soul. And from these conversations of friendship, no man — no man, old or young, went away to remember one word of profaneness, one allusion of indelicacy, one impure thought, one unbelieving suggestion ; one doubt cast on the reality of virtue, of patriotism, of enthusiasm, of the progress of man, — one doubt cast on the righteousness, or temperance, or judgment to come.

"Every one of his tastes and recreations announced the same type of character. His love of agriculture, of sports in the open air, of the outward world in starlight and storms, and sea and boundless wilderness, — partly a result of the influences of the first fourteen years of his life, perpetuated like its other affections and its other lessons of a mother's love, — the Psalms, the Bible, the stories of the wars, — partly the return of an unsophisticated and healthful nature, tiring, for a space, of the idle business of political life, its distinctions, its artificialities, to employments, to sensations which interest without agitating the universal race alike, as God has framed it, in which one feels himself only a man, fashioned from the earth, set to till it, appointed to return to it, yet made in the image of his Maker, and with a spirit that shall not die, — all displayed a man whom the most various intercourse with the world, the longest career of strife and honors, the consciousness of intellectual supremacy, the coming in of a wide fame, constantly enlarging, left, as he was at first, natural, simple, manly, genial, kind.

"I have learned by evidence, the most direct and satisfactory, that in the last months of his life, the whole affectionateness of his nature, his consideration of others, his gentleness, his desire to make them happy and to see them happy, seemed to come out in more and more beautiful and habitual expression than ever before. The long day's public tasks were felt to be done; the cares, the uncertainties, the mental conflicts of high places were ended; and he came home to recover himself for the few years which he might still expect would be his before he should go hence to be here no more. And there, I am assured and fully believe, no unbecoming regrets pursued him; no discontent, as for injustice suffered or expectations unfulfilled; no self-reproach for anything done or anything omitted by himself; no irritation, no peevishness unworthy of his noble nature; but instead, love and hope for his country, when she became the subject of conversation, and for all around him, the dearest and most indifferent, for all breathing things about him, the overflow of the kindest heart growing in gentleness and benevolence; paternal, patriarchal affections seeming to become more natural, warm, and communicative every hour. Softer and yet brighter grew the tints on the sky of parting day; and the last lingering rays, more even than the glories of noon, announced how divine was the source from which they proceeded; how incapable to be quenched; how certain to rise on a morning which no night should follow.

" Such a character was made to be loved. It was loved. Those who knew and saw it in its hour of calm — those who could repose on that soft green — loved him. His plain neighbors loved him; and one said, when he was laid in his grave, ' How lonesome the world seems!' Educated young men loved him. The ministers of the gospel, the general intelligence of the country, the masses afar off loved him. True, they had not found in his speeches, read by millions, so much adulation of the people; so much of the music which robs the public reason of itself; so many phrases of humanity and philanthropy; and some had told them he was lofty and cold, — solitary in his greatness; but every year they came nearer and nearer to him, and, as they came nearer, they loved him better; they heard how tender the son had been, the husband, the brother, the father, the friend, and neighbor; that he was plain, simple, natural, generous, hospitable, — the heart larger than the brain; that he loved little children and reverenced God, the Scriptures, the Sabbath day, the Constitution, and the law, — and their hearts clave unto him. More truly of him than even of the great naval darling of England might it be said, that ' His presence would set the

church-bells ringing, and give school-boys a holiday, — would bring children from school and old
men from the chimney-corner to gaze on him ere
he died.' The great and unavailing lamentation
first revealed the deep place he had in the hearts
of his countrymen."

CHAPTER IX.

Preparation for Service in Congress. — Rank and Acceptance.
— Lost Speeches. — Annexation of Texas. — The Tariff. —
Home Industry and the Mechanical Arts. — Progress. —
Concurrent Views of Other Statesmen.

THE minuteness of investigation shown in Mr.
Choate's professional and classical studies entered
into his preparatory work as a statesman. On his
election to the lower House of Congress in 1830,
and to the Senate in 1841, he took up critically
the great questions which it was expected might
require legislative attention. Few members, certainly no new members, could have trusted more
safely to the information already possessed, and
to the inspirations of the hour in debate. But a
conscientious regard for the duties to be discharged, and a cultivated indisposition to take
that for granted which could be proved, led him
to an extended course of study, and to its faithful
continuance as other questions afterwards arose.

The services of Mr. Choate in the Senate would
seem to have been more important than those
rendered in the House of Representatives. This
may be owing, in part, to the nature of the sub-

jects considered, and, in part, to the better preservation of his later speeches. But many of his
arguments were not preserved. The reiterated request in the "Globe," that members would write
out their speeches, had little effect on him. The
Hon. Alexander H. Stephens recently wrote out
from memory the concluding part of one of Mr.
Choate's speeches which had not appeared in the
"Globe." Professor Brown, always exact in his
statements, says, "Those who heard Mr. Choate's
speech in favor of the confirmation of Mr. Everett as Minister to England considered it one of
the most brilliant ever delivered within the Senate chamber." So, too, one of the regents of
the Smithsonian Institution said that Mr. Choate's
speech before the Board against a departure from
the library-plan "was the most beautiful that
ever fell from human lips." Yet we have nothing of these speeches, nothing of some other
speeches equally commended.

We may well treasure up what remains. His
contributions to the discussion of questions, then
of grave public concern, are so rich and generous,
rise so far "above the penury of mere debate,"
that they may be read with interest by those
whose preconceived notions differ from his views,
and with gratitude by those who find their cherished opinions illustrated and confirmed.

I have to confess that my early estimate of Mr. Choate as a statesman has kindled into admiration with the occasional reading of the debates in which he took part. It was not merely, or mainly, that from the day he was first heard in either House he was regarded as worthy of a place in the front rank of the distinguished men with whom he served; that no imperious member of either party saw in him the mere lawyer, indulging in a style peculiar to another forum, and so, after the manner of Pitt towards Erskine, disdained to reply; that, under his mode of treatment, subjects worn out in debate awakened new interest; or that his views were presented with such zeal and power as to encourage his friends, with such grace and courtesy as almost to persuade his opponents; but, also and especially, that he possessed and exemplified the sagacity, prudence, judgment, and continence proper to the statesman, and the devotion which proved the strength and the purity of his patriotism.

He went into the Senate with reluctance; he withdrew from it as soon as he could do so consistently. But, during his short term of service, questions of special difficulty and importance came up for consideration. Without undertaking to follow him throughout his labors, — the reports before me forbid that, and many of the subjects have long been at rest, — I propose to notice his attitude in respect to some of the topics to which he gave special attention.

It may be observed that those who think that Mr. Choate erred in opposing the annexation of Texas should consider his position at the time, and seek to distinguish what might possibly have been foreseen from what could be learned only by a later experience. If he erred, it is proper to remember that Henry Clay, Martin Van Buren, and Silas Wright erred with him. His views were clouded and his zeal inflamed by no personal considerations. He sought no promotion, could suffer no loss but such as the country might also suffer. Mr. Van Buren failed to receive a nomination for the presidential office and Mr. Clay lost his chance of an election to it by opposing that annexation. Mr. Wright was constrained to decline a nomination for the office of vice-president, as its acceptance would have implied a difference of opinion between his friend, Mr. Van Buren, and himself on that subject. In his " Thirty Years' View," Mr. Benton attempts to show that, by the management of the friends of annexation, Mr. Webster was forced to retire from the cabinet of President Tyler, as his presence there was a hindrance to the negotiation. That those statesmen had considered the question with great solicitude none

can doubt. To finite apprehension, the evils to
flow from that scheme, — war with Mexico, and
a larger voluntary surrender to slavery, — were
imminent and certain; the benefits, — Texas and
California, free and contributing to the wealth
and stability of the Republic, — were remote and
uncertain.

An equal degree of respect, and perhaps on
more specific grounds, is due to Mr. Choate's position on the question of protecting American labor. The expedient of providing the means necessary to defray the expenses of the government
by imposing duties on imports, a mode of indirect
taxation, having been adopted at an early day,
questions as to the rates of duties to be fixed
with regard to the wants of the government, actual and prospective, and to the encouragement or
protection of our manufacturers, vexed the national councils under almost every administration.
That was due to the fact that, for either purpose,
the rate of duties fluctuated with the change of
circumstances, and to the further fact that many
able and judicious men regarded legislation designed to stimulate special branches of industry
into artificial activity as neither politic nor wise.

In March, 1842, Mr. Choate addressed an argument to the Senate to show that, in assessing the
duties which were to yield the desired income,

Congress could discriminate for the protection of labor. He faithfully collated the proofs drawn from many sources, and built up and fortified an argument, legal and historical, which those who agree with him can find little occasion to extend or modify. But, going beyond the mere question of power, he sought, by subtile and delicate inferences and suggestions, to reconcile his hearers to the policy of protection. He appealed to the past, to the maxims of statesmen, and gracefully referred to the opinion of Mr. Madison.

It is not to be denied that our commerce with foreign nations may be regulated by imposing such restraints upon the products of foreign labor brought here as may promote our interests. That power has often been exercised. All that remained, after Mr. Choate's exposition, was the inquiry whether the policy which had led to the exertion of that power for the encouragement of our manufacturers should be continued, and, if so, to what extent.

Mr. Choate took up that question, in some of its aspects, in April, 1844, when opposing a bill hostile to the theory of protection.[1] As a friend of that theory, he was on the defensive; and it must be assumed that he spoke from his knowledge of our manufacturing interests, and of the

[1] *Globe*, Appendix, p. 641.

consequences which might flow from a sudden withdrawal of the protection given them. He opened his argument by claiming that the matter of protection was not an open question except as to the details, the rates of duties to be imposed; declaring, however, that " When the lights of a full and fair experience prescribe the change of a duty, it is to be changed." He says, " And why not open ? Because, Sir, I find such a system of protection in operation *de jure* and *de facto* to-day ; because I know perfectly well, or all our annals are a dream and a lie, that the American people established the Constitution and the Union very much to insure the maintenance of such a system ; because it has been slowly maturing for years ; because so large a concurrence of patriotism, intelligence, and experience has helped to build it up ; because, whether it was wise or unwise to introduce such a system by direct legislation at first, it would be supreme madness now, now when the first stages are past, when the evil, if any there ever was, is all done, and the compensations of good are just fairly commencing, when capital has taken this direction, when prices are brought down, skill learned, habits formed, machinery accumulated, and the whole scheme of things accommodated to it, when its propitious influence is felt palpably upon agriculture, upon the comfort and the standing of labor, upon domestic and foreign trade, upon defense, upon independence, — it would be supreme madness, worthy only of a government nodding to its fall, now to overturn it; because, finally, it is the daily labor and the daily bread of men, women, and children, our countrymen and countrywomen, whom we reckon by millions."

He then goes into particulars, and amplifies the proofs, the inference, the illustrations, but only to establish the thesis laid down at the opening of his speech. A few specific references may suffice to show how, by appeals to the rise and progress of our manufactures, and to the history of our legislation, he seeks to defeat the bill in question.

After having shown that the people, from the first, had sought to be relieved from competition with foreign labor, that the early acts of Congress granted that protection, according to the condition of our manufacturing interests, he says, " And now we are prepared to compare or to contrast with this the second system — the existing system — that which began in 1816 and was matured in 1824 and 1828. Sir, it is exactly the system of 1789, accommodated to the altered circumstances of the nation and the world. The statesmen of the last period followed in the very footsteps of their fathers. The Congress of 1789 found many manfacturing and mechanical arts starting to life, and soliciting to be protected. The Congress of 1816 and that of 1824 found families and groups and classes of manufacturing and mechanical arts, far more numerous, far more valuable, far more sensible also, and with more urgent claims, soliciting protection. In the interval between 1789 and 1816, this whole enterprise had not only immensely enhanced its value but had totally changed its nature. Instead of a few plain, hardy, coarse, simple, household employments, it had become a various, refined, sensitive industry — demanding associated capital, skill long and highly trained, costly and improving machinery — more precious, but presenting a far broader mark to the slings and arrows of fortune, to hostility, to change, to the hotter foreign competitions which its growth is sure to provoke. Now you all praise the husbandry of 1789, which so carefully guarded the few blades just timidly peeping forth in the rain and sunshine of that April day, hardly worth the treading down; will you depreciate the husbandry of 1824, which, with the same solicitude, but at the expense of a higher wall, guarded the grain, then half-grown, and evincing what the harvest was to be ? "

By way of showing the influence of the protective policy, and how, gradually thus fostered, our manufactures had crept into existence, he states some interesting facts drawn from the highest authority. Thus, that in 1789 there was not a cotton spindle in the United States; that in 1805 and 1806 there were only 5,000; in 1810, 80,000; that the first cotton mill was erected in Rhode Island in 1791, another in 1795, and two more in Massachusetts in 1803–04; and that during the next three years ten more were erected or commenced in Rhode Island, and one in Connecticut.

In his desire to elevate his subject above the mere counting of factories and spindles, he says, "The real truth is, Sir, that manufacturing and mechanical and commercial industry is 'the prolific source of democratic feeling.' Of the two great elements which must be combined in all greatness of national character and national destiny — permanence and progression — these employments stimulate the latter; agriculture contributes to the former. They are of those acting and counteracting, opposing yet not discordant, powers, from whose reciprocal struggle is drawn out the harmony of the universe."

He invokes the prudence of the Senate thus: "Sir, let me respectfully recommend cautious and delicate handling of these interests. Vast, various, prosperous as they are, a breath can unmake them as a breath has made. This bill strikes a blow, the extent, degree, and nature of whose injurious effects no man can foresee or limit or cure. That which you certainly do mean to do involves consequences which you certainly do not mean. You begin by saying profits are too high. Then you propose to reduce profits. You begin by saying more foreign manufactures must be imported, because you propose to increase revenue by reducing duties. This demands, of course, enlarged importation. To that extent, to a new and undefined extent, you displace, disturb, diminish the domestic market of your own manufactures. But can you really strike down the general profits and break up the actual market of American labor and yet leave it prosperous, rewarded, and contented ? "

I have thought that, if called upon to consider the policy of such legislation when first proposed, Mr. Choate would not have favored the theory of protection. The conservative character of his mind, his respect for principles, for system, as contrasted with mere expedients, might have held him in restraint. But his relation to the matter came later and in quite another form. As he looked back, he saw that the legislation which began and continued that policy had been favored by statesmen whose wisdom and fidelity he had always held in reverence. As he looked round him he saw that the growth of the mechanic arts was the life of New England, that rough and barren places and lonely waterfalls had been made profitable, and that the inventive genius of the people had been urged forward to countless improvements. So it was that, in representing his State and in studying the interests of other States, he had been brought to believe that the arts, thus nursed into life, should be preserved. He accepted the reasons for protecting them given by statesmen of 1816 and 1824, and declared that, " after the evil is done and the good is beginning," it would be unwise to let them die.

He finds consolation in the fact that his own State had not helped to adopt protection. Thus he says to Senators, " Consider that Massachusetts never made a protective tariff; that she took no leading or influential part in 1816 ; that she opposed that of 1824 with almost her entire vote, and with great zeal and ability ; that she voted against that of 1828 ; that she has done nothing but just to stay where you placed her." Then, as a few passages may show, he clings with pride, to the further credit due to his State. " Certainly, Sir, we are very much in these employments. You may thank yourselves for that. And is it not

an excellent thing for you that we are ? Are we
not a very much more useful member of the part-
nership, more useful to the other partners, than
we could be without ? Is it not a good, honest,
genial, social, ' live and let live ' sort of business
you have driven us into?" "Is it nothing that we
take and consume, within that single State, an annual amount of more than forty millions of dollars
of your productions?" "Is it not a truly national
business which we pursue; national in the surface
it spreads over; national in the good it does; national in the affections it generates?" " Yes, Sir!
Manufacturers and mechanics are unionists by profession; unionists by necessity; unionists always.
Learn to know your friends. The time may come
when you will need them."

In resisting the reduction of duties in so far as
the changes might have brought swift and certain
ruin to manufacturers who had been making large
investments on the faith of what seemed to be the
policy of our government, Mr. Choate was invok-
ing the spirit of deliberation which should attend
legislative reforms. It seems to me that many of
those who could not accept his views as to the influence of such protection upon American labor,
or as to the inherent merit of such an expedient,
would have regarded his argument with respect
if not with favor. But in practice, such protection

admits of neither stability, uniformity, nor repose. It is one of those artificial devices which, in varied forms, return to plague the inventors. When Mr. Choate claimed that the existing duties should be continued, the manufacturers may have needed that protection. They have little need of it now. What they need is a market for their commodities. The transition from one want to the other is the natural result of a policy which gave an artificial stimulus to home industry, but discouraged the exchange of the fruits of our labor for foreign products. It is quite obvious that no tariff has benefited the Southern States or helped our agricultural or commerical interests. When Mr. Choate spoke of New York as " a city which with one hand grasps the golden harvests of the West, and with the other, like Venice, espouses the everlasting sea," he indicates how necessary a liberal foreign commerce was to her prosperity. But it is well to remember that Mr. Choate was not peculiar in his views upon this subject. Under claims less urgent than those of his constituents, other distinguished statesmen have thought and voted as he did. In instances, not to be briefly enumerated, protection of specific articles has been claimed by those not friendly to the theory in its extended application. Thus, for example, Silas Wright wished the duties increased on coarse wool, Thomas H. Benton on lead and indigo. In 1842, Mr. Wright voted for a protective tariff, after having sought to amend the bill, — that being the only mode in which the government could raise the needful revenue. Mr. Benton voted for the protective tariffs of 1824, 1828, and 1832, and in the debates in 1844 declared himself willing to give protection to manufacturers. In the Congress of 1844, Henry C. Murphy gave an exposition of the principles which, as he thought, should be respected in framing a tariff.[1] He believed in a tariff for revenue, with such incidental protection as could be given alike to all sections of the country, — his conception of free trade, — and by a strong array of facts and illustrations sought to show that the existing tariff imposed higher duties on some articles used by the poor than on those used by the rich, and in several respects was sectional and oppressive.

Mr. Murphy and Mr. Choate had like views as to the spirit which should govern legislative reforms. Mr. Murphy, who was, in the usual acceptation, an anti-tariff man, says, "Onerous and unjust as the present tariff is, partial and oppressive as its operation is, I am not for breaking down, at a blow, those establishments which have been brought into existence and kept up by it;

[1] *Globe*, Appendix, p. 414.

for extreme change in laws affecting the industry of the country I hold to be frequently as unjust, both to labor and to capital, as a bad law which is stable, for they may be accommodated to it. We should, therefore, proceed in this, as in other measures of reform, gradually, and with a due regard to the interests which we have nurtured."

The imposition of duties on imports to the extent necessary to defray the expenses of the government gives protection to the manufacturers. It may, as an incident, benefit labor skilled in the mechanic arts. But the benefits do not reach the laborers who clear the forest and till the soil, who dig the canals, make the roads and bridges, open the quarries and build our cities. Such limitations must exist. But, if we have a tariff, we can say, with Mr. Choate, that when the lights of a full and fair experience prescribe the change of a duty, it is to be changed.

CHAPTER X.

Soon after Mr. Choate took his seat in the Senate, he had occasion to defend the policy of President Tyler's administration in a matter of national concern. In December, 1837, during the disturbance in Upper Canada commonly called the Mackenzie Rebellion, the provincial authorities sent over into the State of New York a band of armed men, by whom the steamer Caroline was destroyed, and our government claimed that Great Britain should make reparation. In 1841, Alexander McLeod, a British subject, was indicted in the Court of Sessions of Niagara County for the murder of Amos Durfee, and was held for trial. Great Britain demanded his liberation. Mr. Fox, the British Minister, in his notes to Mr. Forsyth, the Secretary of State in President Van Buren's administration, and to Mr. Webster, as such Sec-

retary under President Tyler, assuming that Mc-
Leod had been thus indicted and held as one of
those engaged in the destruction of the Caroline, claimed that, as that was the public act of
persons obeying the order of their superior authorities, it could not be the ground of legal proceedings against one of them; a theory rejected
by Mr. Forsyth, but accepted by Mr. Webster.

Great attention had been, and continued to be,
given to the affair of the Caroline and to the Mc-
Leod case, in both Houses of Congress. In adopt-
ing the rule of personal immunity suggested by
Mr. Fox, and by his letter instructing the Attorney-General of the United States to attend the
trial of McLeod in New York, and confer with and
advise his counsel, Mr. Webster drew down upon
himself severe and prolonged criticism. Some
able lawyers were of opinion that he had erred in
seeking to apply that rule to one in McLeod's
situation. Mr. Calhoun deliberately stated his
objections to Mr. Webster's course; Mr. Benton
fervently criticised and denounced it; and Mr.
Buchanan took an early and impressive part in
the discussion. It was in answer to Mr. Buchanan's first argument on the subject that Mr. Choate
addressed the Senate on the 11th of June, 1841.[1]

After some preliminary observations, Mr. Choate

1 *Globe*, Appendix, p. 417.

stated with precision the ground on which, and on which alone, Mr. Webster had recognized the rule in question. Thus he said, "What is the concession of the Secretary of State? Why, only and exactly this: that a soldier or sailor, — *de facto* such,— actually engaged in a military or naval enterprise of force, under the authority, in obedience to the command of his government, and keeping himself within the scope of that authority, is not guilty, as the law of nations is administered to-day, of a crime against the municipal code of the country upon which he thus helps to carry on war; that he is not punishable as for such crime by that country ; and that the responsibility rests upon his own government alone to answer, as nations answer for their crimes to their equals. That is the concession. He does not deal at all with the case of a soldier straggling away from his colors to commit a solitary and separate murder. He does not deal with the case of alleged excess of authority. He supposes him to obey the precise directions of his government, and, so doing, he declares him clothed with the personal immunity." "If you turn to the fourth page of his letter, you may see that the murder for which he supposes McLeod indicted 'was a murder alleged to have been committed in the attack,' forming an inseparable, very painful part

of the entire military violence exerted to capture
and destroy the vessel, and not succeeding it. For
the purpose of the concession, he takes as true the
express declaration of Mr. Fox, ' that the transaction on account of which Mr. McLeod has been
arrested and is to be put on his trial,' including
the homicide as an unavoidable incident in it, ' was
a public transaction conducted by Her Majesty's
government.' Such is the concession. I have the
honor to submit, first, that the concession is right
in point of international law, and then that it was
the duty of the Secretary of State to make it, and
of the government to act upon it, exactly as it
was made and acted upon."

Mr. Choate characterized this transaction as an
act of war, — informal, insolemn hostility, — and,
illustrating his subject freely, he proceeded to answer some points of special difficulty which had
been presented by Mr. Buchanan. To show that
no war need be preceded by a declaration, and
that the rule of personal exemption from liability
as for crime extends to actors in wars of the imperfect sort, reprisals or other acts of hostility, he
cited Rutherforth. That the injustice of the hostile attack does not affect the soldier's right to immunity, and that no distinction is made between
regular soldiers and volunteers, he referred to
Rutherforth and to Vattel.

Regarding Rutherforth as an authority in respect to the more modern theory, and wishing to qualify some differences between him and an older author, Mr. Choate said, " Grotius, admirable for his genius, his studies, his most enlarged and excellent spirit, lived too early to witness the full development of his own grand principles, and the accomplishment of his own philanthropic wishes. The existing law of nations has been slowly built up since his time, and to learn it we must have recourse to writers far his inferiors in capacity and learning, but fortunate in being able to record the ameliorated theory and practice of a better day."

In defending his friend, the Secretary of State. Mr. Choate was performing a delicate service. With what prudence, grace, and dignity he performed it, his principal opponent in debate appears to have been conscious. In his reply, Mr. Buchanan said, " I desire to pay a deserved compliment both to the argument of the Senator from Massachusetts, Mr. Choate, and to the feeling displayed by him throughout his remarks."

Having thus called attention to Mr. Choate's relation to the case of McLeod, I would willingly refrain from further reference to it. But as some professional interest, not perhaps well-defined, still attaches to that case, it may be well to state the ground on which, as I conceive, it should have been placed and regarded throughout.

At the time Mr. Webster wrote his note to Mr. Fox, and his instructions to the Attorney-General, this troublesome affair was before the country in two aspects; — one, as to the breach of the amicable relations existing between the two governments, a fit subject for diplomatic discussion; the other, as to the guilt of McLeod, charged with an offense against the laws of the State of New York, a question of which the courts of that State had taken cognizance. It was possible that these two offenses, apparently so unlike, might prove to be one and the same; — that charged against the prisoner merged in and inseparable from the other. But no presumption to that effect could arise. All the facts that Mr. Fox, Sir Francis Bond Head, and Colonel McNabb could lay before Mr. Webster were to the effect that the destruction of the Caroline was deemed necessary in self-defense, and was therefore within the scope of the provincial authority; that the armed men by whom the vessel was destroyed had been sent over on that service; and that the act had been approved by the home government. But whether, apart from that service, McLeod had perpetrated the crime charged, neither Mr. Fox, Governor Head, nor Colonel McNabb could say anything. Indeed, the note in which Mr. Fox told Mr. Webster that McLeod had been charged with having been engaged in the capture and destruction of the Caroline — the death of Durfee a mere incident in the attack — began with the words, " I am informed." But while the indictment against McLeod, a copy of which is before me, has counts for murder and arson, the first counts charged him with having killed Durfee " feloniously, wilfully, with malice aforethought, and with premeditated design." In each of the first counts, it is charged that the crime was committed by him in the Town and County of Niagara ; in neither of them is any reference made to the Caroline affair. It is obvious, therefore, that the information which Mr. Fox had received, and on which he stated to Mr. Webster the charge supposed to have been made against McLeod, was not correct. This error may have arisen from the fact that neither Mr. Fox nor any of those with whom he had conferred had ever read the indictment. In his correspondence, Mr. Webster had not noticed the question whether McLeod might not be guilty, quite apart from the capture of the vessel, nor had that question been suggested in the case that was laid before him. Moreover, there is reason to suppose that Webster himself had never seen that indictment. A member of Congress, a distinguished jurist and statesman, while defending Mr. Webster as warmly as Mr. Choate had done, declared that the case might become proper for a jury. Thus Mr. Caleb Cushing said, " It may be, for instance, that McLeod, if he killed Durfee, did so from private malice, and, if so, he is clearly responsible to the laws of New York for the act; and, if he did so, I cannot but think that the English government, instead of undertaking to protect him, would be glad to see him punished, and the rather if he should have sought purposes of private malice under the cover of simulated obedience to the orders of his government. It may be that these orders did not cover this fact.[1]

The case having been moved into the Supreme Court of the State of New York, and a *habeas corpus* granted by Mr. Justice Cowen, an application for the discharge of McLeod absolutely, or on his own recognizance, or by a *nolle prosequi*, was heard and denied. In his opinion, Judge Cowen considered the law of nations quite at large; and, as the two governments were at peace, no declaration of war having been made, he came to the conclusion that no rule growing out of the usages of nations could be applied to the relief of the prisoner. It must be conceded that this part of the opinion was not necessary to the decision.

[1] *Globe*, 1841, Appendix, p. 422.

But, if the rule suggested by Mr. Fox had been accepted by Justice Cowen, McLeod must still have been held for trial. In no possible view of the case could the application have been granted.

The idea that McLeod should be discharged or be allowed to go on his recognizance could not have been seriously entertained.

As the indictment was for murder, the regular practice was not even to accept bail. That is the rule now, and I trust ever will be. The instances in which bail has been taken after such indictments are exceptional, clearly distinguished by qualifying circumstances from the case of McLeod. As the Governor of the State, Mr. Seward, an able lawyer, had refused to interfere, and as the District Attorney of Niagara County and the Attorney-General of the State were before the court claiming that McLeod should be tried by a jury, a *nolle prosequi* could not have been entered. The power and the duty of the court on the *habeas corpus* were well stated in The People *vs.* Martin, 1 Park. Cr. C. 191, by the Hon. John W. Edmunds, a judge of great learning and experience. In speaking of the McLeod case, that learned judge said, " The question raised there was, whether, after indictment, the court, on *habeas corpus*, would entertain the question of guilt or innocence, and on that question the authorities had been very uniform that it would not; and for the very plain and simple reason that, as the testimony before the grand jury would not be written, and could not be looked into, the court or officer on the *habeas corpus* could not ascertain on what evidence the grand jury had acted, and could not entertain the question without receiving precisely the same testimony which the jury would be obliged to receive on the trial, and thus in fact usurping the province of the jury. Hence it has been the practice of the English courts and our own, which was followed in the McLeod case, not to look into the question of guilt or innocence on *habeas corpus* after indictment."

I have never believed that Mr. Webster wished to have McLeod liberated without a formal trial. He could not have properly moved a step in that direction without an investigation. When, on inquiry, he had learned what the terms of the indictment were, and that, as shown before Judge Cowen, Durfee had been killed when he was at some distance from the Caroline, and, possibly, without his having been engaged in resisting the attack on the vessel, Mr. Webster would have favored a formal trial, or, what would have been most becoming, declined to interfere. His friends, while approving his views on the narrow basis stated, would have admitted that a formal investigation was necessary. That question did not arise in the debate in which Mr. Choate took part, save that, in defending Mr. Webster, he lays stress, as we have seen, upon the fact that he does not deal " with the case of a soldier straggling away from his colors to commit a solitary and separate murder." But, if any argument and admonition were necessary, the observations I have cited from Mr. Cushing's speech would have been sufficient.

It is grateful to remember how happily this affair, in both of its aspects, was disposed of by the general government and by the Supreme Court of New York, each acting in its appropriate sphere, without undue and factitious interference. A few gentle words by Ashburton, in the tone of national regret, were accepted in satisfaction for the forcible intrusion upon our territory ; and, the venue in the McLeod case having been changed to Oneida County, he was tried before Judge Gridley and a jury, and was acquitted.

The testimony against him was as to his silly and repeated boast that he had helped to destroy the Caroline, and " had finished Durfee." But it appeared that McLeod was not one of the party sent over to capture the vessel, and that he was not in the State of New York at the time Durfee was killed. The proof to establish the *alibi* was clear and conclusive.

After the excitement caused by that case had subsided, the power of the United States court was extended by the Remedial Justice Bill, passed July 7, 1842. The purpose was to authorize the removal from the state courts, at an. early stage of an accusation, cases like that of McLeod, and to give to the federal courts power to inquire into contentions likely to create international complications. The measure was just and wise. Mr. Choate gave it his earnest support. He thus stated the practice· under the bill: " The national tribunals interpose so far only as to determine whether the laws of nations entitle the prisoner to his discharge. If they do, he is discharged; if not, whatever the evidence or the deficiency of evidence against him, he is remanded to the court of the State for general trial."

It may be observed that had this law and practice been in full force before the charge against McLeod was made, and had the first counts of the indictment, to which I have referred, been omitted, and it had appeared that McLeod was one of the party ordered over by the provincial authority, and that the death of Durfee occurred as an unavoidable incident in the capture of the Caroline, the prisoner might have been released; but, with the case as it actually existed, McLeod could have had no relief under the Remedial Bill.

Other subjects of importance engaged Mr. Choate's attention while he remained in the Senate. In the discussion of some of them, he took a leading part. Of his three speeches relating to the Oregon Territory, one only has been preserved. It is conciliatory in spirit and of commanding ability. He contributed largely to the confirmation of the treaty between this government and Great Britain, which had been negotiated by Mr. Webster and Lord Ashburton; a treaty by which important claims, long held in suspense, were adjusted, and causes of offense, which threatened to disturb the amicable relations of the two governments, were removed.

In common with the leading members of the Whig party, Mr. Choate was in favor of creating a national bank. It seems probable that if the President, Mr. Harrison, had survived, such an institution would have been established. But upon his death on the 4th of April, 1841, Mr. Tyler became President. When he was chosen Vice-President, it was known that, on constitutional grounds, he was opposed to such a bank. As might have been expected, he held to that opinion.

In the special session of 1841, efforts were

made to create such a bank — a Fiscal Agency — and notably upon a plan which had been reported by the Secretary of the Treasury. To the bill, founded on that plan, an amendment was proposed to the effect that the assent of a State should be obtained before establishing branches of the bank therein. Mr. Choate supported the amendment in a speech [1] from which I take some extracts. He says, " I do not vote for the bill from any doubt of the constitutional power of Congress to establish branches all over the States, possessing the discounting function, directly and adversely against their united assent. I differ, in this particular, wholly from the Senator who moves the amendment. I have no more doubt of your power to make such a bank and such branches anywhere than of your power to build a post-office or a custom-house anywhere. This question for me is settled, and settled rightly. I have the honor and happiness to concur on it with all, or almost all, of our greatest names; with our national judicial tribunal, and with both the two great, original, political parties; with Washington, Hamilton, Marshall, Story, Madison, Monroe, Crawford, and with the entire Republican administration and-organization of 1816 and 1817.

" But it does not follow, because we possess this

[1] *Globe*, Appendix, p. 355.

or any other power, that it is wise or needful, in any given case, to attempt to exert it. We may find ourselves so situated that we cannot do it if we would, for want of the concurrence of other judgments; and therefore a struggle might be as unavailing as it would be mischievous and unseemly. We may find ourselves so situated that we ought not to do it if we could. All things which are lawful are not convenient, are not practicable, are not wise, are not safe, are not kind. A sound and healing discretion, therefore, the moral coercion of irresistible circumstances, may fitly temper, and even wholly restrain, the exercise of the clearest power ever belonging to human government.

" By uniting here on this amendment, you put an effective bank in operation, to some useful and substantial extent, by the first of January. Turn now to the other alternative. Sir, if you adhere to the bill reported by the committee, I fully believe you pass no bank charter this session. I doubt whether you carry it through Congress. If you can, I do not believe you can make it a law. I have no doubt you will fail to do so. I do not enter on the reasons of my belief. The rules of orderly proceedings here, decorum, pride, regret would all prevent my doing it. I have no personal or private grounds for the conviction which holds me fast; but I judge on notorious and, to my mind, decisive indications; and I know that it is my duty to act on my belief, whether well or ill-founded, and however conjecturally derived.

" Let me say, Sir, that to administer the contested powers of the Constitution is, for those of you who believe that they exist, at all times a trust of difficulty and delicacy. I do not know that I should not venture to suggest this general direction for the performance of that grave duty. Steadily and strongly assert their existence; do not surrender them; retain them with a provident forecast, for the time may come when you will need to enforce them by the whole moral and physical strength of the Union; but do not exert them at all so long as you can, by other, less offensive expedients of wisdom, effectually secure to the people all the practical benefits which you believe they were inserted into the Constitution to secure. Thus will the Union last longest, and do most good. To exercise a contested power without necessity, on the notion of keeping up the tone of government, is not much better than tyranny, and very improvident and impolitic tyranny, too. It is turning ' extreme medicine into daily bread.' It forgets that the final end of government is not to exert restraint but to do good.

" Within this general view of the true mode

of administering contested powers, I think the measure we propose is as wise as it is conciliatory; wise, because it is conciliatory; wise, because it reconciles a strong theory of the Constitution with a discreet and kind administration of it. I desire to give the country a bank. Well, here is a mode in which I can do it. Shall I refuse to do it in that mode because I cannot at the same time and by the same operation gain a victory over the settled constitutional opinions, and show my contempt for the ancient and unappeasable jealousy and prejudices of not far from half of the American people? Shall I refuse to do it in that mode because I cannot at the same time and by the same operation win a triumph of constitutional law over political associates who agree with me on nine in ten of all the questions which divide the parties of the country; whose energies and eloquence, under many an October and many an August sun, have contributed so much to the transcendent reformation which has brought you into power?

" There is one consideration more which has had some influence in determining my vote. I confess that I think that a bank established in the manner contemplated by this amendment stands, in the actual circumstances of our time, a chance to lead a quieter and more secure life, so to speak, than a bank established by the bill. I think it worth our while to try to make, what never yet was seen, a popular national bank. Judging from the past and the present, from the last years of the last bank and the manner in which its existence was terminated, from the tone of debate and of the press, and the general indications of public opinion, I acknowledge an apprehension that such an institution, created by a direct exertion of your power, throwing off its branches without regard to the wishes or wants of the States, as judged of by themselves, and without any attempt to engage their auxiliary coöperation, diminishing the business and reducing the profits of the local banks, and exempted from their burdens, — that such an institution may not find so quiet and safe a field of operation as is desirable for usefulness and profit. I do not wish to see it standing like a fortified post on a foreign border, never wholly at peace, always assailed, always belligerent; not falling perhaps, but never safe, the nurse and the prize of unappeasable hostility. No, Sir. Even such an institution, under conceivable circumstances, it might be our duty to establish and maintain in the face of all opposition and to the last gasp. But so much evil attends such a state of things, so much insecurity, so much excitement; it would be exposed to the pelting of such a pitiless storm of the press and public speech; so many demagogues would get good livings by railing at it; so many honest men would really regard it as unconstitutional, and as dangerous to business and liberty, that it is worth an exertion to avoid it. . . . Sir, I desire to see the bank of the United States become a cherished domestic institution, reposing in the bosom of our law and of our attachments. Established by the concurrent action or on the application of the States, such might be its character. There will be a struggle on the question of admitting the discount power into the States; much good sense and much nonsense will be spoken and written; but such a struggle will be harmless and brief; and, when that is over, all is over. The States which exclude it will hardly exasperate themselves farther about it. Those which admit it will soothe themselves with the consideration that the act is their own, and that the existence of this power of the branch is a perpetual recognition of their sovereignty. Thus might it sooner cease to wear the alien, aggressive, and privileged aspect which has rendered it offensive, and become sooner blended with the mass of domestic interests, cherished by the same regards, protected by the same and by a higher law."

At the close of this speech, Mr. Choate was

interrupted by Mr. Clay, and an altercátion, questions and answers, followed. The Washington " Globe " had a full and correct report of the affair. Professor Brown gives a like account. But, in his " Recollections of Rufus Choate," Mr. Whipple has a different version. As he was not present to witness the occurrence, what is said in his " Recollections " to the prejudice of Mr. Choate may be allowed to pass without correction.

In stating his belief that the bill, as reported, would not become a law, Mr. Choate had in view the well-known opinion of President Tyler. That is obvious. He could not with propriety refer directly to that opinion, and says, " Decorum, pride, regret, would all prevent my doing it." Regret for what? Regret for the fact that the President was, as everybody knew, opposed to a national bank. So he judges on what he calls *notorious indications.* What Mr. Choate said would not support the opinion that he had conferred with the President or the Secretary of State on the subject. He stated his own convictions, his right to act upon them, " however conjecturally derived." There was, therefore, nothing to justify the imputation implied in the questions put by Mr. Clay. That Mr. Choate did not lose his temper or self-possession is evident from his last replies to Mr. Clay's demands : —

(1.) " Sir, I insist on my right to explain what I did say, in my own words;" and (2.) "He will have to take the answer as I choose to give it." That Mr. Clay was utterly wrong appears from the fact that the next morning, in the Senate chamber, he made an explanation in the nature of an apology.

Mr. Choate's argument in support of the amendment to the bill was wise and conciliatory. A bank thus created would have been, in a sense, a state institution, its character utterly unlike that of the old United States Bank. His argument, so moderate in tone, so persuasive, would almost lead us to think well of such an agency; to think as well of it as we can of our present national banks.

13

CHAPTER XI.

A FEW words of explanation may be due to the
reader who regrets that a more minute delinea-
tion of Mr. Choate's career as statesman has not
been given. Many of the subjects in the discussion of which he took part in the lower House,
and in the Senate, have lost their significance, or
have become familiar in history. Many of his
speeches have not been preserved, and we cannot, from mere hearsay, outline or estimate the
arguments which gave weight and attraction to
them. His published efforts are widely read,
and he who reads them carefully, catching their
spirit and tone, may claim to know him better
than he who is familiar with the mere acts and
incidents of his life. It has, therefore, seemed

to be sufficient for the present purpose to refer in general terms to the course pursued by him in Congress, and to.call attention to his treatment of some subjects of importance.

In view of Mr. Choate's usefulness in his profession, and of his love of home-life and quiet study, some may regret that he was ever called into the legislative councils. His term in both Houses of Congress, little more than six years, was long enough to impose great sacrifices, but not long enough to secure the highest rewards. No doubt there were some compensations. New channels for exertion were opened to him, and he had the satisfaction of discussing some of the vexed questions of the day before deliberative bodies composed of men of great political sagacity and experience. He must have highly valued the new friends who were thus drawn to him, some of whom ever held him in close and loving remembrance. But to enable a member of either House, whatever be his gifts and attainments, to achieve national fame, and become a vital presence in the memory of the people, he must remain in the service long enough to assume special relations to a great variety of measures of public interest. The mention of such measures would thereafter recall the name of the member, the mention of the name recall the subjects with which he was identified. Such has been the inheritance of Clay, of Webster, of Sumner, of Benton, whose terms ranged from fourteen to thirty years.

It may be inferred that such honors sat lightly on Mr. Choate, inasmuch as he retired from the Senate before the term for which he had been elected had expired, that he might resume with greater freedom his practice in the courts. Indeed, honors and distinctions which he could have gracefully accepted, but which would have changed his relations to the law, were not desired by him. Thus it was that his friends sought in vain to induce him to accept the position, informally tendered, of professor in the Cambridge Law School, a place made illustrious by the services of Judge Story. So, also, he declined the office of judge of the Supreme Court of Massachusetts, offered him by Governor Briggs; and the yet higher distinction of justice of the Supreme Court of the nation, as successor of Judge Woodbury.

I have thought that Mr. Choate had a modest estimate of his own powers. In the trial and argument of causes, he had had no occasion to doubt his ability to perform his whole duty. But he may not have been satisfied that he could in equal degree discharge his duties as judge. The notion prevailed in the profession, and perhaps was credited by him, that, wanting the judicial temperament, the greatest advocate, whose modes of thought and of reasoning peculiar to the bar could not be easily qualified, might not be a great judge. He must have regarded the late Benjamin R. Curtis as an exception to that theory, since he favored his appointment as justice of the Supreme Court, the place Mr. Choate himself might have accepted. He seldom erred in estimating the qualities of other minds, and did not err in this instance; the great advocate became preëminent as a judge.

But there were serious objections to Mr. Choate's acceptance of judicial office. By years of study, devotion, and work suited to his taste and genius, he had secured a position and an income that might have satisfied the ambition of almost any man. It would have required a great effort to cast aside the robes he had with honor worn so long. In that service, without being hard or exacting, without wronging any man, he had secured the means necessary to support his family in a manner suited to his position, to educate his children, to collect the books he loved, to promote the interests of schools and of moral and literary associations, and, in a generous spirit, to relieve the wants of others, — even of those who had no claims upon him. But it remained for him to lay up more securely a competence for his family. To that end he must continue his professional work. He did so until his desires would seem to have been fulfilled.

The qualities of Mr. Choate's nature, his habits, the incentives which moved him, and the principles which he cherished have been illustrated by my correspondents. From first to last he appears to have been true to his own nature. Early in life he saw his vocation, and, without faltering or repining, accepted it, — the representative of those who, being dumb, need an advocate. Had he been proud, austere, or imperious in tone and manner, no one would have wondered; but he was neither. In his courtesy to his brethren at the bar, in his kindness to his juniors, — too sovereign to seem like condescension, — in his fidelity to his clients, in his genial spirit and sweetness of temper, in his freedom from egotism, and in his love of study and submission to labor, he gave grace and dignity to a weary and a useful life. What more could he do to perfect a character which the student may regard as an example? What more to inspire us with love and gratitude?

Mr. Choate continued his professional work after his physical strength had begun to fail. He was

before the Supreme Court, in Gage *vs.* Tudor, in
March, 1859. The next month he attended at
chambers on a mere motion. Later in the month,
and at Salem, he took part in a contention as to
the validity of a will, but was not able to remain
in court until the case had been fully heard.[1] We
are told that he never went to his office again.

I have few words to add. I put aside letters,
in which friends have given many particulars as
to his sufferings for some weeks after he had left
the court for the last time. As I am not writing
the life of Mr. Choate in detail, I spare myself
and the reader the pain of such recitals. It is
grateful, however, to learn that, to the last, his
mind was clear and active; that the cheerfulness
which had been a sovereign trait of his character remained; and that the lessons — fragments
of favorite authors — which his daughters and
his son read to him, were heard with a lively interest, the old interest, and were soothing to his
spirit.

After much consideration, and upon medical
advice, he undertook a voyage to Europe to improve his health. But, alas! it was too late. He
left Boston on the Europa, on the 29th of June.
Not being able to continue the voyage, he landed

---

[1] My friend, Benjamin E. Valentine, Esq., having examined the
records, assures me that this was Mr. Choate's last case.

at Halifax, where, on the 13th of July, 1859, he died.

From his studies and convictions, Rufus Choate was conservative. He had a profound regard for our organic laws. To him the Constitution was sacred, to be observed, or to be amended in the orderly methods appointed. He saw that slavery was a state institution, under the control of, and to be abolished by, the States where it existed; and that Congress had no power to touch the question whether it should be continued or not. He deprecated our feverish and fruitless discussions as to the duties of the Southern States, — our attempts to regulate, as a matter of sentiment, an evil which we could not cure or even modify. This drew down upon him the reproach of a party which claimed to represent the spirit of higher and more humane laws than those which had been, or by our instrumentality could be, enacted. Yet it cannot well be suggested that the man who is now loyal to the Constitution and to our laws is entitled to more respect than was **Mr.** Choate, who ever cherished such a spirit.

Mr. Choate sought to inspire the people with such love for the Constitution and the Union as might make secession impossible. Had he lived, he would doubtless have continued that instruction, in the hope that free men, acting faithfully and with patience, might devise means for the cure of all the evils of the body politic. I believe that, had the sentiment of the North and of the South been ripe for it, his plan would have been to purchase the freedom of the slaves. But there was no hour in his life when such a scheme could have been suggested. He foresaw the trouble which at last came, and with an anxious heart, solicitous for the preservation of the Union, gave no uncertain indication of what he would do, should he live until the day of wrath and conflict.

Edward Ellerton Pratt, Esq., gives me the substance of a conversation which he had with Mr. Choate in the summer of 1856. They were sitting on the rocks at Marblehead, and looking over the waters in which the frigate Constitution was chased by British cruisers in the war of 1812–14. Mr. Pratt says, " In speaking of that war, the question arose as to the next struggle in which this country might be engaged. Mr. Choate said, ' I shall not probably live to see it, but I fear there will ere long be a civil war between the North and the South.' I expressed my horror at such an idea, and asked how that could be possible. Said he, ' It is a very easy thing to get up such a conflict when one large section of the country, inflamed by interest, pride, and resentment, is hostile and united. We at the North, if we wished, could bring it about; so could they at the South; and the adverse feeling is getting so bitter that one side or the other may provoke the issue. If the Democrats, now about to elect Buchanan, have prudence and good temper, they can tide the trouble over for a while, perhaps until there may come a better understanding and more friendly feeling. But I fear they will not show such moderation and prudence.' Mr. Choate appeared to think it probable that within ten years a civil war would break out, and told me that it would be my duty, the duty of all, to do what was possible to maintain the Union whether war could or could not be averted."

The war came, and, when the sound of the guns at Fort Sumter awakened the North, Rufus Choate, Jr., then a young lawyer in Boston, and Joseph M. Bell, a lawyer of large reading and experience, who had married Mr. Choate's eldest daughter, entered the service; in a sense they gave their lives for the suppression of the Rebellion.

Rufus Choate, Jr., served in the war with great distinction. He was in several engagements; and, though ill at the time, took part in the battle of Cedar Mountain. His exposures brought on the neuralgia, and he was compelled to resign his commission as captain, and return home. After

MT.AUBURN, MASS

could bring it about; so ⸻ they at
and the adverse feeling ⸻ so
one side or the other ⸻ th
the Democrats, now ⸻ elect Buc
prudence and good ⸻, they ca
trouble over for ⸻, perhaps until
come a better understanding and mo
feeling. But I fear they will not show
eration and prudence.' Mr. Choate a
think it probable that within ten years
would break out, and told me that it w
duty, the duty of all, to do what ⸻
maintain the Union ⸻
not be averted."

The war came, and, when the
guns at Fort Sumter awakened ⸻
Choate, Jr., then a young lawyer in l
Joseph M. Bell, ⸻ lawyer of large r
experience, ⸻ married Mr. Cho
daughter, entered the service; in a
gave their lives for the suppression of
lion.

Rufus Choate, Jr., served in the war
distinction. He was in several engagem
though ill at the time, took part in the
Cedar Mountain. His exposures ⸻
neuralgia, and he was compelled ⸻
commission as captain, and ⸻ be

Eng'd by Geo. E. Perine from Phot

MT. AUBURN, MASS.

a long illness, he died on the 15th of January, 1866.

Major Bell was a member of General Butler's staff at New Orleans, and acted as provost judge with great acceptance. After returning to Virginia, he was stricken with paralysis while presiding over an important trial at Norfolk. After a time he was brought home. He remained an invalid until his death on the 10th of September, 1868.

By a merciful dispensation, it was thus given to those loyal and devoted men to die in the presence of loving friends. Thus also it was given to Rufus Choate himself, who had in the spirit of his life fought for the Union, to be represented in the final struggle for its preservation. Had he been alive, what more could he have done, what other sacrifice could he have offered up, for that Union and the Constitution ?

CHAPTER XII.

Rufus Choate and Lord Macaulay: a Contrast.[1]

THE double relation which distinguished men have held to other men often excites curiosity and regret. Their public life and service may be well known, their private life and character, however worthy, may remain unknown. The information is generally sought for in biographies. But the veil which separates those conditions, or states of being, may intervene even between friends, and limit or qualify the most faithful revelations. We may well be grateful, however, for delineations by writers of taste and judgment, who knew, as well as could be known, the men whose genius and character they have earnestly and lovingly sought to commemorate. Thus could Professor Brown write of Rufus Choate, and Mr. Trevelyan of Lord Macaulay.

The work by Trevelyan was necessary. It was well that something more definite and personal than had been learned from Carlisle, Arnold, and

---

[1] This paper was written before the previous chapters and for separate use.

Cockburn should be known of Macaulay. Beyond casual references, some sketches, and a few anecdotes, grown so familiar that no prudent diner-out would venture to repeat them, we knew him from his speeches and course in Parliament, his Essays and Reviews, his services in India, and from the History. But the inferences to be drawn were general; the veil behind which lay his private life remained undisturbed. As an author, he came to us after elaborate preparation, as if in state dress, and took the reading public by storm. His writings had a fascination strong enough to divert students from their lessons, the readers of romantic tales from their dissipations. At the time when he was expressing to Mr. Everett his surprise that any but "a few highly educated men" in this country were interested in his History, our wives and daughters were reading it. It seems incredible that he could have thought his work too profound or "insular in spirit" for general readers; a history which, though dealing with principles in large relations, appealed strongly to the imagination, gave the romantic side of events, and, in highly wrought and felicitous descriptions, called, from the depths of the past, forms regal in their adornment and beauty. But in calmer hours, Mr. Macaulay may have had a just estimate of his labors. He must have known

that his services in Parliament had been of less
value and importance than those of Brougham;
that he had lacked the almost prophetic apprehension, the logical precision, the harmony of
thought and expression of Edmund Burke; and
that his Essays, rich in poetic sentiment and illustration, his criticisms, more acrid to the taste than
the invectives of Junius, could not take deep root
in firm soil. But, in the retrospect, he was, no
doubt, satisfied with the policy which had led him
to seek relation with the names of some of the
men who had helped to shape history, as well as
with an interesting period of the national life of
England. In that he was wise, as the conservative element, respected by time, lies in the nature of the subject rather than in an author's
mode of treatment. Macaulay's verses will be
read, as they are the " Lays of Ancient Rome; "
his History will be known when most of his other
writings are forgotten. In the coming generations, none will care whether Croker was a bad
fellow, and ignorant of Greek; whether Barère,
when he ceased to write trifles, began to write
lies; whether Robert Montgomery was a poet or
not.

But Macaulay's strongest claim to remembrance
rests on his services in India. He thus won a
place in legal history. But for that service, we

should have no pride in the fact that he was a lawyer, and be less ready, perhaps, to recognize the resemblances and the contrasts which existed between some of his characteristics and those of Rufus Choate. Not that they had anything in common, as lawyers, save in their mastery of legal principles applied by the one in his labors in India, illustrated by the other in the labors of his life. Mr. Choate never had occasion to frame a code for a peculiar people. Mr. Macaulay, having been called to the English bar, held a short and silent flirtation with his mistress, the law, and, finding her coy and cold, gave her up. He had, indeed, one case in court and but one. There was, therefore, nothing like professional brotherhood between him and Mr. Choate. The likeness and unlikeness, material to our purpose, are to be found elsewhere.

They were fortunate in their lineage; each came of good stock. They had admirable training at home, cherished great love for those related to them by family ties, and were blessed in the return of that love. With a poetic temperament, exquisite sensibility, and a fondness for the romantic, were united loyalty to the truth, and aversion to everything like duplicity, or artifice in life and conduct. They also had great industry, devotion to study, and desire to excel. But nature, as if to perfect her work, and set these, her favorite children, quite apart from others, gave to each of them great, indeed marvelous, powers of memory. In their boyhood they became so familiar with Bunyan's Pilgrim that they could recite most of it. Later in life, they apprehended and retained the sense of what they had rapidly or casually read, and could recall the dates and the relations of events. Instances illustrative of such powers, when suddenly called into exercise, have been given by their biographers. In speaking of his knowledge of certain books, Mr. Macaulay said that if, by some miracle of Vandalism, they were destroyed off the face of the earth, he could, from memory, reproduce them. It is quite possible that Mr. Choate could have made a like boast, if he had allowed himself to speak of the extent of his own acquisitions. It appears that what he had read, and considered worthy of attention, he remembered to a remarkable extent, and could use with precision, ease, and celerity. That is clearly shown in some of his speeches delivered in the heat and pressure of debate. The powers of memory possessed by Choate and Macaulay challenge our admiration, however, not simply because they were marvelous in sudden and signal display but because of their healthy origin and growth; they were held to the last in perfect coordination with their other powers. Both were ardently devoted to classical studies, had an intimate acquaintance with the Latin and the Greek, and knew something of some other languages. They did not take up the German early in life; — Mr. Choate studied it with his daughter, Mr. Macaulay on his return voyage from India, and after his method of beginning with the Bible, which he could read without a dictionary. In some respects he was more fortunate than Mr. Choate. He had more leisure, a larger acquaintance with learned men and with society, and should have attained a higher and broader culture. He had access to many books which could not be found in this country, but was a mere reader of some works of importance, which Mr. Choate studied, and in parts translated. He wrote out his speeches, and revised them for the press, and with care treasured up his thoughts and words. Mr. Choate let his thoughts and words — many speeches and arguments which had excited unbounded enthusiasm in learned men and severe judges — go to the winds as uttered. That economy and the want of it bore their appropriate fruits. Mr. Macaulay's name became familiar in every household. Mr. Choate's merits, if not his name, would have passed out of mind, but for the zeal of his friend and biographer, who illus-

14

trated his virtues, and collected mere fragments of his works.

But, now that Mr. Trevelyan gives us the letters, diary, and journal of Macaulay, as Professor Brown had given us those of Choate — the same forms of literary labor, representing more truly than other forms the habits of thought, and modes of expression peculiar to each of them — the reader may consider their relative merits. After lingering over and seeking to compare their work, our conviction is that in the simplicity and unstudied grace of his letters, in the earnest purpose and profound study disclosed in his diary, in the descriptions, criticisms, and suggestions recorded in his Journal, in tone and spirit, in the use of clear, compact, nervous, beautiful, yet simple English, Mr. Choate appears to greater advantage than Mr. Macaulay.

Mr. Choate's suggestion, that one who would write well should write slowly, had respect to the example of some great authors — Sallust, Virgil, Tacitus — as well as to the instructions of Cicero and of Quintilian. The virtue of such deliberation was recognized by Mr. Macaulay. When the materials for his History had been collected and arranged, his task was to write two pages daily; and, in one instance, after having been engaged nineteen days on thirty pages, he was not satisfied with the character of his work. The habits of Burke, Bossuet, Gibbon, and others, in correcting their compositions, are well known. Macaulay bettered the instruction. He was constantly revising his work. Having stated in his diary the time by which the third volume of his History might be written — " rough-hewn " — he adds, " Of course the polishing and retouching will be an immense labor." Of that care and industry, great certainly, and worthy of commendation, Mr. Thackeray, with characteristic extravagance, said, " He reads twenty books to write a sentence ; he travels a hundred miles to make a line of description."

By his example, Mr. Macaulay has happily put in a protest against the free use, by English writers, of words and phrases from other languages. With reasonable success, he resisted the temptation to indulge in such quotations. That was no slight victory as, with his well-stored and active memory, such words and phrases, often laden with a delicacy and fragrance not to be retained in any translation, must have frequently occurred to him. Mr. Choate had not, in equal degree, that power of resistance. In pages of his Journal, and in some of his arguments, we do not find him using foreign words, nor need he ever have used them. But, when he did so, it was the well-accepted aphorism, the ripe fruit of ancient experience, to which he stood related as an heir, that he wished to appropriate. The maxim or precept pressing upon his mind had been so familiar that he was led to take it in its old attire, as an imperial hand might accept tribute in a foreign coin. But he applied freely, and in simple English, the teachings of the old masters. The foreign word or phrase, when used, was a mere adjunct, an additional rap of the hammer after the nail had been driven, — the argument complete without it, the terms luminous, the sense transparent. He was, therefore, always understood even by those who knew nothing of Latin or Greek. It may be inferred from the directness and ease with which he continually expressed in English the most subtle thoughts and distinctions that he never could have been conscious of anything like poverty in our language. It served him in a spirit of entire obedience. He illustrated its strength, contributed to its wealth and dignity. His pride in it would seem to have been intense, his faith in its mission unfaltering, his ideal of it akin to that perfection which Cicero may have had in view, when he extolled the discourse of an old philosopher as a river of flowing gold. Mr. Choate has left us some of the best specimens of modern English. But he had not, like Macaulay or Virgil, the leisure to give a day to the writing of two pages, or of two verses, or even to revise and polish much that he had written. Some of his best lectures and arguments were prepared in the short intervals of professional toil. The wise counsel, the profound deduction, the brilliant thought and illustration, the exceeding grace and beauty of expression, " skiey sentences, aërolites, which seem to have fallen out of Heaven," were conceived while the pen was doing its rapid work, or in the excitement of the moment when he was speaking. A friend found him in the night sitting up in bed, writing.[1] He could only thus make up for delay which other duties had imposed. He was preparing the eulogy of Daniel Webster, to be delivered at Dartmouth College. When, some days later, before an audience representing the highest culture known among us, he had set forth the life and character of Mr. Webster, according to his conception of them — the profound study and discernment, the long, patient, patriotic service, the great example, the loss " incapable of repair," the love and reverence due to his memory then and evermore, — the audience drawn into profound sympathy with the subject, strong men in tears, — Mr. Choate, as if the fervent thoughts that possessed him demanded more free utterance

[1] Edward Ellerton Pratt.

from the heart, cast aside his notes, and gave his peroration without them.

Some significant words as to the relation of our language to the Bible deserve attention. After a conversation with Lady Holland, in which she had condemned the use of such words as " constituency," " talented," " gentlemanly," Mr. Macaulay says, " I did not tell her, though I might have done so, that a person who professes to be a critic in the delicacies of the English language ought to have the Bible at his fingers' ends." Speaking of the Bible in schools, Mr. Choate says, " I would have it read not only for its authoritative revelations and its commands and exactions, obligatory yesterday, to-day, and forever, but for its English, for its literature, for its pathos, for its dim imagery, its sayings of consolation and wisdom and universal truth." [1] He read it daily. Something of the spirit of it pervades his speeches suggestively, giving tone and an air of authority to the argument. That is especially so in those speeches in which he illustrated the character of our Pilgrim Fathers, their faith and endurance, the blessings of peace, of education, and of the law. In his references to favorite authors, his admiration great, if not amounting to hero-worship, he

---

[1] See Dr. Spear's *Religion and the State*, as to the Bible in our public schools.

yet assigns them a subordinate place. Thus, in noting in his Journal his morning's study, he refers to Milton. " I read, besides my lessons, the temptation in Matthew, Mark, and Luke, in the Greek ; and then that grand and grave poem which Milton has built upon those few and awful verses — ' Paradise Regained.' I recognize and profoundly venerate the vast poetical luminary ' in this more pleasing light, shadowy.' Epic sublimity the subject excludes ; the anxious and changeful interests of the drama are not there. It suggests an occasional recollection of the book of Job, but how far short of its pathos, its agencies, its voices of human sorrow and doubt and curiosity, and its occasional, unapproachable grandeur ! Yet it is of the most sustained elegance of expression. It is strewn and burning with the pearl and gold of the richest and loftiest and best instructed of human imaginations."

Mr. Choate had faith in the inspiration of the Scriptures and in the scheme of redemption. He had a profound reverence for " the foolishness of preaching." He attended faithfully, for years, the church of the Rev. Dr. Adams in Boston. On the hearing of the last case in which he appeared as counsel at New York, Mr. Choate was ill, and the court adjourned over from Friday morning to Monday, when he proceeded with his argument.

But on the intervening Sunday, I met him at the old Brick Church; where, though nervous and suffering, he listened devoutly to a plain sermon by the Rev. Gardiner Spring. If Mr. Macaulay had like faith, he had not like reverence. He regarded ecclesiastical matters "exclusively from the standpoint of the state;" a sermon as an intellectual performance. If the discourse was learned and fine, it was well to be in church. He leaves a record of two occasions when he was there — the one on a day appointed for national humiliation and prayer — and he says, "Nothing could be more solemn and earnest than the aspect of the congregation, which was numerous. The sermon was detestable; ignorance, stupidity, bigotry. If the maxims of this fool," etc. On the other occasion, the preacher was dull, and Macaulay says, "I withdrew my attention and read the Epistle to the Romans. I was much struck by the eloquence and force of some passages." "I know of few things finer than the end of the first chapter and the 'Who shall separate us from the love of Christ?'" We do not pause to inquire when and where he knew the finer things, however few, being in turn much struck by the deference he so loftily pays to "the eloquence and force of some passages." We recall nothing so exquisitely complaisant in Hume or

Gibbon, and confess that no such generous criticism could have been conceived or perpetrated by Rufus Choate.

A sensible man always respects the delicacy of the situation in which he may be placed, quiets a difficulty, and smoothes over an impertinence. Mr. Choate was so fortunate in observing the "due temperance" that his life never rose to the dignity of a single quarrel; yet his patience was often severely tried in the courts, in the Senate, and in popular assemblies. But it may be well to observe how easily Macaulay could get up trouble by evading or answering a simple question. At a public meeting, an elector in the crowd asked what his religious creed was. Macaulay cried out, "Let that man stand up where I can see him." It was a Methodist preacher. They hoisted him up on a form, and Macaulay, inveighing against bigotry, poured out a torrent of reproaches, and finally declared, "Gentlemen, I am a Christian." The poor preacher, about to be roughly handled by the fellows near him, slid down and crept away. The crowd cheered, perhaps because of Macaulay's virtuous indignation, perhaps because of the vital discovery that had been made. We think Mr. Choate would have answered such a question without heat or irritation.

At an early day, Macaulay was admonished to

improve his temper. Later, Disraeli said, "He must get rid of his rabidity." Sydney Smith told him that his "great danger was that of taking a tone of too much asperity and contempt in controversy." As we are contrasting him with one who never needed such advice, who never had a revenge to gratify or an enemy to pursue, the flower and fruit of that rabidity, asperity, and contempt, as shown in Macaulay's treatment of others, deserve notice. We do not pause to ask whether the studied denunciation of Mr. Croker or of Robert Montgomery, running through a dozen pages or so, had or had not some justice to qualify the apparent malignity. All that could be allowed to pass as belonging to, even if not dignifying, criticism. But not until Mr. Trevelyan had unrolled the record for inspection, did we know that Macaulay could go so far beyond the office of the critic as to treasure up bitter personal animosities, and that, writing in quiet hours, he could illustrate that evil temper by unbecoming words. He calls Croker, then in Parliament, a "varlet;" and says, "I detest him more than cold boiled veal." We also learn that Montgomery, finding the article denouncing him republished and hawked about, the bitter cup ever held to his lips, was in great distress, and wrote again and again to Macaulay and his publisher, asking "to be let out of the pillory," and that Macaulay put on the record, "Never with my consent." While we turn with repugnance from much that he wrote of Lord Brougham, we quote a few words. Macaulay says of him, "He has outlived his power to injure." Again, "Strange fellow! his powers gone; his spite immortal; a dead nettle." The grounds of his hatred of that great man were trivial, such as most persons would have passed over in silence. We are told by Macaulay that Lord Brougham thought that the seat given to him in Parliament should have been given to another; that Brougham professed not to have read the "Essays;" had not complimented him on his speeches when others had done so; and that he aspired to too much control over the "Edinburgh Review." Thus Macaulay states his grievances, *distempered dreams,* and rejoices over Brougham's supposed mental as well as political decline, although Brougham had been the friend of Macaulay's father, and had favored his projects. How much more graceful and becoming if Macaulay had been silent, or had treated Brougham with something of the respect Choate always manifested for Daniel Webster!

In speaking of Rufus Choate, Mr. Charles G. Loring said, " He rarely permitted himself to indulge in personalities, and never in those of an offensive and degrading nature." Mr. Richard H.

Dana, Jr., asks, " Who ever heard from him an un-
kind word ? " And Professor Brown says, " He
never spoke ill of the absent, nor would suffer
others to do so in his presence." We contrast
with such concurrent testimony what Macaulay
deliberately wrote of other members of Parliament. In a letter to Ellis, as to the close vote on
a reform bill, he says, " And the jaw of Peel fell;
and the face of Twiss was as the face of a damned
soul; and Herries looked like Judas taking his
necktie off for the last operation."

Since Lord Coke announced that two leaks
would drown any ship, we have learned that the
principle admits of extended application; that a
single flaw will spoil a mirror, too much alloy the
largest coin in the realm, and that a spirit of rabidity and asperity being cherished in the heart,
other evil spirits will enter in and take possession.
We must confess, however, that we always regarded Macaulay gratefully until we began to read
his letters, diary, and journal, and that from
thenceforth we have felt great concern as to his
taste, style, and manners.

In a letter to his sister, Macaulay mentions his
introduction to Lady Holland, and her gracious
invitation to Holland House. In other letters, he
refers to his visits there after this fashion: " I
dined yesterday at Holland House; all lords ex-

cept myself." He met there many distinguished persons; for the first time heard Talleyrand, then famous, talk, and tell stories. The reader of the " Life of Sydney Smith," by his daughter, will recall his estimate of the honor conferred upon him when, young and poor, he was received into that society, and of the kindness shown him by Lord and Lady Holland, — a grateful and beautiful picture. As the doors of Holland House were thrown wide open to Macaulay, and as he was treated by Lord and Lady Holland as a son might have been, that sovereign courtesy should have been sufficient to inspire in one fit to be introduced a grateful respect, a decent degree of reticence. But what record does Macaulay leave? The little household flurries are depicted; the unguarded chat and prattle of the most gracious hostess that ever smiled a welcome to her guests are given; her freaks, fears, superstitions, lamentations, and " her tantrums" are described, even to the extent of saying that she was hysterical about Macaulay's going to India, and had to be soothed by Lord Holland. No zealous attorney was ever more faithful in getting up a bill of particulars.

Macaulay's sorrow for the dead and dying dignifies a pathetic letter to his sister. Thus he writes: " Poor Scott is gone, and I cannot be sorry for it. A powerful mind in ruins is the most heart-breaking thing which it is possible to conceive. Ferdinand of Spain is gone, too; and I fear old Mr. Stephen is going fast. I am safe for Leeds. Poor Hyde Villiers is very ill."

How considerate the transition from the want of hope for others to his own flushing hope in the coming election! Through the dark shadows, the light breaks in so naturally, — "Don't fret, sister, I am safe for Leeds."

Mr. Choate read with discrimination the authors of his day. Mr. Trevelyan says, " Macaulay had a very slight acquaintance with the works of some among the best writers of his own generation." But his reading seems to have been incessant, fragmentary, and capricious. He says, " I walked the heath in glorious weather, and read ' The Mysteries of Paris.' Sue has quite put poor Plato's nose out of joint." Again, he says, " Read ' Northanger Abbey '; worth all Dickens and Pliny together. Yet it was the work of a girl. She was certainly not more than twenty-six. Wonderful creature! Finished Pliny. Capital fellow, Trajan, and deserving of a better panegyric." Most scholars have been satisfied with the picture drawn of the Emperor. Choate commended Pliny as " one who seldom colored too highly."

Mr. Choate was never severe as a critic; his

dissatisfaction was always expressed in becoming terms. Mr. Macaulay's criticisms, as we now have them, were often crude, mere freaks of fancy, rashly and rudely stated. Thus he says, " Looked in the ' Life of Hugh Blair,' — a stupid book, by a stupid man, about a stupid man." Blair was not a great man, but he was always, and especially in his style, respectable. His first volume of " Sermons " was published on the advice of Doctor Johnson. Macaulay refers to two of Gibbon's critics thus: " That stupid beast, Joseph Milner." " But Whitaker was as dirty a cur as I remember." This may excite surprise, as Macaulay remembered so many curs. He puts down some men as beasts, several as asses, others as curs. The association brings to mind what Coleridge said of Burke, in his public character, to wit, " That he found himself, as it were, in Noah's ark, with a very few men and a great many beasts." But neither of those critics was stupid. Mr. Choate thought well of Milner, and we turn poor Whitaker over to Mr. Charles Butler, a lawyer, a great controversialist, one who always wrote as became a gentleman. He says, " Dr. Whitaker's criticism of his (Gibbon's) history is rough, but powerful."

We do not pause to illustrate Macaulay's egotism and vanity ; the proofs cropping out in many

pages of his letters and diary would be burden-
some.   As compared with Macaulay's self-lauda-
tions, — from the " My speech has set me in the
front rank," on down to the " How white poor
Peel looked while I was speaking," and to the two
damsels who, having paid their shilling to see the
hippopotamus, abandoned the show to get a look
at Macaulay, — Mr. Choate's record would seem to
be poor indeed.   Not a shade of egotism or vanity
was ever imputed to him.   Nor need we, after our
quotations from Macaulay, enforce our conviction
that his style, unlike the style of Mr. Choate, had
caught no grace from Grecian studies, no strength
from biblical reading.

The spirit of grace and courtesy which indicates social and literary refinement in a man not
morbidly selfish shines forth in his words, spoken
or written, and in his enforced intercourse with
decent strangers.   Mr. Macaulay has given us
some evidence of the amenity of his manners,
when he was approached respectfully by persons
wishing to do him honor.   He says, " What odd
things happen !   Two gentlemen, or at least two
men in good coats and hats, overtook me as I was
strolling through one of the meadows close by the
river.   One of them stared at me, touched his hat,
and said, ' Mr. Macaulay, I believe.'   I admitted
the truth of the imputation.   So the fellow went

on, 'I suppose, sir,' " etc. · But he soon got rid of the fellow. Macaulay was at Rome, and says, "Yesterday as I was looking at some superb portraits by Raphael and Titian, a Yankee clergyman introduced himself to me ; told me that he had heard who I was ; that he begged to thank me for my writings in the name of his countrymen. I bowed, thanked him, and stole away, leaving the Grand Duke's picture a great deal sooner than I had intended." In contrast with these exhibitions, the statement of the Rev. Dr. Adams may be cited. He said that Mr. Choate "Treated every man as though he were a gentleman ; and he treated every gentleman almost as he would a lady."

The poverty which often attaches to biographies qualifies, in some aspects, these works of Professor Brown and Mr. Trevelyan. This was unavoidable. It is quite apparent that no one could fathom the mystery of Mr. Choate's genius, or state its precise character. His friends could only wonder and admire, — seek to measure its power in the intellectual performance. Mr. Macaulay had, from first to last, been so silent in respect to a matter of the most vital concern, as to the life that now is and that which is to come, that his nearest friends could make no discovery, his biographer no revelation.

15

But no one who had considered Macaulay in his works previously published, and who now considers him in his other writings, will doubt the uses of biography. If one who is supposed to give tone to society has an artificial voice full of melody when abroad, a natural voice full of discord when at home, that should be known. If an author, who has beguiled us into a high estimate of his merits, appeared as a poet in prose as well as in verse, his words and sentences polished and full of measured sweetness, — " a burnished fly in the pride of May," — was, in reality, weak in tone and sentiment, bitter and unforgiving, ungrateful for social service and distinction, often rude in manners, and as a writer, and in his natural, every-day style, was diffuse and ungraceful, if not rough, all that should also be known. If such a character appears in its true light when contrasted with one whose life, open as the day, was a perpetual benediction, full of beneficent influences, inciting to everything that was just, loyal, noble in sentiment, beautiful in speech, uniform and exemplary in conduct, we may well be thankful that biographies could be written.

LETTERS.

LETTER FROM JOSHUA M. VAN COTT.

MR. JOSHUA M. VAN COTT, having, in casual conversation, mentioned an interesting occasion when he heard Mr. Choate, had the kindness, at my request, to send me this note — he calls it " a scrap."

In December, 1843, the New Englanders in New York celebrated the anniversary of the landing of the Pilgrims, Rufus Choate being the orator, and his theme, " The Age of the Pilgrims, our Heroic Period." [1] The oration was delivered in the old Broadway Tabernacle, then the largest auditorium in the city. The great building was crowded to hear the famous speaker. Mr. Webster and other distinguished public men were on the platform. Mr. Choate was then in his prime, and his presence was hardly less striking than that of the great expounder. He was tall, thin; his complexion a rich olive; his eyes large, liq-

[1] See the oration in vol. i. of Brown's *Life and Writings of Choate.*

uid, glowing; the face oriental, rather than that
of an American, and generally rather sad than
eager and passionate. His voice was a rich bari-
tone, sonorous, majestic, finely modulated, and inimitable in the expression of pathos. He philo-
sophically developed the rise of Puritanism and
the causes of the Pilgrim emigration, and came
down to the Mayflower, to Miles and Rose Standish, to the landing at Plymouth, the severity of
the winter, the famine and the sickness, and the
many deaths — fifty out of a hundred, including
that of the beautiful Rose Standish. Pausing,
with a sad, far-off look in his eyes, as if the vision
had suddenly risen upon his memory, and with a
voice inexpressibly sweet and pathetic, he said,
"In a late visit to Plymouth I sought the spot
where these earlier dead were buried. It was on
a bank somewhat elevated, near, fronting and
looking upon the waves, — *symbol of what life
had been to them,* — ascending inland behind and
above the Rock, symbol also of that Rock of Ages
on which the dying had rested in that final hour."
I have never seen an audience more moved.
The orator had skillfully led up to this passage,
and then, with a voice surcharged with emotion, he
thus symbolized the stormy and tumultuous life,
the sudden and sad end, and the heroic faith with
which, resting upon the Rock of Ages, they had

lain down on the shore of the Eternal Sea. As Choate approached the climax, Webster's emotion became uncontrollable; the great eyes were filled with tears, the great frame shook; he bowed his head to conceal his face in his hat, and I almost seemed to hear his sob. The audience was flooded with tears, a handkerchief at every face, and sighs and sobs soughed through the house like the wind in the tree-tops. The genius of the orator had transferred us to the spot, and we saw the rocky shore, and, with him, mourned the early dead.

We have had but one Rufus Choate; alas! we shall never have another. We have had powerful dialecticians, such as Hamilton and Pinkney and Webster; we have had great stump speakers, such as Senator Corwin and Sergeant S. Prentiss, but none who could sway the soul like the great lawyer, scholar, statesman, and orator of New England.

> " So on the tip of his subduing tongue
> All kinds of arguments and question deep,
> All replication prompt, and reason strong
> For his advantage still did wake and sleep:
> To make the weeper laugh, the laugher weep,
> He had the dialect and different skill,
> Catching all passions in his craft of will."
>
> SHAKESPEARE'S *Lover's Complaint.*

LETTER FROM REV. A. P. PUTNAM, D. D.

WHEN the Rev. A. P. Putnam, D. D., was about leaving Brooklyn for his summer vacation, knowing that he was a native of Danvers, and that he proposed to remain for some time in the vicinity of Mr. Choate's early dwelling-place, I asked him to keep in mind the subject to which these articles •have been devoted, and to favor me, at his convenience, with such impressions as occurred to him and such facts as he might learn. I gratefully acknowledge the kindly and generous spirit in which he has complied with the request.

MY DEAR JUDGE, — I beg you to accept my thanks for the copies which you have kindly sent of "The Albany Law Journal," containing your exceedingly interesting and timely articles illustrative of the life and character of Mr. Choate. I rejoice that your efforts to rescue so much valuable testimony to his worth and so many facts concerning his habits and history, before those who from their personal friendship or acquaint- ‹

ance are best qualified to furnish such material have quite passed off the stage, are so widely and gratefully appreciated. Though a native of Danvers, where he began the practice of the law, yet, while he was there, I was too young to see and hear him as many of the older residents were wont to do. But I recall how frequently he was a favorite theme of conversation with my father, who was associated with him not a little in political and town affairs, and who had the greatest respect and admiration for his talents and virtues. After he removed from Salem to Boston, the charm of the man and of his eloquence lingered long in the minds of all classes of people in Essex County, and stories of his early successes at the bar and predictions of his brilliant future continued to be rife in and about the scenes of his opening professional career. I well remember how, on one occasion, when, thirty or forty years ago, he came from Boston to Danvers to try a case of local interest, a most eager desire to see him was manifested by the villagers, who assembled about the hotel to witness his arrival, and then crowded into the hall to listen to his argument. I was myself but a boy in the thronged apartment, and have no very distinct recollection of what he said at the time; but I shall never lose the impression which his look, manner, and voice made upon me.

In form, feature, and expression he was then the perfection of manly beauty, while he had already won an enviable fame as an orator and advocate. Long afterward it fell to me to go to the city to engage him for a lecture. I found him at home, seated in a soft, comfortable arm-chair, and suffering severely from neuralgic pains in his head. The brief interview is precious to me in memory, as well because it was the only opportunity that was ever permitted me to exchange words with him as because he seized the moment to pay a tender tribute of esteem and affection to one who had recently died, and who was yet dearer to me than to himself. I always, however, sought to hear him whenever it was announced that he would speak in public, and whenever it was possible for me to be present. Some of his later political speeches found no response in one of my anti-slavery convictions; but there was magic in his spell, and there was also truth in the man. For, however questionable his reasoning may now seem, in view especially of all that has since occurred in our national history, who can for a moment doubt that a soul so sensitive and conservative, yet so patriotic and unselfish as his, must have been deeply in earnest, as he foresaw and dreaded the conflict that was near at hand, and did all that he could to stay the storm. One of the ablest utterances I ever heard from him was, I think, his speech on the judiciary question, July 14, 1853, in the Massachusetts convention, held during that year in Boston, for revising and amending the state Constitution. It was an exceedingly powerful argument, and it was as captivating in style and delivery as it was sound and irresistible in its logic. The hall of the House of Representatives was crowded in floor and in gallery, and the attention of all was riveted to the end. The peroration was a splendid tribute to the people of Massachusetts, and ended thus: " They have nothing timorous in them as touching the largest liberty. They rather like the exhilaration of crowding sail on the noble old ship, and giving her to scud away before a fourteen-knot breeze; but they know, too, if the storm comes on to blow and the masts go overboard, and the gun deck is rolled under water, and the lee shore, edged with foam, thunders under her stern, that the sheet anchor and best bower then are everything! Give them good ground tackle, and they will carry her round the world and back again till there shall be no more sea." The effect of such a speech, with these concluding words, may be better imagined than described. Immediately as he finished it, he put on his wraps, even though it was summer, and like some mysterious personage walked out of the assembly, followed by the gaze of the impressed and admiring multitude.

His judgment respecting one of the notable men of the convention is interesting. The towns and cities of the Commonwealth seemed to have vied with each other in electing as members their leading statesmen, politicians, lawyers, jurists, scholars, authors, editors, teachers, reformers, clergymen, merchants, or farmers. It was a very remarkable body of men, and among them were Rufus Choate, Charles Sumner, R. H. Dana, Jr., Marcus Morton, Otis P. Lord, Henry Wilson, Charles W. Upham, Benjamin F. Butler, William Appleton, J. Thomas Stevenson, John C. Gray, Sidney Bartlett, N. P. Banks, Anson Burlingame, Charles Allen, Samuel A. Elliot, George N. Briggs, George S. Boutwell, Henry L. Dawes, F. B. Crowninshield, George S. Hillard, and many others of state, if not of national, reputation. But Mr. Choate told a friend of mine, who was a member from Roxbury, that the man who was the ruling genius of the body, most powerfully controlling its deliberations and shaping its proceedings, having the most thorough knowledge of all his associates, and most fertile of methods in adapting means to ends, always carrying the whole business of the Convention in his mind, ever watching his opportunity, and never failing to accomplish his purpose, was Henry Wilson. Such testimony from such authority, with regard to the "Natick Cobbler," giving him so proud a preëminence amidst the assembled wisdom of the State, was a tribute indeed.

While spending my summer vacation at Beverly a few months ago, I took the cars one day for Essex, in order to visit the spot where the great advocate was born. On reaching the village, I went with a friend to the head of the creek where the ship-builders launch their barks, and there joining two of Mr. Choate's nephews, Rufus and William, we rowed together down the winding stream for about two miles, until we came to the small bay whose waters inclose the island on which he first saw the light, and which is itself shut in by the enfolding arms of the white sand beaches that project from, or lie along, the shore. The land on either side, as we proceeded on our way, was mostly level and marshy, but about midway, on our left, it rose into a gentle swell, and was largely shaded by a noble growth of walnut trees, presenting a lovely site for a summer residence. It was long a cherished dream of Mr. Choate's — to which his biographer makes a passing allusion — that he should one day build himself a house here, where he might each year

come and rest a while from his arduous profes-
sioual toils, and refresh himself with the cool sea
airs and the old familiar scenes of his infancy and
youth. Yet it was too lonely a spot for the
younger members of the family, and the project
was never realized. Also at the left, and within
the little bay, is what is known as Dean's Island.
It is a small extent of land, covered with trees
and entirely uninhabited. One could easily believe concerning it that it was never the abode
of any living creature. Mr. Choate was one day
gliding past it, in company with the nephew who
bears his name, and was hearing the latter tell
how he had visited the silent and unfrequented
spot. It was at a time when the cholera was
raging in various parts of the country, and was
the subject of general and anxious remark, and
the uncle, affecting a great horror of the scourge,
asked with a touch of his subdued yet delicious
humor, " And Rufus, did you find any cholera
there ? "

The island on which Mr. Choate was born is
just opposite the mouth of the creek, and is sep-
arated from the mainland by a wide channel of
water at high tide, but may with some difficulty
be reached with a horse and wagon when the tide
is out. Its surface consists of about three hundred
acres, and the whole rises into a well-rounded em-

inence, whose summit must be about two hundred feet above the level of the water. Its bald, naked aspect is quite unrelieved by trees or vegetation, except as the more southern slopes are brought under some degree of cultivation by those who occupy the three farm-houses situated there. In one of these houses Rufus Choate was born; but when he was only six months old the family removed to the village where he grew up to early manhood. The house is painted white, and has latterly received a piazza on the front, which faces the south. The larger part of the island has been in the possession of the Choate family for seven generations. Its proper name is "Choate Island," a name to which the facts of its original and continued proprietorship well entitled it, and which is actually given it in the maps of the Coast Survey. A considerable portion of the land is now owned by the nephew, Rufus. His illustrious uncle always turned to his birthplace with fond affection, and was wont to go thither in the summer for a time, taking with him some books and friends. It is reasonable to suppose that the spot and its surroundings must have exercised more influence upon his mind and character than those who have written about him have been wont to trace. Who can tell how much of the marvelous beauty of his lost lecture on "The Romance of the Sea," or

how much of the pathos or witchery or eloquence
of many another of his productions must have
been due to what, in youth, as in maturer life, he
thus often saw and felt there at his " native isle."
From the brow of the hill, he could discern, in
clear weather, far away at the north, the mountains of Maine and New Hampshire. Beyond the
marshes and the village that lay immediately at
the west, he could see not a few of the towns and
villages of Essex County, numbering many a glittering spire, and delight himself with a richly diversified and most pleasing landscape. Just at
the southeast, the great cape extended its lofty
ridge far out toward the sea, while close along the
nearer shore lay various larger or smaller islands
or sand-bars, with their white cliffs and shining
levels, washed on the one side by the waters of
several rivers that poured down their currents
from the interior, and on the other by the waves
of the ocean, whose vast expanse, broadening to
the view, specked with sails, and fascinating with
its ever-changing hues, completed the circuit of the
range. In all this scenery there was a breadth
and a variety, a certain lonely grandeur and perpetual revelation, which, for one who was such an
ardent lover of nature, and who was so susceptible
and imaginative as Mr. Choate, could not have
failed to possess an indescribable charm.

We drank at the well from the "old oaken bucket, the iron-bound bucket," whose water was as cool and reviving as that which at Salisbury, N. H., once evoked from Mr. Webster, in his old age, the fervent ejaculation, "This water of my father's well, it is sweeter than the nectar of the gods." And then we entered the house, saw the room where the infant Rufus made his advent, and the other apartments which have been so familiar to successive generations of his name, listening to many an interesting story of the lives of those who have there had their home. A fresh breeze had sprung up as we returned to our boat, and we were borne gayly up the stream down which we had been rowed. We took tea with the family of the late David Choate, at the homestead to which Rufus was taken when an infant, and which was from that time his abode until he went forth into the wider world. It was pleasant to talk with such of the nearest relatives of the departed as are still living in Essex, hear them speak of one of whom they are so justly proud, and see the memorials and keepsakes that tell of their love for him.

Some of the early letters of Mr. Choate have come to light since Professor Brown published his "Memoirs." These, in view of the fact that they were written, chiefly, in his school-day life, and in consideration of the paucity of such materials as

16

are illustrative of his history, may be regarded as of some interest and importance, though there is nothing in them of very remarkable significance. I was permitted to take them for a time and make such use of them as I might see fit. A few extracts from them may prove welcome to the readers of these pages as showing more fully his habits of study, his tastes and predilections, and his peculiarities of mind in that formative period of his life. It is possible that one or more of these letters may have been partly given in some form to the public before, but I am not aware that such has really been the case, and I am told by his nephew that, as a whole, they are quite unknown beyond the immediate circle of his friends or relatives. Some of them abound in fun and absurdities. Others are thoughtful and sad. Nearly all of them indicate an original cast of mind, an earnest love of knowledge, and a strong determination to conquer, with a tender and ardent affection for his home and the dear ones who were there.

The first is dated June 17, 1815, and was written to his brother David from Hampton, N. H., where he was fitting himself at an academy to enter college. He refers at the outset to a charge which he had received from the " combined powers," or " the folks," at home, that he should write immediately " a long, solid letter."

Then he proceeded thus: "Did you ever see a definition of the word *solid?* If not, I will give you one from Bailey's Dictionary. 'Solid (F. *solide,* L. *solidus*), massive, hard, firm, strong, real, substantial, sound, lasting.' How," he asks, "can I build a 'solid letter,' then, with such materials as these; viz., thin paper, no bigger than a four and a half penny, shallow brain, and no life at all?" Instantly he dashes off into a strain of bombast, interspersed with quotations about the storms and desolations of winter and the sunshine and loveliness of the season that had succeeded, suggesting that it may all serve to "fill up" what he evidently means as a sort of burlesque of the thing his family have asked for. Toward the end of the letter, he writes that he has begun the "De Oratore," and hopes soon to be "fit." But he depends much on spending a month or two at home "before the Dartmouth 'Scrape' comes on." He is now in the sixteenth year of his age.

Then there is another of these letters from Hampton, dated July 20th of the same year, and addressed also to his brother David, in which he debates the question, in lawyer-like fashion, whether he shall go home before the end of the quarter, the disputants being "*Rufus & I.*" The reasons for his going prevail. "The die is cast." He says, "I want some time for relaxation and delivery from purgatory previous to besetting Dartmouth College."

He entered college in the summer of 1815, and in a letter written from Hanover and dated December 5, 1815, he gives an account of his expenses, which certainly were small enough, and arranges with his brother for a visit home early in January. He adds, " Only about ten or twelve of my class remain. The rest have taken schools. How thankful ought I to be that I am not *obliged* to resort to this for assistance. We who remain have a chance to improve in the languages particularly."

Early in the following March he had returned to Dartmouth, and he writes to David, " Should I have my health, my acquirements ought to be great. Whether the measles are hanging about me or not is uncertain. I feel rather unwell, but a few days will decide. Respecting the affairs of the college, everything is at present in dread uncertainty. A storm seems to be gathering, the sky lowers, and ere long may burst on the present government of the college. What the event may be time will discover. If the State (and there is no doubt of it) be Democratic, a revolution will take place. Probably President Brown will be dismissed. In that case the college will fall. However, say nothing — all may yet be well, and if not, we are not to blame." . . . "The class is ambitious; and to be among the first, in one which is pronounced the best in college, will be an arduous undertaking. Good health will be absolutely necessary for a candidate."

"These hints about *health* may make you uneasy, but you must not mind it. I sincerely hope to be able to study hard, but shall never injure myself in that way. I suppose Washington[1] is getting through with the "Reader." He must attend closely to Latin and Greek. Two years would make a thorough scholar out of anything, and if this college should fail, the more he must study to enter at Cambridge." He says he has paid Mrs. D. for his board, has "discharged all debts" and has "some left;" but as certain necessary expenses will soon absorb what little money remains to him, he half sportively adds, "I don't know what more to write, but suppose in about a month you send me a little money." And again, "I will now close, requesting you to write immediately and pay the postage."

On November 3, 1816, he again writes from Hanover to David, who had evidently been very sick, "My dear brother, my feelings, on receiving another letter from you, I shall not pretend or

---

[1] A younger brother who was born January 17, 1803, and died during his senior year at college.

attempt to describe. You can conceive with what anxiety I was waiting news from home and the joy I must have felt in recognizing your well-known hand — the hand indeed of one, as you observe, ' almost literally raised from the dead.' How grateful ought we both to feel. And, if I know anything of myself, I do feel so. These gloomy forebodings that distracted my waking hours, and the dreams that haunted my sleep have now left me, and I can think of home without its appearing dreary and melancholy; but I will only add, my heart's desire is that the cure may be perfected. Respecting my own situation, I would tell you that it is in the highest degree pleasant. My room is good, and room-mate agreeable, and our fellow students in the house, seven in number, mostly seniors, friendly and familiar. Compared with last term, my eyes are well, though I do not attempt studying evenings, this circumstance rendering application in the daytime necessary. I have too much neglected exercise, and my head suffers for it. Since conversing, however, with Dr. Mussey, I have altered my habits and regularly exercise once a day. The instruction we enjoy is most excellent. President Brown hears us in Horace, and Professor Shurtleff in Algebra; and it is our own fault if we do not make suitable advances. By abridging hours of recreation, I have made myself master of the French grammar, and read, without a translation, one or two pages in the original of Telemachus as an exercise every morning. We have a task assigned the class, of rather a singular nature, and such a one as will with difficulty be well performed — it is the rendering into English poetry one of the Odes of Horace, and this, with two or three other exercises which fall upon us, will I fear oblige me to hurt my eyes by application in the evening. I forgot to observe, when speaking of instruction, that Professor Adams corrects our compositions."

Yet again, he writes from Hanover to David, under date of December 16, 1816, "I have been unavoidably prevented, till this moment, from answering your last, and expressing my joy at its contents. You will be sorry to hear what I have to tell you respecting affairs of the college. Intelligence has just reached us, that another act has passed both branches of the Legislature, and become a law, authorizing nine of the new trustees only to do business, — a number which, it is supposed, can very easily at any time be assembled. That this body will convene immediately, perhaps before the end of the term, and remove the whole of the present government of the college, and supply their places with men of their own party,

is what the best amongst us confidently expect.
The situation of the institution is, you perceive,
critical in the extreme; 'Consternation turns
the good man pale.' You may judge better of
the singular state of the college, and of the confusion which prevails, from the following circumstance. It is customary for the sophomore class
to take on itself the business of getting the catalogue of officers and students annually printed.
It was, as usual, done by my class this fall, with
the introduction, if I may so express it, 'Catalogue of the Officers and Students of Dartmouth
College.' The few Democrats and fellows of 'the
baser sort' amongst us immediately employed our
Hanover Democratic printer to strike off an edition in this form: 'Catalogue of the Officers and
Students of Dartmouth University, together with
the Trustees (old and new) and Overseers of the
same!' So much for affairs of college. . . . I
have been exceedingly troubled with headache,
and my eyes have become somewhat weak. I,
therefore, look with impatience for the close of
the term. I would, however, observe that, if my
health is continued, I shall employ the coming
vacation in diligent and profitable study; and,
excepting the Londonderry visit, which I heartily
dread, I shall shut myself up. I have secured
'Smith's Botany' and 'a 'Telemaque' of Dr.

Mussey, to which my attention will this winter be devoted."

The last of these letters which I have in hand was written to Mr. Choate's sister Hannah, while he was studying law under Mr. Wirt at Washington, and is dated September 29, 1821. It begins thus: " We sent you such a storm of letters two or three weeks since that somehow we hardly thought to be turned off with but one in answer, however full and excellent it might be, and so have waited and waited, unreasonably, you will say, in daily expectation of another or two. But I have taken hold at last, and a letter you shall have, — with nothing in it though, but very much love to you all, very much joy at David's so gratifying recovery, and the word ' *all's well.*' " A little farther on he writes, " M. and E. went to Mount Vernon yesterday, and have brought back leaves, acorns, etc., plucked from the grave that hallows that place and makes it a spot so dear to the heart of every American. Sister S. and I hope to go down next Saturday." Besides his regular study of the law, he tells us that he is " engaged every other day in the week, three hours, in a school of young ladies, as a *portant,* — all for cash, of which the Doctor does not manage to have any very great abundance, or for which I do not choose to ask him." He continues, " I

have some trifling debts which it is my determination you at home never shall pay; and, seriously
as I regret the inroad on my hours of study, I
cheerfully resign from 11 to 2. You can hardly
imagine how much I long to go back to you, and
look around once more on our family circle, and
on the hills, dales, and waters of our much-loved
birthplace. Sometimes I almost determine to return this fall, but then what shall I do for money,
and how shall I dispose of my professional studies?
So, on the whole, I must stand by, I think, till
June, 1822. In the mean time, as soon at least
as the session begins, we must contrive to hear
from each other oftener, and when D., who I hope
is nearly well enough already, has so recovered as
to write, once a week must be the word. I like
this city very little, and hope and believe I never
shall make up my mind to stay here for life. That
question as to the place of my future residence
begins at last to be a very serious one, and I think
of it daily and nightly. Still there are more than
two years to me yet before I need decide, and all
I ought to wish to do is to improve them to the
very utmost." Again, as often in the course of
these letters, his fond affection for his brother
David finds its wonted expression. "You don't
know how it delights me to hear of D.'s recovery,
and how we want to see it under his own hand
and seal."

This David, who died about five years ago, at the age of seventy-six, was, I scarcely need add, a man of much prominence and great usefulness. He possessed, in no small degree, many of the extraordinary natural gifts that distinguished his more celebrated brother; and, though he had had less favorable opportunities for early culture, he nobly justified the bright hopes that clustered about his promising youth by the solid and lasting service which he rendered, through all his manhood, in the interests of education, law, and religion.

Among several scraps which I have in Mr. Choate's handwriting, is a letter which he wrote from Washington, when he was no longer a law student there, but about twelve years later, February 4, 1833, while he was a member of Congress. A short extract affords us a glimpse of what some of the national representatives were thinking about and doing. "Things stand pretty dubiously yet. However, the Union is well enough. The tariff we may save by a bargain." The last law case which Mr. Choate was ever engaged in has been referred to in a previous communication. A brief, written at the time with his own hand, is also in my possession, and is a curiosity in its way. Its chirography makes quite credible the story, — which, however, comes to me from very good au-

thority, — that a now deceased member of the
Middlesex bar once received from him a letter
respecting a suit in which the two were associated;
and, being unable to read it, or to find any one
else who could do so, he took it back to the writer,
who was actually unable to decipher its strange
characters himself. And were the latter to re-
appear amongst us, after this lapse of years, I
fear he would be equally unsuccessful in making
out the brief I have mentioned.

I have often heard Massachusetts lawyers speak
of the strong prejudice which Mr. Choate soon encountered from the older and more conspicuous
members of the profession after his advent at the
Boston bar. The way he had of gaining victories
by his brilliant style, his captivating eloquence,
his wonderful power over juries, and his new and
novel methods of procedure, was deemed an im-
pertinent departure from the long-established rule
and routine. Few could understand his tactics,
and more than a few persistently disparaged his
talents and attainments, ridiculed his efforts and
peculiarities, and sought to annoy and perplex
him in court by unusual rudeness. On one occasion, when he had borne patiently many an unfriendly interruption and bitter taunt, some one
who was near asked him why he endured such
treatment, and why he did not retort. " I shall

retort," he said, " by getting the case." And he
got it.

Others fitted for the task have already, perhaps,
given us a satisfactory analysis of Mr. Choate's
mind and character. It is not for me to attempt
it, and my letter is even now too long. But I
cannot forbear adding a word about what has always seemed to me one of the very finest of his
traits. During my summer sojourn at Beverly, I
was a near neighbor of the venerable Dr. Boyden,
whose testimony, as that of the only surviving
college classmate of the great lawyer, you gave to
the public in connection with your last article. In
several interviews I had with him, he dwelt much
upon the many rare virtues and excellences of his
distinguished and life-long friend, and touched
particularly upon his generous appreciation of
whatever was good in others, and his absolute
freedom from all envy and jealousy. Rufus
Choate always wished and aimed to excel, but he
was glad to see his companions and competitors
excel also, and was ever ready to help them in
their struggles and toils. He coveted no preëminence that must be purchased at the cost of those
who were striving with him for fame and glory.
He had no habit of disparaging his associates or
rivals at school, at the bar, in legislative hall, or
in the political arena. I can think of only one in-

stance by way of exception. When Charles Francis Adams, during the early years of the Free Soil movement, was pointing the people to the one straight path of duty and safety, Mr. Choate, whose honest views and sympathies and actions took a very different direction, indulged in the sarcasm of referring to John Quincy Adams as the " last of the Adamses." He did not live to see, to the full extent, how unfortunate was the word. For, when the awful conflict came which no oratorical gifts or skillful compromises could avert, and the peerless magician of the courts and of popular assemblies had himself forever quit the stage, it was that same son of the " old man eloquent " who, through long and perilous years, rendered his country a service abroad which history will claim as scarcely inferior, in measure and value, to any that was performed by the wisest and best of our statesmen at home.

Yours, very truly,

A. P. PUTNAM.

LETTER FROM HON. ENOCH L. FANCHER.

THE following was received from the Hon. Enoch L. Fancher : —

MR. CHOATE AND THE METHODIST CHURCH CASE.

One of the most important cases of my early practice was the so-called Methodist Church case. It was brought by Henry M. Bascom and others, as commissioners and representatives of the M. E. Church South, against the commissioners of the M. E. Church and the agents of its Book Concern in the city of New York.

The suit was tried at New York, in the United States Circuit Court, before Judges Nelson and Betts, in May, 1851.

Previous to the trial, I went to Boston to engage Mr. Choate as counsel for the defendants, and to acquaint him with the facts and questions involved in the case. After a brief interview at his office, an appointment was made by Mr. Choate, according to which the Rev. Dr. George Peck, one of the defendants, and myself were to meet him at his residence at four o'clock in the afternoon.

Dr. Peck and myself were punctual to the engagement, and Mr. Choate received us in his library, which comprises the entire second story of his residence, shelved to the ceiling, with transverse cases, all filled with books, through which you wound as in a labyrinth. There were all the Greek authors, most of the Latin, a large collection of law books, and a well-selected collection of miscellaneous works of every description.

In one of the passages between the cases stood a high desk, at which Mr. Choate stationed himself, drawing his hand and arm, as he wrote, as high as the shoulder. On a lounge, near by, my companion and myself were seated, and from four till ten o'clock, deducting an interval of about thirty minutes for tea, we were plied with questions from Mr. Choate, while he scrawled in quaint hieroglyphics what we supposed he intended as answers to the queries propounded. His eye dilated, his voice grew tremulous, his lips quivered, and his great frame seemed to shake with the thoughts whose symbols were so strangely recorded. He would at times cry out, "Stop there," holding up his left hand till he had written what he desired; then, dropping the hand, would say in tones as musical as a flute, "Go right on, give me all of that view." Occasionally pausing, he would add, "This is the greatest case I ever studied; I want you to leave with me every scrap of brief you have made." I left him with no doubt that he fully understood the whole case, and had enlisted in it strange enthusiasm.

Subsequently he visited me at my residence in New York, when he reviewed, with masterly ability, the general features of the great controversy between the Church South and the M. E. Church; and asked further questions concerning the case, which seemed to arouse his ardent energies.

During the long trial of the case he became ill; and one day was obliged to leave the court-room and go to his hotel. He charged me to take down every word of Mr. Lord's argument, and to bring to him the notes of it in the evening. I found him in bed with a physician present, who told him he should prescribe calomel. "How large a dose have you been accustomed to?" asked the physician. "I don't know," replied Mr. Choate, "but give me the largest dose you ever gave a man in your life!"

On account of his illness, the court was adjourned from Friday to Monday; and, on the morning of the latter day, Mr. Choate came into court looking wan and showing signs of his indisposition. He began to speak, evidently in weariness, but growing stronger as he continued; and, thenceforward, all that day and for the most of the next day he poured forth strains of eloquence and argumentative power that I have never heard rivaled. His brief was a mass of loose letter sheets, on which, in his peculiar chirography, he had jotted down in dashes, trammels, hooks, quavers, and quail-tracks, such memoranda of the case as seemed, from his argument, to cover the whole controversy. The rain fell from his bushy locks; his voice (I never heard such a voice) kept tone to the rhythm of his eloquence and power of his argument. No man living could have excelled him in that speech.

In his opening remarks, full of pathos and beauty, he deprecated the events of " sad and singular interest " that had led to the dismemberment of the great Methodist Church, and ventured the expression of the hope that if the steps the plaintiff had taken should turn out to be " unprofitable as well as devious," it would be easier to retrace them. " Many times," said he, " I remember the historian tells us, many times, the alienating states of Greece had all but made up their minds to discontinue the common consultation of the Oracle of Delphi, and seek for the will of Jove in divers local temples; and they would have done so had not the impracticability of partitioning the treasures which the piety of so many generations had gathered on the charmed, neutral ground necessitated a salutary delay."

His whole argument was one of triumphant vigor; and had it been made thirty years later, when the sentiments that ruled courts and judges on the Southern question had come to a sounder basis, it would have been successful. No judge, with his eye on the presidency, could, at that day, be convinced by the eloquence of a Choate or the logic of a Plato, if that conviction resulted in a judgment against the South. The great North was, however, right that day, though the Court gave the palm of victory to the South.

After the stenographer had written out the speech of Mr. Choate, I mailed it, directed to him at Boston, with the request that he would correct and return it, as it was intended to preserve a full history of the case and of the arguments as well. He returned it without the correction of a word, writing me a humorous and interesting letter. A filibuster, named Lopez, had, just before, set sail with an expedition against Cuba. Mr. Choate wrote that he had not found time to correct the speech, and probably would not find time to do so, "until Lopez hoisted his piratical flag over Havana!"

When the question of what should be the char-

acter of the Smithsonian Institution was under
discussion in the Senate of the United States, Mr.
Choate, who had been lately made a senator for
Massachusetts in place of Mr. Webster, promoted
to the cabinet, took part in the debate. He
made, as I was told by the late Dr. Bishop, who
was present, the great speech of the occasion.
He ranged over the field of literature, and por-
trayed the beneficent influence of literary institutions, and claimed for the Smithsonian a foundation of broad character. Senators crowded around
him to listen to the new wonder; and, as he resumed his seat, Calhoun, who stood near, leaning
on the back of a chair, exclaimed to some senators, "Massachusetts sent us a Webster, but, in
the name of heaven, whom have they sent us
now?"

I do not shrink from recording my deliberate
opinion that Rufus Choate was the greatest lawyer and the most eloquent orator of his time.
Probably, as a *belles lettres* scholar he had no
superior; while the vast range of his rich and
copious vocabulary was equaled only by the vocal
music that charmed it, and that wonderful play
of thought that set both in motion. Under his
magic wand,

> " A brighter emerald twinkled in the grass,
>   A deeper sapphire melted in the sea."

LETTER FROM HON. GEORGE W. NESMITH.

THE Honorable George W. Nesmith, late one of the justices of the Supreme Court of New Hampshire, who was in college with Mr. Choate and was his confidential friend afterwards, has had the kindness to send me this paper: —

MY DEAR SIR, — I confess it would be a hopeless task for me to delineate the character of Rufus Choate. You have given, in your own finished style, a concise, yet comprehensive, view of what he was and did, and you have been aided by those who saw and heard him more frequently than myself. Yet I will place my memory at your service.

I knew him well while at college. Our acquaintance commenced in 1816. He was one year in advance of me in collegiate standing and in age. I belonged to the same literary society with him for three years, and remember with pleasure his leadership there. During my last year at college he was a tutor.

After graduation we lived a hundred miles apart. I frequently saw him when I visited Boston, had interviews with him, and occasionally heard him in courts of justice. I was with him in the Whig presidential conventions at the nominations of General Taylor, at Philadelphia, and of General Scott, at Baltimore. At both conventions we supported Mr. Webster as a candidate. I afterwards heard his famous eulogy upon Mr. Webster. A short time before his death, I had an interesting conversation with him, in which he announced the unwelcome intelligence that his physicians had notified him to quit all labor and to take a sea voyage, as this offered the only hope of recruiting his feeble bodily frame.

The only reminiscence of his college life which occurs to me as not already narrated by your correspondents was an amusing practical joke perpetrated by him and some other students. They exchanged potatoes for apples in the sole remaining sack of a farmer of the name of Johnson, from Norwich, and then induced Johnson to offer the contents of the sack for sale at the college. A purchase was made by the students who had been notified of his approach, and then, upon opening the sack, an outcry was raised against Johnson for attempted imposition. Protestations of innocence were met with ridicule, and suggestions of the interference of the Evil One. Choate, standing in front of Johnson, amused at the perplexity depicted upon his countenance, exclaimed, " Would that Hogarth were here!" Johnson caught at the name with suspicion, and afterward offered to reward us if we would tell where Hogarth was to be found.

One of Choate's most eloquent and effective speeches was delivered in his senior year at college, in the autumn of 1818, while acting as president of our literary society. It was upon the occasion of the introduction of many members from the Freshman class. The custom of presidents of the association had been to make a brief formal speech, setting forth the objects of the society and the duties of its members, and that was all we expected. We were surprised by a well prepared and eloquent address of considerable length. At that time he was in vigorous health and full of energy. The silvery tones of his voice, resounding through our little hall, kept the assembly spell-bound while he discoursed upon those elements of character essential to the formation of the ripe scholar and the useful citizen. The late Chief Justice Perley was one of the young men then made members of the society of " Social Friends." In after-life I often heard him allude, in terms of high commendation, to that perform-

ance.   On the following day I undertook to note
down in a little scrap-book some of the thoughts
to which Choate had given utterance, although
I could not reproduce the brilliant language in
which they were expressed.   I give some of those
memoranda : —

"To make the successful scholar, patient, constant, well-directed labor is an absolute requisite."
"He must aim at reaching the highest standard
of excellence of character.   Good mental endowments must be allied to conscience, truthfulness,
manliness.   In the affairs of life, brains are essential, but truth, or heart, more so."   "Not genius
so much as sound principles, regulated by good
discretion, commands success.   We often see men
exercise an amount of influence out of all proportion to their intellectual capacities, because,
by their steadfast honesty and probity, they
command the respect of those who know them.
George Herbert says, 'A handful of good life is
worth a bushel of learning.'   Burns' father's advice to his son was good, —

> 'He bade me act the manly part,
>   Though I had ne'er a farthing,
> For, without an honest, manly heart,
>   No man was worth regarding.'

"A critic said of Richard Brinsley Sheridan,
that, if he had possessed *reliableness* of character,

he might have ruled the world; but, for want of it, his splendid gifts were comparatively useless. Burke was a man of transcendent gifts, but the defect in his character was want of moral firmness and good temper. To succeed in life we must not only be conscientious, we must have also energy of will, — a strong determination to do manly work for ourselves and others. The strong man channels his own path, and easily persuades others to walk in it." "When Washington took command of the American army, the country felt as if its forces had been doubled. So, when Chatham was appointed Prime Minister in England, great confidence was created in the government." "After General Greene had been driven out of South Carolina by Cornwallis, having fought the battle of Guilford Court House, he exclaimed, 'I will now recover South Carolina, or die in the attempt.' It was this stern mental resolve that enabled him to succeed." "Every student should improve his opportunities to cultivate his powers. He owes this duty to his friends, his instructors, and his country. Our learned men are the hope and strength of the nation. 'They stamp the epochs of national life with their own greatness.' They give character to our laws and shape our institutions, found new industries, carve out new careers for the commerce and labor of society;

they are, in fact, the salt of the earth, in life as well as in death. Constituting, as they do, the vital force of a nation and its very life-blood, their example becomes a continual stimulant and encouragement, to every young man who has aspirations for a higher station or the higher honors of society. Now, my brethren and young friends, we beseech you to strive earnestly to excel in this honorable race for just fame and true glory, and in your efforts to mount up upon the fabled ladder do not be found, in the spirit of envy, pulling any above you down, but rather, in the exercise of a more liberal spirit, holding out a helping hand to a worthy brother who may be struggling below you. Be assured you exalt yourselves in proportion as you raise up the humbler ones."

The second part of his discourse was specially devoted to the pleasure and rewards derived from an intimate acquaintance with classical learning. His suggestions were valuable and impressive, and urged home upon our attention with great rhetorical force. If this speech had been published, it would have furnished the young student with a profitable guide in his pursuit of knowledge.

Mr. Choate has been rightly described to you as an *original nondescript.* He was like no other person in his style of writing, or in his oratory. He perceived quickly and 'acquired rapidly. He possessed a retentive memory, appropriating to himself readily the thoughts of others. To his able reasoning powers he united an imagination " richly perfumed from Carmel's flowery top," powerful, soaring, unbounded. He seemed to have been fashioned for a poet. He remarked to me one day that he loved poetry, but poetry did not love him.

As to temper, he was always indulgent and kind, speaking evil of none. In his daily intercourse with others, he was courteous and liberal to a fault. He was naturally gentle ; but, when pressed hard, was capable of inflicting blows that left an impression. I once heard him deal with a bad witness in court. He did not call him hard names, but covered him over with an oily sarcasm so deep that the jury did not care to look after him. In other words, the witness was slain politely, and laid out to dry.

Not far from the year 1845, the Hon. Levi Woodbury was invited by the literary societies of Dartmouth College to deliver an oration at the annual Commencement in July. Going thither, I had a seat in the stage coach with Mr. Webster, Mr. Woodbury, and Mr. Choate. A good opportunity was presented of witnessing their conversational powers. Mr. Webster and Judge Woodbury had for many years resided in Portsmouth, N. H., and topics relative to men and scenes there were much discussed by them. Of course I could not but be an interested listener. The early history of our State, the character of the settlers, their leaders, their privations and sufferings by reason of Indian warfare, the character of our early governors, and the growth of the State, with historical reminiscences and anecdotes, were introduced. I was surprised to find that Mr. Choate was so familiar with our early history as to give dates and events with accuracy. By easy transitions they passed to the judiciary of the State and the members of the bar, discussing their respective merits. On these local subjects the New Hampshire men, of course, had the vantage ground. Wishing to give new direction, therefore, to the conversation, I asked Mr. Choate as to his later reading. He answered that he had recently been occupied in the perusal of Milton's prose and poetry. Mr. Webster said to him, " As you are so recently out of Paradise, will you tell me something about the talk that Adam and Eve had before and after the fall?" Mr. Choate asked, " Do you intend that as a challenge to me?" Webster answered, " Yes, I do." Choate hereupon recited promptly portions of the addresses of Adam to Eve, and Eve to Adam, much to the edification of his audience. Webster rejoined with the 'description of the conflict between Gabriel and Satan, from the sixth book of "Paradise Lost." His recitation was received with applause. John Milton himself, had he been present, would have been satisfied with the performers on that occasion. We had seen celebrated actors on the stage, but none before like those in the stage.

At my last interview with Mr. Choate in Boston, after alluding to his incessant and severe labor at the bar for many years, he said he was literally worn out, and added, in a melancholy way, "I have cared much more for others than for myself; I have spent my strength for naught." I reminded him that he had gained high reputation in his profession, and also as a scholar, and that this was his reward. He said, "We used to read that this kind of fame was but an empty bubble; now I know it is nothing else." Such was Mr. Choate's estimate of human glory when consciously near the termination of his eventful and honored life. He added, "My light here is soon to be extinguished. I think often of the grave. I am animated by the hope of that glorious immortality to be enjoyed in a kingdom where sin and sorrow cannot come."

I remain, very respectfully, etc.,

GEO. W. NESMITH.

To Hon. Jos. Neilson.

LETTERS FROM HON. WILLIAM STRONG.

———◆———

ALTHOUGH not written for publication, I am permitted, upon my special request, to give the following portions of letters received from the Hon. William Strong, Associate Justice of the Supreme Court of the United States.

EXTRACTS FROM LETTER OF JANUARY 30, 1877.

"I read twice, carefully, Trevelyan's 'Life of Macaulay' immediately after its publication in this country. I had previously read Mr. Brown's charming biography of Mr. Choate, and read it, I believe, more than once. Until your article in the 'Albany Law Journal' appeared, it had not occurred to me to compare the two men, and even now I find it difficult to compare them. In my judgment, they were very unlike. Undoubtedly there were some particulars in which they resembled each other. Both had remarkable powers of memory, but Macaulay's was rather the memory of words, while Choate's was that of ideas as well as of words. Each of them had a large element of the dramatic. Each was a natural poet. Each was a man of great industry and of brilliant accomplishments. But here the resemblance seems to me to cease. Considering that Macaulay was free from the cares and pressures of a profession, and, indeed, from any demands that interfered with his entire devotion to any subject that interested him, he gave comparatively little to society and to the world. He made a few speeches (not many) in the House of Commons. He wrote a few reviews and essays. He wrote some pretty poetry, and he wrote his ' History of England.' He prepared also (with much help) his Indian Code. All these things were well done; most of them were brilliant. They were, and they will long continue to be, very readable. But every one of them was the product of long and uninterrupted labor; written and re-written again and again, and never permitted to go from him until he had expended upon it his best culture and his highest power. We see, therefore, in Trevelyan's Life, Macaulay at his best, and only on the very *apices* of his powers. Choate never had time for such expenditure of labor, and he was less careful of his posthumous reputation. Yet he was at least equally brilliant, more versatile, and far more logical. His style, undressed, is as beautiful as that of Macaulay arrayed in its best costume, and his oratorical powers seem to me to have been much higher. His ability to influence and sway other minds has never been surpassed. But I have no time to go into an analysis of Macaulay's and Choate's mental powers, acquisitions, and culture."

"In moral traits the two men are not to be compared. Though Macaulay was tender and loving to his mother and sisters, perhaps also to Ellis, he loved himself supremely. Beyond this narrow circle there can hardly be said to have been any who had a place in his heart. He was conspicuously vain, envious, jealous, and lastingly malignant. Yet he was a great and brilliant man. But how unlike the great and brilliant American!"

"I shall wait for the completion of your articles with much interest, and perhaps I should not have thrown out the crude observations I have made. Yet I will add one remark. Perhaps the mellowing influence of a cordial acceptance of Christianity will account for the superior loveliness of Mr. Choate's character over that of Macaulay. Can there be anything more touching than the former's conduct at the baptism of his dying daughter?"

EXTRACTS FROM LETTER OF JUNE 16, 1877.

"I have read with great interest all you have said of Mr. Choate in the ' Albany Law Journal.'

You certainly have no reason to regret the work you have done in bringing before the thought of the country the most remarkable man (in some particulars) who in modern times has appeared in the legal profession. I have admired your analysis of his character and endowments. You have done a work I should have feared to attempt. There was so much to admire in Mr. Choate, from whatever stand-point one looked at him, that it is difficult to speak the truth of him without exposure to the charge of exaggeration. His affection and his domestic life how charming! His sense of honor how keen! His subjection to the control of high moral principles how complete and constant! His imagination how brilliant and chaste! His logical power how masterly! His memory how tenacious, and his industry how untiring! He seems to have united in himself the highest excellences that are generally considered inconsistent with each other; for illustration, the power of exact reasoning and of sharp discrimination, with the most playful fancy; and a devotion to his professional engagements, apparently disdainful of rest, with a ceaseless and demonstrative outflow of the best affections of the heart. He proved that these virtues are not necessarily incongruous. And then where could he have found time for so much classical reading? Macaulay had no profes-

18

sion to which he was tied. His business was to be a reader and a general student. Mr. Choate had enough for a life's work which demanded his first attention, and that work was always done."

LETTER FROM REV. R. S. STORRS, D. D.

In this paper the Rev. Richard S. Storrs, D. D., LL. D., pays a becoming tribute to the genius and personality of Mr. Choate. With a profound sense of the harmony that exists between the written and the suggested eulogy, I may be allowed to say that, while I have often heard old friends of Mr. Choate speak of the magnetic attraction of his voice and manner, of the fascination with which others were drawn to him as by some spell not to resisted or forgotten, I never before had so clear a conception of the power of such sovereign qualities. By this paper we are led to think of Mr. Choate as in his old manner; and, through the mazes of life, study, and service, catch glimpses of him everywhere. We are also reminded that, beyond the skill which may be taught and learned, more natural, vivid, subtile, and enduring; richer, higher, and holier far than mere outward manifestation, was the influence which Mr. Choate exerted in forming the taste and style, strengthening the loyalty, faith, devotion, and judgment of those who were brought into communion with him. It may also be understood how one thus favored and impressed can write as if the voice of his long-lost friend could still be heard, as if the clouds and shadows of the intervening time were swept aside, and what is told had occurred but yesterday.

MY DEAR JUDGE NEILSON, — I wish that it were in my power to send you such reminiscences of Mr. Choate as would be worthy to be associated with your excellent articles, and with the interesting and valuable letters which you are gathering from others. But so many years have passed since I had frequent occasion to meet him, and my thoughts in the long interval have been so closely occupied with the incessant duties of a different profession, that I could hardly hope to furnish anything of incident which other pens have not anticipated, or to add a needed line or tint to your careful picture. It is a pleasure to me, however, and the impulse of a sincere gratitude to one who was kind to me in my youth, and whose genius and spirit were full to me then of a fine inspiration, to record my sense of the extraordinary gifts of the man, and of his beautiful and unselfish temper. It will hardly be worth while to print what I write. If it shall give you any suggestion as to how he appeared from my point of view, it will have fully served its purpose.

I saw Mr. Choate for the first time at Amherst, nearly forty years ago,[1] — I think in 1838, — when he tried a case there before referees, his opponent being Hon. Isaac C. Bates, then of Northampton. Mr. Bates was a man of great personal dignity and grace, as well as of commanding ability, whom it was always delightful to see and to hear; but one of the faculty of the college had incidentally said to me that this Mr. Choate was a man who should have been a Greek professor, but who somehow had wandered into the law, and my curiosity was keenly excited to see one who read Plato or Demosthenes "with his feet on the fender," and who still condescended to argue questions of contracts, usury, and the title to lands. The details of his argument have long since passed from my recollection; but I remember, as if it had been yesterday, the power which he showed in the cross-examination of some specially shrewd and stubborn witnesses, the vigor and rapidity of his argumentation, the force of his invective, and the exceeding beauty of two or three swift touches of description with which he fairly illuminated the landscape, with some of whose crooked boundary-lines his argu-

[1] Written in 1877.

ment was concerned. Tones of his voice which I
then heard are still in my ear; and the unique
and mysterious enchantment of his presence — his
curling locks, dark as the raven's wing; his weird,
sad, unworldly eyes; a certain remote and solitary
air which seemed to invest him — stirred my imagination, fastened to him my wondering thought.
I was reminded of the personal effect then produced on me, when standing, many years after, in
the Florentine chapel, before the darkening mar-
ble of the famous statue of Duke Lorenzo, whose
face

> " Is lost in shade; yet, like the basilisk,
> It fascinates, and is intolerable."

Mr. Choate's appearance, at that time in his
life, was potent as a spell over young imaginations. It chained the eye, and haunted the memory. One longed, yet almost feared, to know him.
He appeared to my fancy a sort of Oriental emir,
hardly at home in our strange land, who would
have spoken with more abundant natural freedom
in one of the great Semitic dialects, and among
whose treasures there must be no end of jewels,
spiceries, and inestimable mails.

I afterwards heard him many times: in his
eulogy on President Harrison, for example, in
Faneuil Hall, in 1841; in several of his political
speeches, at one of which, in Boston, I remem-

ber still his glancing description of the recent nomination of Briggs and Reed for governor and lieutenant-governor of Massachusetts, as fitly representing the State in its completeness, — " Berkshire and Cape Cod, the mighty backbone and the strong right-arm of the old Commonwealth." I heard him on one Fourth of July at Concord, when he followed Webster, Berrien, and others, in an address of extraordinary force and splendor, which fairly whirled upon its feet one of the most exacting assemblies that I remember to have seen. I not infrequently heard him in court, though not, as it happened, in any one of the *causes célébres* with which his public fame is conspicuously connected. I heard his magnificent eulogy on Webster, at Hanover, in 1853; and I met him for the last time, I think, at Salem, in 1856, when his genius, wit, and kindly courtesy were as abounding and delightful as ever, though the shadows on his face and the unfathomed pathos of his eye were as impressive as anything ever seen on countenance or canvas.

In the autumn of 1840, I was received by Mr. Choate as a student in his office, though circumstances forbade, at the time, my residence in Boston. Early in 1841, he was elected to the national Senate, as the successor of Mr. Webster; and I thenceforth saw him only occasionally, though for the following year and a half I was all the time pursuing my studies under his direction, and at intervals reporting my progress to him. I really knew him better, I think, after this transient connection with his office had ceased than while it continued; and the thought has been a pleasant one to me that the church of which I have long been the pastor took an impulse to its formation from that transcendent address of his in New York, in 1843, of which Mr. Van Cott has eloquently written.

The instant and eager boyish admiration with which I at first regarded Mr. Choate gave place, as I knew him, and as my own mind advanced toward maturity, to a more discriminating yet more profound sense of his varied and prodigal intellectual gifts. I can but repeat what others have said. My only excuse for repeating it at all is that you have asked me, and that my impression is not copied from others, but was individual and received at first-hand.

He was a scholar by instinct and by the determining force of his nature. All forms of high intellectual activity had charm and reward for his sympathetic and splendid intelligence. He especially delighted, however, in history, philosophy, eloquence, and the immense riches of the ancient literature. His library was peopled to him with living minds. The critical and august procedures in history were as evident to him as processions in the streets. No inspiring and majestic voice had spoken from Athenian *bema*, in Roman forum, in English Parliament whose vital words, even whose tones, did not still echo in his ear. He would have made a Greek professor, elegant in scholarship, rich in acquisition, energetic and liberal in instruction. I am not aware that he ever made special study of theology. He simply took it up, I think, with a literary interest, when its great discussions came in his way; yet Professor Park once said of him, after a half day's conversation, that "If he had not been the first lawyer of his time, he might have been its most eminent theologian." (It is only fair to add that Mr. Choate, knowing nothing of this remark, said to the same gentleman — Mr. Lawrence, then of Andover, — that "If Professor Park had not been the great theologian that he was, he would have surpassed any man whom he knew at the American bar.")

His relish for thought, and for the powerful expression of thought in the most fit and admirable words was only matured by his life-long habit. From the crowd in the court-room, the pressure of cases, the pursuit of clients, and all the elements and the incidents of suits, still quivering with the excitement which had searched every nerve in his throbbing frame, he retreated to the authors, ancient and modern, in whom he delighted; and it was as if he had changed the noisy world for another, more serene and exalting. There were the bloom and the music that he loved, the clearer lights on statelier shores, the spirits that touched his to expand and renew it. He could not go to the White Mountains, on a four-days' journey, without taking with him a trunkful of books. He was simply true to his consciousness in saying that, if he were to go to Newport for pleasure without his books, he should hang himself before evening.

Yet, with his instinctive delight in learning, and in the commerce with illustrious minds to which it introduced him, with the accumulating acquisitions with which it enriched him, and the constant impressions upon his own intellect which came from eminent orators and thinkers, he retained, absolutely, the native peculiarities of a genius as genuine, and certainly as striking, as has anywhere appeared among American public men. You have contrasted him with Macaulay. But in one respect they were certainly alike. Both " carried lightly their load of learning." His mental eye was as fine as a microscope for almost imperceptible distinctions. He penetrated instantly, with affirmative insight, to the secret of entangled and

complex matters. His logical faculty was as keen
and expert as if he had never done anything else
but state and argue questions of law in the courts.
His memory had a grasp, which was utterly relentless, on any principle, fact, or phrase; while
his judgment was as prompt, within its limits as
sagacious, as if he had never heard of Greek par-
ticles and never had read a Latin page. But the
imagination was certainly supreme in him; while
his fancy was also as sparkling and exuberant as
if no argument had ever been wrought by him in
its constraining and infrangible links. This made
his mind not only stimulating but startling, abundant in surprises, suddenly radiant on far themes.
He said nothing in a commonplace way. A flash
of unfamiliar beauty and power was in his slight
and casual remarks. The reports of some of them
are still, I suspect, as current in court-rooms as
when he lived; while, on the larger historical or
philosophical subjects, his sentences, now and
then, were as literal sunbursts, enlightening half
a continent with their gleam. He said as little,
I should think, as any man who ever lived, of
like culture and equal eminence, on the supreme
matters of God, destiny, immortality; but I can
easily understand, what I used to be told, that,
when in rare and preëminent moods he touched
these topics, among intimate friends, his words

were to the usual words of men on similar subjects as superb, tropical passion-flowers among the duller, common growths, purple and golden in their hues, while inclosing at their heart memorial signs of the Divine sadness.

With this sensitive, vigorous, and various genius, and these large acquisitions, Mr. Choate threw himself, with all the energy of his strenuous will, into his chosen profession of the law. He loved it, and he idealized it. He was proud of its history; he exulted in its great names. The law was to him the expression of the highest justice of the state, enlightened and directed by its instructed and intuitive reason. It essentially concerned, therefore, the moral life of communities and of centuries. It had immense historical relations. As obtaining among us, for example, it was the impalpable, vital presence which connected our recent, fragmentary history, our circumscribed American life, with the great life of England, and with its renowned and crowded annals, back to the time of Edward the Confessor and " the common folk-right of the realm; " back, indeed, to the days of King Alfred. He meant to be master of it, by the most exact, profound, indefatigable study of statutes, cases, and the principles they involved. I perfectly remember how this sovereign and far-reaching view of the law impressed my thought, and stirred my enthusiasm, when I first talked with him; how fundamental it was in the scheme of study which he outlined before me; how incessantly it reappeared, whenever I met him. He was at one time, certainly, a most searching and systematic student of the vast Roman law; and no novel ever fastened the eyes of its readers as did any book which illustrated the principles, the practice, or the history of the law, the eyes and mind of Mr. Choate. He loved to regard it as radically grounded, with whatever imperfections, in the enduring cosmical equities, deriving from them its virtue and validity. The country had to him historical importance as the home of a matured and ubiquitous law, guarding the weak, avenging the humble, restraining while protecting the wealthiest and highest. The colonization of the country was impressive to him, not so much for its picturesque incidents as because it had brought hither this great inheritance of rights and of rules, acquired through ages. The magistrates of the law were venerable to him, however plainly inferior to himself in ability and learning. The courts were temples of order and justice. He spoke only the feeling of his life when he said before the legislative committee, " I never read, without a thrill of sublime emotion, the concluding words of the Bill of Rights, — ' to the end that this may be a government of law, and not of men.'"

The application of the law to cases requiring careful adjudication was, therefore, to him a matter of real and serious importance. In connection with it he recoiled from no labor, and was impatient of no details. The most trivial incidents became critical and grave when they furnished occasions for declaring and administering those permanent rules of social order which had been elaborated through centuries of years, for which brave men had fought and suffered, and which had their fruit in the peace of the state, as they had their life in the supreme ethical harmonies.

I do not at all mean to imply that he was not intensely ambitious of success, in whatever cause he undertook. Certainly he was; and the fervid passion grew with his growth, was more eager after each victory, became most intense when his famous successes had prejudiced juries, made judges wary if not hostile, and rendered future similar victories almost impossible. Indeed, his normal rule of practice distinctly was, that each party should present his case in its fullest strength, with whatsoever could make it persuasive; so that out of the sharpest possible collisions of argument and of testimony the final result might be deduced. He thought of his client, and of no-

body else, when he stood for him before a tribunal. Everything that could possibly serve that
client commanded, thereby, his zealous approval.
Everything that threatened him was somehow
or other to be overcome. If the floor of the
court-room had fallen beneath him, unless it had
stunned him, I am sure that it would not have
beaten from his mind the thought of his case for
more than a minute. But in spite of this he had,
when I knew him, an ideal sense of the majesty
of the law, of its moral dignity, and its historical
office, which gave an undertone, delicate and
grand, to all his common professional work. He
could not have labored with that intensity which
was constant with him, except for this inspiriting
force; yet I have no idea that he ever knowingly
misrepresented a principle of the law to serve the
client, who was to him, for the passing moment, as
his own life. Governor Bullock once mentioned to
me an incident which came under his notice when
Webster and Choate were antagonists before the
court. Mr. Choate had lucidly, with great emphasis, stated the law. Mr. Webster — than whom
a greater master of attitude, gesture, and facial
expression never lived — turned on him the gaze
of his great eye, as if in mournful, despairing remonstrance against such a sad and strange per-
version. "That *is* the law, may it please your

Honor," thundered Mr. Choate, catching the glance, advancing a step, and looking full in Webster's face, "That *is* the law, in spite of the admonishing, the somewhat *paternal* look in the eye of my illustrious friend."[1] And it was the law, as affirmed by the court.

The fervent enthusiasm with which Mr. Choate devoted himself to the trial of his cases could only be understood by those who recognized the genius of the man, craving exercise and excitement, his culture supplying him with unmeasured resources, and the admiration which he felt for the law, with its magistrates and tribunals. It had little to do with fees or with applause. It was sometimes shown in the unnoticed case, in the small back-office of some referee, with no audience present, as fully as in the echoing court-room, on a grand field-day. I never heard of a mind of such compass as his, so energetic and so affluent, which heated so quickly. It was like a superb Corliss engine, driven for days with a bushel of coal. The mere attrition of any case, where the

---

[1] Such dainty and humorous use of words was constant with him. "When I had been two days on the Rhine," he said to me at Hanover, "I knew the whole river perfectly; could n't have known it better if I 'd been *drowned in* it." A reputation which had been damaged in the courts was, "to make the best of it, sadly tenebrious." His "overworked participle," his description of the witness testifying, in a case where a tailor was concerned, "with an eye to pantaloons in the distance," etc., are well-known.

facts were in doubt and the principles obscure, was enough to set his whole force in activity. And the enthusiasm, so easily enkindled, was as enduring as it was instantaneous. It almost literally knew no limit. It saw every difficulty, faced every juridical danger, snatched every instrument of impression, watched the face of every juror, took instant suggestion from the eye or even the attitude of the judge, felt the subtile force of the general feeling pervading the court-room, kept all the facts and all the principles incessantly in mind, transfigured them all in the radiance of genius, and shot his vivid interpretation of all upon the jury, in the most plausible, deferential, captivating, commanding utterance which even lips so skilled and practiced could attain. Weakness, languor, sickness itself vanished before this invincible spirit. Haggard, wan, after a night of sleepless suffering, his throat sore, his head throbbing, swathed in flannels, buried under overcoats, with wrappings around his neck, a bandage on his knee, a blister on his chest, when he rose for his argument all facts reported by witnesses in the case, all the related and governing precedents, all legal principles bearing upon it, all passages of history, letters, life, that might illustrate his argument or confound his antagonists seemed visibly present to his mind. He thought of nothing but

jury and verdict. His eloquence was then as
completely independent of technical rule as are
screams of passion, or the shouts of a mob. He
was after a favorable decision of the case, as if
his own life depended on it. Short, sharp, shat-
tering words rattled like volleys before and after
resounding sentences. Language heaped on his
lips. Images, delicate, homely, startling, blazed
upon his pictured words. The common court-
room became a scene of the most astonishing
intellectual action. Judge Shaw looked at him
as he might have looked at the firm-set heavens,
glittering with meteors. The farmers, mechanics,
traders, on the jury, were seized, swept forward,
stormed upon, with an utterance so unbounded in
variety and energy, sometimes so pathetic, sometimes so quaint, sometimes so grotesque, always so
controlling and impellent, as only his hearers ever
had heard. The velocity of his speech was almost
unparalleled, yet the poise of his mind was as
undisturbed as that of the planet; and each vague
doubt, in either mind, was recognized and com-
bated, unconscious prejudices were delicately con-
ciliated, each tendency toward his view of the
case was encouraged and confirmed, each leaning
toward his opponent was found out and fought,
with a skill which other men toiled after in vain,
which seemed in him a strange inspiration.

No wonder that he sometimes wrenched the verdict from unwilling hands, in cases which looked to outsiders as desperate as Bonaparte's charge upon the bridge of Arcola! No wonder that his profession loved and admired him with a fervor of feeling which twenty years have not diminished, and that " grace and renown " were felt to have departed from darkened court-rooms when his incomparable mind and mien were no more present! No wonder that Mr. R. H. Dana said, in substance, at the meeting of the bar after his death, " The great Conqueror, unseen and irresistible, has broken into our temple, and has carried off the vessels of gold, the vessels of silver, the precious stones, and the ivory, and we must content ourselves hereafter with vessels of wood and stone and iron ! "

I have spoken, my dear Judge, simply of Mr. Choate's intellectual endowments, and of his rare mental equipment, as these impressed me more than thirty years ago. Of the sweet courtesy of his feeling and manner in social life, of his constancy to his friends, his generosity toward his juniors, his unfeigned deference toward the bench, of his unresentful spirit toward assailants, his utter want of political ambition or pecuniary greed, his chivalrous devotion to what he esteemed the best public policy, though it severed him from friends and added new shadows to his last years, of his blamelessness of life, especially of his habitual respect for the Divine Revelation, and for the house and the ordinances of worship, — of these I retain such happy recollections as all those must who chanced then, even slightly, to know him.

But I have immensely outrun already the intended limits of my letter, and other pens must delineate these. I have said enough, I am sure, to show you why I am grateful for his influence upon me, which was far greater than he knew, and why — though I see the limitations of his mind, and was never in sympathy with some of his opinions — I retain his image with a fondness and a regret that never will cease. I cannot think of him to-day without being braced against any temptation to languor in study or remissness in work; without feeling afresh the vastness and the charm of that world of thought and of elegant letters in which his spirit rejoiced to expatiate; without being consciously grateful to God that, at the age when I took impressions most readily from others, I was brought for a time into contact with a mind so remarkable as his, so rich in knowledge and so replete with every force, with a temper so engaging, with an intellectual enthusiasm so incessant and inspiring.

Ever, my dear Judge, faithfully yours,

R. S. STORRS.

LETTER FROM MATTHEW H. CARPENTER.

THIS letter from the late Matthew H. Carpenter, formerly United States Senator from Wisconsin, is important not only by reason of his high character as a lawyer, but because he had been a student under Mr. Choate.

DEAR SIR, — Returning from Washington, I have just found yours of the 18th. I have read your two articles in the "Law Journal" on Rufus Choate. Your articles are an excellent and truthful generalization of his character, professional and political.

He was more than a father to me, and I loved him next to idolatry. I studied law with him in 1847 and 1848. The most striking of all his characteristics was his regard for the feelings of others. Whatever he might say in the excitement of a trial in regard to the opposite party, or even of witnesses whom he disbelieved, he was, in his office, and in all professional and social intercourse, most considerate of the feelings of others.

I never heard him speak an impatient or angry word in my life. Especially to young men did he show this tender consideration. Webster's presence overawed a young man; Choate impressed the young man with his greatness, but he did so by lifting him for the time up to his own level. His genius seemed to be an inspiration to every young man who entered his presence; and those who had the honor of his acquaintance regarded him with an admiration akin to hero-worship. Even the old man who tended the fire in the office never entered Mr. Choate's room without receiving some kindly salutation. His name was John — John *what* I never knew. But Mr. Choate always called him *Johannes,* with a tone of tenderness and affection which delighted him, and which lingers in my ear to this day.

One of Mr. Choate's characteristics was to idealize everything. His perception of subtile analogies tinged his mind, and appears in his utterances; in his mental atmosphere all things, however common or even unclean, became transformed, beautiful.

Another feature was his charity. From those who would borrow he turned not away. I remember an occasion when he was exceedingly driven in the preparation of a brief that had to be printed for use the next morning. He was examining the authorities, and dictating to me as his amanuensis. By some inadvertence, his door was not locked, as it usually was, and a squalid beggar made his way into Mr. Choate's presence. He had all day refused to see lawyers, doctors, authors, and others. But, seeing the old man, he turned to me and said, "My boy, charity is a privileged subject, always in order. Let us hear what the old man has to say." After listening for a while, he determined to give him three dollars, and made faithful search through his pockets without finding the amount. He then borrowed the money of me, and gave it to the old man; and the next morning, when he came into the office with three or four overcoats on, he had three dollars in his hand, which he threw down on my table saying, "There is nothing quite so mean as borrowing a *small* sum of money and forgetting to pay it."

He always stood in awe of Webster, and spent nights in preparation when about to contend with him at the bar. This I never could understand; as a mere lawyer, I think Choate as much the superior of Webster as Webster was the superior of lawyers generally. His knowledge of the law, his readiness in using all his resources, legal, literary, historical, or poetical, his power of advocacy, the magnetism of his presence and the absolute enchantment in which he wrapt both court and jury never were equaled in any other man, I believe. I remember an instance of one of Choate's clients coming into his office in great glee, and informing Mr. Choate that he had just met his antagonist, who had said he expected to be beaten in the case, because he had nobody but Mr. Webster, who would pay no attention to the case until it was called for trial, while Mr. Choate would be thoroughly prepared on every point. Mr. Choate seemed to be rather displeased than flattered, and, turning to his client in a solemn, almost tragic, manner, he said, " Beware of any hope that rests upon undervaluation of Mr. Webster. He will be there on the morning of the trial with one case from the Term Reports exactly in point; and, if we escape with our lives, so much the better for us."

I think he had formed the resolution that no man should leave his office except in a pleasant mood, if not in a roar of laughter. I remember that on one occasion a clergyman came to consult him about a matter full of sorrow. During the consultation, Mr. Choate was very much affected, and I knew from his tremulous tone, without looking at him, that his eyes were filled with tears. I thought at that time that the old clergyman would be an exception, but I was mistaken. Mr.

Choate followed him to the door and opened it and made some remark which I did not hear, but which literally convulsed the old clergyman.

Mr. Choate's wit and humor were all the more effective from the fact that God never put upon a man, except perhaps Lincoln, so sad a face.

During all the time I was with him, his health was more or less disturbed, and his face was eloquently expressive of constant anguish. Many a time I have seen him come into the office from the court-room, the personification of weariness and sorrow, so much so that often merely looking in his face has forced the moisture to my eyes. But the tear never reached my cheek before he would set me laughing with some quaint remark. I remember his coming into the office and telling me that the Supreme Court of Massachusetts had just decided an important cause against him, evidently to his great surprise. He threw down some books and papers on his desk, and after telling me of the decision, added in a half-serious, half-playful way, " *Every judge* on that bench seems to be more stupid *than every other one;* and if I were not afraid of losing the good opinion of the Court I would impeach the whole batch of them." Yet, notwithstanding such badinage, his reverence for the Court, and especially for Chief Justice Shaw, was unbounded. As a further instance of such pleasantry, Stevenson, the sculptor, told me that he was once engaged in carving a lion of exaggerated size; that, while he was engaged on the head and mane, Mr. Choate took the liveliest interest in the work, calling every morning as he came down, and every evening on his way home, to mark its progress. Stevenson, being curious, asked Mr. Choate why that work interested him so much. " Why," said Mr. Choate, " that is the best likeness of Chief Justice Shaw that I ever saw."

His complete mastery over the melancholy, the gloomy emotions of human nature, has reconciled me to Shakespeare's representation of Richard the Third's making love to Anne in the funeral procession of her husband. Had Mr. Choate thus met her, he could have lifted the shadows from her heart.

I could go on much longer without being weary of the subject; and, although this has been dictated in haste, it may be some confirmation of the view of Mr. Choate's character which you have so admirably set forth.   Yours truly,

MATT. H. CARPENTER.

To Hon. J. Neilson.

LETTER FROM JAMES T. FIELDS.

It was fortunate that the late James T. Fields was able to leave this record of his love and admiration of Mr. Choate : —

My dear Sir, — I thank you for those numbers of the "Albany Law Journal" containing your interesting papers on Mr. Choate. Everything with reference to that great man is most attractive to me, and I could not resist the impulse of writing a lecture not long ago on his brilliant career, that I might say something to young students, inadequate though it might be, that would perhaps incite them, by his example of untiring industry, to a more enthusiastic pursuit of knowledge, and a more earnest study of the art of eloquence. That lecture has already been delivered in various colleges and law schools, and I hope has led some of my listeners to read Professor Brown's memoir of our great advocate, your own papers in the "Law Journal," and the reminiscences of Dr. Storrs, Mr. Carpenter, and others, who knew and appreciated him.

I wish I had the opportunity to comply more closely with your kind request, and send a better response to your invitation. I can only, before getting off for the summer, send you this fragmentary epistle.

Mr. Choate is now, to employ Landor's significant line,

"Beyond the arrows, shouts, and views of men,"

and his supreme qualities are only beginning to be apparent in their grander aspects. As a lawyer, ranking among the highest; as an eloquent advocate, second not even to Lord Erskine, whom he far surpassed in scholarship; as a patriot, devoted to public duty solely; he is now taking his place without a rival and without a cavil. Years ago I hung up his portrait in the little room we called " our library," for a constant reminder of the long-continued enjoyment it was my own good fortune to have derived from the kind-hearted Mentor and friend. To have had the privilege of living in the same city with him for so many years, of hearing the sound of his voice in public and in private for a quarter of a century, was indeed of itself an education. To the young men of my time, who lived so much under the spell of his eloquence, he was an inspirer, an initiator; for he taught us by his example to reverence and seek whatever was best in learning, and excellent in thought and

character. As young students of literature, eager
to listen and acquire if we could, we found a new
power created within us by *contact* even with such
a teacher and guide. To follow him, to wait upon
his footsteps through the courts of law, the Senate,
or the lecture-room, was in a certain sense to be

"From unreflecting ignorance preserved."

His own great acquirements taught us to nurse
that noble self-discontent which points and leads
to a loftier region of culture, and impelled us to
aspirations we had never dreamed of until his affluent genius led the way. Like Charles Fox, he
was born with the oratorical temperament, and so
he magnetized all the younger men who flocked
about him eager to be instructed. I do not believe
the "high-placed personage" ever lived in any
community who had more affection and reverence
from the youth of his time than Mr. Choate.
There were about him habitually that diffusive
love and tenderness which make idolatry possible
even among one's contemporaries. While he electrified us, he called us by our Christian names;
and when he beckoned us to come, we dared and
delighted to stand by his side and listen. His willing and endearing helpfulness made him beloved
by his inferiors as few men of his conspicuous eminence ever were before, and one could not approach him and remain unmoved or only partially

attracted.   You could not meet him on the street, even, without having a fresh impulse given to your circulation.   During the period when he took early morning walks, some of us, mere boys at that time, loving the sight of the man and the music of his voice, used to be on his track, watching for him on his matutinal rounds.   As he came sailing into view

> " On broad, imperial wings,"

with that superb and natural gait so easily recognized by those who knew him,

> " Far off his coming shone."

As he swung himself past, he would drop into our greedy ears some healthy, exhilarating quotation, fresh from the fount of song; some golden sentence suited to the day and hour; something ample and suggestive that would linger in our memories and haunt our young imaginations years afterward, influencing perhaps our whole lives onward.

Happy the youth who was occasionally privileged to walk with him on such occasions,

> " Under the opening eyelids of the morn,"

for then he would discuss, perhaps in his deep and never-to-be-forgotten tones of admiration, the lofty Homeric poems; quote the divine, and to him familiar, words of Plato; dilate with a kindred rapture over some memorable passage of Plutarch;

or hold up for counsel and admonition some of the sublimest inspirations of the Bible. Well might a young man, thus enchanted, exclaim with Comus,

> " Oh, such a sacred and home-felt delight,
> Such sober certainty of waking bliss
> I never heard till now!"

He seemed ever on the alert to quicken and inspire thought in the heart and understanding of the young. I remember, on the eve of sailing on my first brief visit to Europe, he passed me on the stairs at a crowded reception, and whispered as he went by, "Don't fail, my young friend, if you go near it in your travels, to pause at the grave of Erasmus for me."

It was dangerous for any young man, not a student at law, to hear him discourse of the profession as he fully and solemnly believed in it, accepting as he did the splendid metaphor of Hooker, — " Her seat the bosom of God ; her voice the harmony of the world; all things in heaven and earth doing her homage ; the very least as feeling her care, and the greatest as not exempted from her power." One of Choate's former office students once said to him, " The more I get into practice the more I like the law." " Like it!" said Choate, " of course you do. There is nothing else for any man of intellect to like." This was said in that fine frenzy of exaggeration which he sometimes delighted in, but no young man could hear him discourse of jurisprudence and not wish to join the ranks. Law was the banner of his pride; the flux and reflux of party strife were distasteful to every fibre of his intellect; and he always gave us to understand that he considered his profession worthy of all the hope of ambition, and all the aspirations for excellence. At the bar Mr. Choate towered superior to every kind of jealousy, of suspicion, of malevolence, to every narrow and sordid motive, to all the meaner trepidations of mortality. He was by nature a gentleman, and he had no petty vanities, either public or private. He was indeed an inspired orator. What power, what tenderness, what magnetism pervaded his utterances! His voice vibrated with every sentiment, every impulse of beauty and wisdom. He ran over the whole gamut of expression at will. When he spoke of flowers, his words seemed to have the very perfume of flowers in them; and when he painted the ocean, which he loved so fondly, his tone was as the scent of the sea when the wind blows the foam in our faces. As Churchill said of Garrick, he also had indeed

> " Strange powers that lie
> Within the magic circle of his eye."

If he habitually composed for the ear more than for the eye, it was because his victories were to be won face to face with his fellow-men. I have heard him argue a hundred cases, perhaps, large and small, and he always seemed alike invincible, as if no mortal power could take his verdict from him. His manner to the opposing counsel was full of courtesy and conciliation; but if that counsel became arrogant and insulting he would slay him with a sentence so full of suavity and keenness that the unmannerly victim never knew what killed him.

There were uninstructed and unsympathetic listeners, of course, who described Mr. Choate as declamatory, and accused him of being over-worded and over-colored, — "driving a substantive and six," as they called it, — but those same platitudinous dwellers in the twilight of the mind would no doubt quarrel with the tints in Milton's "L'Allegro," and find Collins's "Ode to the Passions" highly improper. Mr. Choate was no doubt rich and exuberant in his style, but who would not prefer the leap of the torrent to the stagnation of the swamp? It was truly said by Mr. Everett, in Faneuil Hall, at the sad hour of our sharp bereavement in 1859, that with such endowments as Mr. Choate possessed he *could* fill no second place. Thinking of the magic orator, the profound lawyer, logician, and scholar, I recall Ben Jonson's memorable words on the wonderful power of Lord Bacon, for they are all applicable to Mr. Choate, — "There happened in my time one noble speaker, who was full of gravity in his speaking. His language (where he could spare or pass by a jest) was nobly censorious. No man ever spoke more neatly, more pressly, more weightily, or suffered less idleness in what he uttered. No member of his speech but consisted of his own graces. His hearer could not cough or look aside from him without loss. He commanded where he spoke, and had his judges angry and pleased at his devotion. No man had their affections more in his power. The fear of every one that heard him was lest he should make an end." And that was just the fear we all had when Choate was speaking, — lest he should stop, lest the sound of his perfect voice should cease, — lest he too should make an end. I cannot but lament that those who have more recently put on the legal robes, and whose steps are yet on the threshold of life, can have no chance of ever hearing those magic tones which so thrilled the young students of my time, and realized to us that sovereign genius which unites the faculty of reasoning with the faculty of imagination.

My letter is already too long. Pardon my prolixity, and believe me, dear sir, most cordially yours,

JAMES T. FIELDS.

To Judge Neilson.

LETTER FROM DR. BOYDEN.

Dr. Boyden, of Beverly, Mass., an intimate friend of Mr. Choate's, had the kindness to send me the following: —

We entered college together in 1815. He was between fifteen and sixteen years of age, very youthful and engaging in appearance, modest and unpretentious in manner. He had been fitted for college in a rather desultory way, his preliminary studies with the minister, the doctor, and the schoolmaster having been interrupted by seasons of work on his father's farm. He had spent a short time at Hampton Academy just before coming to Dartmouth. Several students, fresh from Andover, entered at the same time. They were more fully prepared than he, and, at the start, showed to better advantage in their recitations. But by and by some of these began to fall from their first estate, and it was remarked about the same time, that "That young Choate in the corner recited remarkably well." Before the end of the first term he was the acknowledged leader of the class, and he maintained that position until graduation, without apparent difficulty. No one pretended to rival him, nor did he invite comparison. He paid little attention to the proficiency of his fellow-students. His talk was of eminent scholars of other countries and of former times, and they seemed the objects of his emulation. One European scholar being mentioned as having committed to memory the Greek primitives, Choate seems to have accepted the suggestion as a valuable one. A few weeks afterward I was in his room, and he asked me to hear him recite. I took a book and heard him repeat page after page of Greek primitives, without ostentation, but merely, to all appearance, to test himself.

He did not limit his studies to the curriculum. After the first year he read a great deal beyond the prescribed course, especially in Cicero, of whose works he thus went over several, and took up, besides, some of the Greek authors.

He neglected athletic exercises almost entirely. His chief relaxations from study were of a social character. He would get half a dozen of the students into his room, and, refreshments being obtained, would give himself up with them to having a " good time."

In the public exercises of the college he attracted much attention. If he had an oration to deliver, the audience was always eager to hear it, and generally was rewarded by a masterly effort.

As we adopted different professions, he the law, and I medicine, I had, much to my regret, few opportunities of witnessing the displays of his maturer powers. But our personal intimacy was very great, and continued through life.

I had, from the first, no doubt that he would strive for, and attain, the foremost rank in his profession. When he commenced practice in Salem, we had two or three old lawyers, of whom Mr. Thorndyke was one. I said to him, "Mr. Choate is not in the Superior Court yet (his time not having expired in the Common Pleas); but I know him very well, and he will be at the head of the Essex bar as soon as he can get there." The old lawyer looked at me with surprise and incredulity; but I had the pleasure of hearing him, before many years had elapsed, admit the fulfillment of my prophecy.

During the earlier years of his practice, he sometimes spoke to me of his aspirations, one of which was to be one of our chief justices. He was offered a judgeship afterward, but never could afford to accept.

His professional income he spent lavishly. He gave away a great deal, and neglected, in many instances, to collect or to charge for his services. He was careless in payment, too, but never to the point of injustice. Having borrowed a sum of money when a young man, he retained it for many years, always paying interest, though it is certain he could have repaid the principal many times over if it had been necessary. Finally I, as the representative of one of the heirs of the lender, had occasion to ask for the money, and it was paid at once. When paying the interest, he said to me on one occasion, " You have had some trouble about this, I will give you your law;" and he did, both advice and service, when needed. I had occasion to know much of his benefactions, as I was sometimes his almoner. Some instances of his generosity I communicated to Mr. Brown, when he was preparing his book.

His love of study lasted through life, and he accounted it as one of his chief blessings. In speaking to me of his son one day, he held up his hand and said, " I would give that finger if it would make him love study as I do."

The humorous side of his character has been, to so great an extent, that on which the public attention has been hitherto fixed that it needs no illustration. But the evenness of his temper is worth remarking. He was always agreeable, genial, companionable, playful even, toward those with whom he was intimate. I could never be long in his company without hearing some enlivening pleasantry.

I do not think Mr. Choate was fitted to be a leader in politics. He was constitutionally timid and conservative. Given a leader, like Webster, he was a useful and zealous supporter. Let him have a question to argue, and, if he felt that the country was his client, he waxed eloquent and sought eagerly for victory. During Webster's lifetime he initiated no policy. The latter, on his death-bed, told Choate, " You have a great future before you if you go with the party and direct them." Choate could go with the party — he could even go against it; but the instinct of leadership was weak in him; to control the party was work to which he was not fitted, an up-hill labor.

It is exceedingly difficult to describe or to characterize such a man. He was unlike any other I have known. Webster seemed to be a good deal like other folks, only there was more of him. But Choate was peculiar; — a strange, beautiful product of our time, not to be measured by reference to ordinary men.

LETTER FROM EMORY WASHBURN.

THE late Emory Washburn sent me this tribute to the memory of Rufus Choate : —

DEAR SIR, — It is with much hesitation and misgiving that I enter upon the attempt to comply with your flattering request to give you some of my recollections of Mr. Choate. Aside from the difficulty in describing a man of such varied and peculiar characteristics and qualities, it is to be borne in mind that it is already seventeen years since his death, and that, during that time, impressions originally strong have been growing fainter, and the incidents and events of his life becoming less distinctly defined, and that many things which were worthy of notice at the time they occurred have lost their interest for want of surrounding circumstances. All I shall attempt will be to recall general impressions rather than distinct incidents.

While I have no right to claim any special intimacy with Mr. Choate, I met him too often, after our first meeting in the Legislature of 1825, in private and social life, as well as at the bar and in the courts and in public assemblies, not to receive and retain pretty decided impressions of the power and qualities for which he became so widely known and admired. He was about four months my senior in age.

In stature Mr. Choate was nearly, if not quite, six feet in height, strong and muscular, without being in the least gross. His head was finely formed, and covered with a profusion of very dark, curly hair. His complexion was dark, his features regular, his lips thin, and, when his countenance was at rest, were generally closely shut, giving his mouth an expression of contemplation rather than firmness. His eye was dark, was mildly piercing, and, at times, had a pensive cast, which was in harmony with his whole expression when by himself. His movements, without being awkward or abrupt, indicated nervous energy rather than muscular power. When in company with others, his face assumed as many shades of expression as he had changing moods of thought. From the quiet rest of deep contemplation it would light up by a sudden flash of playful humor, or an expression of intense interest, when he gave utterance to some new or inspiring thought. But although a ready humor, thus modified, was perhaps one of the most characteristic marks of the amiable temperament for which he was distinguished, it never degenerated into boisterous mirth nor broke out into laughter. I doubt if any one ever heard him laugh aloud, though no one ever had a keener sense of the ridiculous, or loved fun more heartily.

While such was the general temperament of the man, as he appeared to others in the ordinary intercourse of society or business, to his more intimate friends, as often as leisure or opportunity offered, this playful habit of thought and fancy manifested itself in a great variety of forms. When in such a mood, it was delightful to see him unbend, and give conversation free play. He would indulge in such extravagant forms of expression, such exaggerated statements, such absurd opinions, and conclusions so utterly at variance with his well-known sentiments, half gravely uttered, and yet understood by all, that it was an occasion of constant merriment; in which, without even descending to drollery, he was often carrying on graver discussions, or attacking some popular whim or error, mingling wit with logic, and fun with graver realities of life.[1] There would be no end to the anecdotes illustrative of

[1] It was thus, perhaps in more extravagant forms, with Sydney Smith.   J. N.

this phase of his mind, if any one had taken the pains to preserve them. One has been often repeated, of his opinion of Chief Justice Shaw, for whom, by the way, he had a profound veneration for his qualities as a judge, and between whom and Mr. Choate there was a mutual admiration and respect. No man had a kinder nature than the Chief Justice, and no man would have sooner shrunk from saying or doing anything which could wound the sensibilities of another; and as for conscious partiality in favor of any one, because of his rank or position in society, no man even suspected it. But, unfortunately, he had a way of expressing his disapproval of what seemed to him a fallacy in an argument, or a questionable mode of proceeding in a cause, which sounded very like reproof, and often gave pain to the subject of it, from the manner in which it was done. Nor did Mr. Choate escape. On one occasion, after listening with respect to one of those rebukes, as he did to everything which fell from the Court, Mr. Choate turned to two or three of his brethren who had heard it, and quietly remarked, with that expression upon his countenance which always told the mood he was in, " I do not suppose that any one ever thought the Chief Justice was much of a lawyer, but nobody can deny that he is a man of pleasant manners." On one occasion he was engaged in a very important case in a remote county, when it fell to me to hold the term of the court. He gave up two days to the preparation before the commencement of the term, but found one sufficient, so that the other day was lost in waiting. To one who could not tolerate an idle hour this was inexpressibly irksome. I arrived in town in due time, and met Mr. Choate at the door of the hotel, and was greeted with "I am glad you have come at last, for I have been waiting for you just fifty thousand years;" which, considering his impatience in losing time, was hardly an exaggerated expression of his estimate of it.

In the composition of Mr. Choate's nature, the prevailing element was sweetness. Bitterness was entirely left out. His spirit, like the action of his mind, was quick and easily aroused; but he could not carry anger, nor keep alive a feeling of resentment. He had no false pride of opinion, and could laugh at his own mistakes as readily as others. After witnessing in court, one day, with two or three others, the queer rulings of a certain judge, who had made himself somewhat conspicuous in his mode of conducting trials, one of them turned to him and said, "Let us see, did you not join in a petition to have this man appointed?" "Headed it," said Mr. Choate, with the quietest possible humor, and went on with his conversation.

In his family no one could be more delightful, ministering to the happiness of the circle of which he was the special centre, and in which his conversation was full of pleasant humor and profitable instruction. So, in his intercourse with his friends, though free from everything like restraint, he never talked without some purpose or aim, or without saying something that might be remembered. His voice was pleasant and well modulated; and, though clear and resonant, never loud or harsh, even when excited before a popular audience. His command of language was literally wonderful. No man had a richer vocabulary of choice and apt words. He was never at a loss for the right form of expression, nor did he obscure a vigorous thought by the beautiful drapery in which he clothed it.

In his manner of addressing an audience, especially a jury, he made use of a great deal of action, but without rant or violent gesticulation. He grew animated by the very effort of speaking; every muscle seemed to be brought into play, and his whole person gave signs of emotion. The perspiration would fall in large drops from his hair and run down his face; which, at times, grew pale and haggard while he poured out, in one unbroken current, language full of thought, emotion, or rare illustrations, of which his public addresses largely partook. But, though a casual listener might be dazzled by the brilliancy of his rhetoric and the charm of his eloquence, no one who followed his train of thought, when desiring to convince his audience of some interesting truth, could be more impressed by the beauty of his oratory than by the clear statement and logical arrangement of his argument, which carried with them the conviction of his hearers. One peculiarity marked his style, whether oral or written, and that was the continuous and unbroken train of thought upon which he sometimes entered; which, instead of being exhausted by being pursued to any given extent, seemed to gather new exposition and illustration as he proceeded, until there seemed no place left at which to arrest it. If some important idea or proposition presented itself to his mind, it seemed to call up so many kindred and associated ideas, and one thought came crowding so closely upon another, that there was left him no place for pause or suspension, and he would go on through an entire page without a space for a punctuation mark, beyond an occasional dash to hold its parts together.

Whenever he spoke, he played upon his audience as a master with the tones or harmonies of an organ, at one moment delighting them with his humor, at another moving them to indignation at some unmerited wrong, and touching at another a shade of delicate sensibility, leading them, it might be by a train of profound thought and subtile reasoning, to the conclusion which he was aiming to reach. And it was not easy, at times, to say in which of these exhibitions of moral and intellectual power he was most to be admired.

And yet, when one recalled the grave or even sad cast of his countenance when at rest, and remembered the change that came over it as it lighted up almost to inspiration when he was dealing with reasons and the passions of his fellow-men, in masses, and saw how he moulded and gave form to the opinions of others by the mere force of his powers of persuasion, he could not fail to perceive that his true strength lay in the region of sober dialectics rather than in that of brilliant oratory.

In the management of his own affairs, Mr. Choate was careless in charging or collecting moneys, while he was generous, almost to a fault, in his contributions to the necessities of others. But in no way was this readiness to bestow the fruits of the labors, by which he earned his livelihood, more marked than in the frequent devotion of his time to the preparation or delivery of orations, lectures, and addresses on occasions of literary, patriotic, political, and commemorative gatherings, for which he could expect no other compensation than the consciousness of its being a means of directing and controlling the thoughts and opinions of others. This constant strain upon his mental and physical energies, in connection with a frequent recurrence of severe headaches, began, at last, to tell upon his constitution as well as upon his looks. The lines and furrows of his face grew deeper and more visible; his countenance began to bear a worried and haggard look, except when animated in debate; and age, while it spared the lustre of hair, gave signs of premature progress. But whatever he lost of muscular activity seemed to be more than made up by an added supply of nervous and intellectual energy, till both gave way before the approach of the disease which terminated his life. His sweetness and kindness of manner, however, remained with him till the last.

I can speak of his qualities as a senator only from the published accounts of the day. Nor would I venture to speak of his scholarship with confidence, except from the testimony of others. No one, however, could be with him any length of time without perceiving his familiarity with classic authors and their literature. In his public addresses, and even in his arguments before juries, he not infrequently resorted to quotations from these authors, when he wished to give some happy thought an epigrammatic force. And those best capable of judging were unqualified in their high appreciation of the extent and accuracy of his attainments in classic learning. I remember his showing me at his own house, with a kind of affectionate pride, a beautiful copy of Cicero, and remarking with considerable emphasis that he never suffered a day to pass by in which he did not read one or more pages in that volume. I have no doubt that, if his memory had rested upon his attainments as a classical scholar, it would have associated his name with some of the first in the land; yet he did not limit himself to the literature of the ancients, but was equally thorough in that of his own language.

But the sphere in which Mr. Choate was most ambitious to excel, and in which he achieved his most signal success, was that of the bar. To that he gave his best energies, and in its service he wore out the physical powers of a vigorous constitution. He cultivated the law as a broad and liberal science, while, in applying it to the practical questions cognizable by the courts, he spared neither time nor labor to make it serve the purpose of equal justice. To this end he applied great

quickness of apprehension, patience in research, a
generous pride in his profession, and an aptitude
for labor which shrunk from no degree of diligence or requisite amount of exhaustion. Nor
were these qualities displayed occasionally only.
Whether his case was small or large, whether his
cause was upon the civil or the criminal side of
the court, whether his client was rich or poor, or
his fee was a large or a small one, he went into it
thoroughly prepared, and ready at all points;
and, when in, he gave to it his whole energy, and
spared nothing which could insure success. Nor
were his arguments confined to the details of the
more technical points of his case; he made free
use, at will, of that store of learning and illustration which his memory was at all times ready to
supply. I heard him, on one occasion, address the
court, when I presided, upon a motion to dismiss
an indictment, charging embezzlement upon an
officer of a bank, on the ground that the statute
prescribing the *form* of stating the charge, and
under which the indictment had been drawn, was
ex post facto, it having been passed subsequently
to the alleged act of embezzlement. It was purely
a constitutional argument, and the point lay within a narrow compass. But, for beauty of diction,
aptness of illustration, and force of reasoning, it
was one of his best efforts.. He dwelt, among

other things, upon the history of our Constitution, and showed how its provisions, many of them at least, had their origin in the events of English history. He spoke of the Star Chamber, the bills of attainder, the progress of English liberty during the Commonwealth and at the Revolution, and of the last struggle of prerogative with the free spirit of the Constitution in the attainder and execution of Sir John Fenwick, and brought these all to bear upon the danger, as a precedent, of holding a man to answer for a crime under an act of legislation passed subsequently to the commission of the deed, especially where, as in this case, a popular odium had been awakened against him as a public officer.

Nor was his skill in conducting the trial of a cause less remarkable than the ability with which he presented it, in the end, to the court and jury. In the cross-examination of witnesses, he seemed to know intuitively how far to pursue it and where to stop. He never aroused opposition on the part of the witness by attacking him, but disarmed him by the quiet and courteous manner in which he pursued his examination. He was quite sure, before giving him up, to expose the weak parts of his testimony, or the bias, if any, which detracted from the confidence to be given it. On the other hand, he never allowed himself to appear surprised or disconcerted by anything in the way of evidence or argument which might come out in the course of a trial, however damaging it might seem to the case. To the jury it seemed to come as a matter of course, and nothing on his part served to give it any special importance. Anecdotes of this character were often told of him, — one of which I give, as it was told to me, to illustrate his coolness and self-possession, as well as his adroitness in warding off what he could not meet. In giving his testimony, a witness for his antagonist let fall, with no particular emphasis, a statement of a most important fact, from which he saw that inferences greatly damaging to his client's cause might be drawn, if skillfully used. He suffered the witness to go through his statement; and then, as if he saw in it something of great value to himself, requested him to repeat it carefully, that he might take it down correctly. He as carefully avoided cross-examining the witness, and in his argument made not the least allusion to his testimony. When the opposing counsel, in his close, came to that part of his case in his argument, he was so impressed with the idea that Mr. Choate had discovered that there was something in that testimony which made in his favor, although he could not see how, that he contented himself with merely remarking

that, though Mr. Choate had seemed to think that
the testimony bore in favor of his client, it seemed
to him that it went to sustain the opposite side,
and then he went on with the other parts of his
case.

In the trial of his cases, Mr. Choate took full
notes of the testimony, to which he often seemed
to refer, though to one who looked on it was difficult to see anything there that was legible or
could be deciphered. His handwriting, at best,
was a puzzle, little better than hieroglyphics.
His minutes of testimony were far worse, being
made up of words and symbols and, now and then,
a spiral curve longer than the rest, which he
seemed to be able to read and interpret, though
no one else would think of attempting it.

In his manner to the Court, he was always deferential and respectful, even when the judge was
his junior in years or his inferior in learning or
ability. Indeed, courtesy, a kindness of manner,
was a part of his nature, which he uniformly exhibited in his intercourse with the bar as well as
with others.

When he died, therefore, he left no wounds for
time to heal; no resentments for injuries un-
atoned for; and when, with what he might have
regarded as still many years of brilliant success
before him, he died at the age of fifty-nine, every

one felt there was a void, which no one could fill, within the circle in which he had moved; while to such as knew him in the more intimate relations of private life it was the loss of a companion, a friend endeared by the qualities which men love and admire.

I stop here, not because I have exhausted the subject, but because I have found it is not within my power to treat it as it ought to be. But you asked me " to recall facts, incidents, and events, personal, professional, and domestic," and I hope you will accept this as an earnest of good intentions.   Yours truly, etc.,

                                        EMORY WASHBURN.

JUDGE J. NEILSON.

Mr. E. D. Sanborn, professor in Dartmouth College, sends me the following reminiscence of Mr. Choate : —

My acquaintance with Mr. Choate began as early as 1831, when I was a student in college. He was warmly attached to Hanover, where the happiest days of his life were spent in study and in teaching. Here, too, he found his wife; and the old home, where the young tutor and the beautiful girl who won his heart met to enjoy the passing hours and make their plans for coming years, was peculiarly dear to him. The late Cyrus P. Smith, at the commencement dinner of 1875, recited a little incident in the history of Mr. Choate's tutorial life. The students knew that their teacher often passed some of the small hours of the night in Mr. Olcott's parlor. Mr. Smith and a few of his associates used to serenade the young couple occasionally. One night they took their stand on the deck of the steeple near the house, whence the whole village could hear. In their song they substituted the names of the parties for classic names, and made the refrain loud and long. In the morning Mr. Choate sent for Mr. Smith, whose voice he had recognized, and admonished him to select a humbler stand, and a more seasonable hour for his musical exhibitions. Thus ended the farce.

My first introduction to Mr. Choate was in the library of " The United Fraternity." His conversation was of books. He called my attention to some good authors for a young man to read. Among others he took from its shelf an old folio, much worn and defaced, and said that he had found great benefit from the careful reading of that work. It was Dr. William Chillingworth's work, entitled " The Religion of Protestants a Safe Way to Salvation." Hallam says, " This celebrated work, which gained its author the epithet of immortal, is now, I suspect, little studied, even by the clergy." Mr. Choate pronounced the author the greatest reasoner, in that age of giants, in logic. He said he knew no work to be compared with it, except " Edwards on the Will." He had read Chillingworth with great profit, and advised all young men to study it who desired to become good logicians. From that time to the day of his death, I never met Mr. Choate without gaining instruction from his conversation. His discourse was always of lofty themes.

I once had an opportunity to spend a few hours in his library by his invitation. His books were the latest and best editions of standard authors. I was then interested in the classics. That department of his library I carefully examined. I found there the most recent and most approved editions of Greek and of Latin authors. I took the books from their shelves, one by one, to learn, if possible, what use the owner had made of them. In some of them I found traces of his study through the entire work, in others the leaves had been cut, and marginal notes made in one third or one half of the work. I happened then to be staying at a house opposite that of Mr. Choate. I woke about midnight and saw, across the street, Mr. Choate standing at a high desk by the window, evidently employed in reading. So, after the fatigues of the day, he refreshed his mind with good books at night.

Once I was invited to meet his pastor, Rev. Dr. Adams, and a few other friends, at dinner. It was at the time when Dr. Adams was so severely censured for his book called "The Southside View," in which he ventured to recite his personal recollections of some good men at the South. The friends of Dr. Adams had held a public meeting to express their confidence and affection for the author of that famous book. Mr. Choate made a speech, commending his pastor for preaching the gospel instead of politics, and remarked that, after spending six days in controversy at the bar and on the platform, he was rejoiced to have his attention called to religion on the seventh. This speech gave birth to a new party cry, " The Gospel according to Choate," which was as widely printed and commented upon as his famous phrase, " glittering generalities," applied to the Declaration of Independence. At the dinner-table, Mr. Choate, in a quiet, confiding, deferential tone, called out his guests on their own specialties. His twinkling eye, pleasant smile, and genial comments made the occasion one long to be remembered.

At the funeral of Daniel Webster, I walked with Mr. Choate to the cemetery. He made many considerate and thoughtful remarks on Mr. Webster's life. He spoke of him with filial sadness and reverence. Mr. Webster was " his guide, counselor, and friend." I felt almost abashed at his appeals to me for my opinions, as though I could possibly know anything of the great orator which he did not know; but that was his mental habit. He made those with whom he conversed feel that he regarded them as equals, to whom he could often show deference.

After multitudes of orators had eulogized the deceased statesman, Mr. Choate came to his old haunts in Hanover, and in the old church uttered his memorable eulogy, — perhaps the most brilliant and appreciative tribute to departed worth ever made by mortal man. If any one can name a greater, let him " speak, for him have I offended."

Mr. Choate prepared a speech for the Webster dinner at Boston, a short time after Mr. Webster's death. He was too ill to deliver it; it was never published. Fletcher Webster was permitted to read it. One paragraph he copied, and sent to me. It was as follows : " Sometimes Mr. Webster incurred the lot of all the great, and was traduced and misrepresented. Sometimes he was pursued, as all central figures in great triumphal processions are pursued, as all glory is pursued, by calumny; as Demosthenes, the patriotic statesman; as Cicero, the father of his country; as Grotius, the creator of public law; as Somers and Sidney, as Burke, as Grattan, as Hamilton, were traduced. Even when he was recently dead, the tears and prayers of the whole country did not completely silence one *robed and reverend backbiter.*" The shade of Theodore Parker, it is hoped, will receive with such candor as marked the living man, this *honest* tribute to his ministerial labors.

Mr. Abbott Lawrence once said to me, at his house, that, when he was Minister at the Court of St. James, he frequently met eminent lawyers who were very desirous of learning everything they could about Mr. Webster and Mr. Choate, especially their personal appearance, habits, and opinions. They questioned him respecting their interpretations of great questions of law. Mr. Lawrence ventured to propose several of their questions to Mr. Choate, and his replies were received with great respect by English lawyers.

Mr. Choate was religiously educated, and the instructions of his parents modified and controlled his whole life. Mr. James W. Paige, of Boston, informed me that Mr. Webster and Mr. Choate often met at his house, where they sometimes discoursed of " high and holy themes." One evening allusion was made by one of them to the custom of committing to memory devotional poetry in childhood. Mr. Webster challenged Mr. Choate to recite Watts's psalms and hymns from memory, to ascertain which could hold out longest. They continued the exercise for a full hour, till the ladies cried " Hold ! enough ! " because they desired to hear these gentlemen talk on other subjects.

Mr. Choate was once walking, on Commencement Day, in Hanover, when a lady attempted to pass him in the crowd, wearing one of those elegant shawls whose knotted fringe always catches the button of the pew door of country churches, when suddenly he found himself caught by the button of his coat. He turned and said, " Madam, I beg pardon; I should be delighted to go with you, but I have an engagement in the opposite direction." I remember an amusing incident recited to me by one of the students, showing how much he was absorbed in a case he was studying, "*totus in illis.*" A client was consulting him whose name was Stoughton. At that time a popular nostrum, called " Stoughton's Bitters," was everywhere advertised. Mr. Choate had seen the advertisements, and, during all the interview, he addressed his client as " Mr. Bitters."

Yours truly,

E. D. SANBORN.

LETTER FROM EDWARD B. GILLETT.

A DISTINGUISHED member of the Massachusetts bar, residing at Westfield, who was much at the bar with Mr. Choate, writes me : —

MY DEAR SIR, — I take pleasure in trying to comply with your request to furnish some personal reminiscences of Mr. Choate. Perhaps, by way of illustrative notes to your articles, you may utilize some of them.

I called upon Mr. Choate when he was confined to his house by a lame knee. He was always in his library, surrounded by his five or six thousand silent friends, covering the walls of the second story of his dwelling on Franklin Street.

On one occasion I found him before his table turning the leaves of Macaulay's History. I inquired if he was revising the judgments recently expressed in his lecture upon that subject. He replied, No, that he was reading Cowley's poems, which always greatly interested him ; that he had just discovered in the volume an expression similar to that found in the first book of "Paradise Lost," "The height of this great argument," which he thought a fine and extraordinary phrase. He had thereupon begged his wife, the gracious purveyor to his infirmities, to hand down Macaulay to him that he might detect whether Milton had "hooked" from Cowley, or Cowley from Milton. "But," said he, "Cowley has got him. It is, however, only the equitable thing. Milton had a right to forage the whole intellectual world in the way of reprisal, for his *disjecta membra* are scattered thick through all literature."

I have in my possession his copy of Cowley's works. The pencil marks along the margins of pages suggest the remark he once made to me, that he "often found a single 'winged word' as suggestive as the most germinant thought." This may explain what is said to have been his habit of frequent reading and study of the dictionary "by the page."

Upon a mantel in his library, as I now somewhat indistinctly remember, were placed, at one end, a bronze bust or statuette of Demosthenes; at the other end, a similar one of Cicero. Over Demosthenes was suspended a small engraving of Daniel Webster; over Cicero an engraving of Edward Everett. Upon my speaking of the appropriateness of the juxtapositions, he drew some parallels and contrasts between the great orators, and in a few minutes said more memorable things, by way of characterization, than I have ever heard compacted into the same number of sentences. I remember that he pronounced Cicero to be " the greatest master of speech who had ever lived."

I was associated with Mr. Choate in the trial of a railroad case before a committee of the Massachusetts Legislature. He was then preparing an address upon Macaulay's " History of England," to be delivered before the Mercantile Library Association in Boston. On the morning of the day he was to give his address, he said that it was not nearly written. I suggested that he would be compelled to extemporize a portion of it. He replied that he would " cut out " from the hearing and go into an adjoining lobby and write while the witnesses were being examined in chief, if I would call him so that he could be present at the cross-examination. This arrangement was carried out, and it was wonderful to note how intuitively and instantly he gathered the scope of the direct testimony given in his absence. On one occasion, I followed him almost instantly from the committee room to the lobby, and found him already writing at the top of his speed. He said that his only way of making preparation for such occasions was to postpone it until the last possible moment, and then work *totis viribus ;* that he had been already writing since three and a half o'clock that morning.

Mr. Choate, on one occasion, came into the court-room of the District Court in Boston, while I was trying a case before a jury. He was accompanied by Mr. B. R. Curtis, their object being to discuss before Judge Sprague, then presiding, some interlocutory motion during the recess. Mr. Choate drew his chair to my side, and placed his hand on my shoulder in that magnetic way of friendly confidence which did so much to endear him to younger members of the profession. He then inquired with a sort of comical eagerness, " Pray tell me whose witnesses are all these women ? " I answered, " Part are mine and part are the plaintiff's." Then he said, " Pray tell me which side has the majority ? " I said that I had. He replied, " I will give you my word the case is yours. But now," said he with humorous solemnity, " let me give you my dying advice, — never cross-examine a woman. It is of no use. They cannot disintegrate the story they have once told; they cannot eliminate the part that is for you from that which is against you. They can neither combine nor shade nor qualify. They go for the whole thing, and the moment you begin to cross-examine one of them, instead of being bitten by a single rattle-

22

snake, you are bitten by a whole barrel full. I never, excepting in a case absolutely desperate, dare to cross-examine a woman."

His library was especially rich in ancient classics. He pointed out that department to me with evident satisfaction; one shelf was filled by different editions of the Greek Testament, some in elegant modern binding, and others in " old vellum." I alluded to this. He then said, " You recall a visit I once received in my room from Mr. Webster, when I was Senator at Washington, endeavoring to impose upon the people of this Commonwealth the delusion that I was an eminent statesman. I saw Mr. Webster's wonderful black eyes peering over my books, as if in search, and asked him what he would please to have. He turned to me with one of his smiles, such as never transfigured the face of any other man or of any woman, and said, " I observe, brother Choate, that you are true to your instincts in Washington, as at home, — seven editions of the Greek Testament, but not a copy of the Constitution."

You cannot, my dear sir, fail to see that I have written very hurriedly; but, as you have the choice both of excision and exclusion, I do not hesitate to send you my meagre materials. I beg leave to thank you that you are willing to freshen our memory of that wonderful man, whose profound and precise learning as a lawyer was hardly surpassed by his marvelous genius for advocacy, but who was nowhere more delightful or amusing than in private conversation. Carlyle is right when he tells us that " Great men, taken in any way, are profitable company."

With very great respect,

EDWARD B. GILLETT.

To Judge Neilson.

LETTER FROM HON. NATHAN CROSBY.

—◆—

The Hon. Nathan Crosby, one of Mr. Choate's early friends, who has been for more than thirty years in judicial service, writes the following letter. The reader will think it natural, as well as fortunate, that old college friends, in writing about Mr. Choate, should recur to those early days.

A short time before the death of the Rev. Joseph Tracy, D. D., he had written an article on the religious character of Mr. Choate, intended for publication in some religious magazine. But the article was not given to the public. Judge Crosby has been kind enough to obtain it from the family or representatives of the writer and send it to me.

After stating the fact that much had been written about Mr. Choate, and suggesting that much yet remained to be written, Dr. Tracy asks, "But what have the orthodox reviewers to do with Rufus Choate?" and answers, "Much, on many accounts. In all the religious or ecclesiastical relations which he sustained, he was one of us. He was educated from his earliest infancy in our faith. He studied it, understood it, was convinced of its truth, avowed and defended it on what he deemed proper occasions, public or private, to the end of his life."

He proceeds to illustrate that view by references to Mr. Choate's example, opinions, and addresses, making special use of his remarks on the occasion of the twenty-fifth anniversary of Dr. Adams's pastorate of the Essex Street Church, in which — the last public address ever made by Mr. Choate — he avowed his faith in the doctrines there taught.

MY DEAR JUDGE, — Mr. Choate was one year before me in college. When I entered, he had already acquired the reputation of leader of his class. My earliest personal knowledge of him was obtained through two of his rivaling classmates, Heydock and Tracy, who had been with me in Salisbury Academy. Mr. Choate came to Hanover at an opportune period, as, in fact, we all did. The college difficulties had just divided the old residents into two partisan, though quite unequal, bodies, both of which changed the former limited courtesies extended to students into open blandishments and friendly alliances. President

Brown was young and enthusiastic, and desirous, not only that the students should acquit themselves well as scholars, but that they should be kindly received and should make friends for themselves and the institution in the village, and so carry with them to their homes good accounts of the college and the people. Mr. Choate found an old and valuable friend in Dr. Mussey, the head of the medical school. Dr. Mussey had practiced in Essex during the childhood of Mr. Choate, and had boarded in his father's family. Upon being appointed to a professorship, he had given up his practice to Dr. Sewall, who afterward married Mr. Choate's sister, and first taught Latin to Rufus.

He was fortunate, therefore, in his surroundings at Hanover, but more fortunate in his eagerness to learn and his aptitude for study. His ambition, which we saw in his acts and habits, appears now, by confession, as it were, in the letters of his college life, recently furnished by your correspondent, the Rev. Dr. Putnam. The amenities of the people and the absence of rowdyism on the part of the students were alike notable during President Brown's administration; and many who were there at this period, besides Mr. Choate, owe much to the graceful influences of the cultured ladies of their early acquaintance.

Mr. Choate was sociable as well as studious, but did not care for play. He found exercise in walks over the hills around the college, and up and down his room while pursuing his studies. His most frequent out-door companion was his classmate Tenney, who furnished a ready laugh to Choate's equally ready wit. Tenney was a jolly, light-hearted youth, well suited to clear the cobwebs from an overworked brain, and as such, doubtless, he ministered, perhaps unconsciously, but none the less beneficially, to his friend. Choate's room was of ready access to his mates, and was a sort of centre of mirth and wit; but when sport was over he turned to his studies with avidity. He possessed a wonderful power of concentration, and studied with great intensity. I roomed near him for a year, and could appreciate this somewhat, as he studied very much aloud, making his voice and ear and his gestures, too, probably contribute each its power of impression upon the memory. He dropped into study readily as a habit, and thus, at brief intervals, doubtless, through life, added much to his stores of knowledge. We boarded together for a while at Professor Adams's; and when in the dining-room, before the bell called us to take our seats at the table, Mr. Choate would stand at the sideboard, where lay a large reference Bible, and turn over the leaves from place to place, as if tracing out some chain of theological inquiry.

Mr. Choate by ardent, if frequently interrupted, labor became the ideal scholar and the pride of the college. No one had ever more completely won the admiration of the faculty, of his fellow-students, and of the people of Hanover. Not a lisp of irregularity, of incivility, or neglect was heard against him from any quarter. But toward the close of his college life he became an invalid, was emaciated, walked feebly, his place in the recitation-room was often vacant, his condition a source of anxiety and alarm. Dr. Mussey took him to his house, and watched over him by day and by night. At length the appointments for Commencement were made, and Mr. Choate was set down for the valedictory. Great fears were entertained that he might be unable to participate in the exercises. As the day drew near, the leading topic of inquiry and discussion was his condition, — the last report from his chamber the most important news; — and old graduates, as they arrived from day to day to participate in the proceedings, came to share in the anxiety, and feared that they might not hear him whom they perceived to be so universally admired and beloved. The day came at length, and with it uncertain reports intensifying the anxiety, and casting doubt not only on the probability of his appearance on the platform, but as to the duration of his life. The procession was formed without him, and moved to the church, amid general gloom, for the public exercises. The place was crowded; the graduating class responded to the orders of the day down to the valedictory. Then a few moments of hushed suspense, and Mr. Choate was called. He advanced slowly and feebly, as if struggling to live and to perform this as a last scholarly duty. Tall and emaciated, closely wrapped in his black gown, with his black, curly hair overshadowing his sallow features, he tremblingly saluted the trustees and officers of the college, and proceeded in tremulous and subdued tones with his address, which was full of beautiful thoughts, couched in chaste and elegant language. When he came to say the words of parting to his classmates, his heart poured forth treasures of affectionate remembrance, closing with swelling fervor and inimitable power as he exhorted them not to slacken or misapply their intellectual energies and tastes, but to press on to the highest attainments in the domain of learning. "The world from this day and place opens wide before you. You are here and now to drop the power and aid of the association and emulation of our happy days, and strike, single-handed and alone, into the manly struggles of life. You may sow and reap in whatever field or realm you choose, and gather the glorious rewards of intellectual culture of pure minds and diligent hands. Go, go forward, my classmates, with all your honors and all your hopes. You will leave me behind, lingering or cut short in my way; but I shall carry to my grave, however, wherever, whenever I shall be called hence, the delightful remembrance of our joys and of our love." I can only give a faint and imperfect impression of his loving words; but my memory of the scene is fresh and vivid. The great congregation, from admiration, excitement, and grief, found relief in a flood of tears.

Mr. Choate remained in Hanover one year as tutor, and was the central figure of a set of linguists then connected with the college. James Marsh and George Bush, distinguished scholars, just before him; George P. Marsh and Folsom, of my class; and Washington Choate, brother of Rufus, Perley, and Williston, two classes next after mine, gave an impulse to the study and love of classical literature unknown before or since in that college. Friendly emulation and student pride led to the daily canvassing of books published, authors read, and works studied. Folsom, W. Choate, and Williston died early; the other scholars named became eminent men. Washington Choate was regarded as equal to his brother in scholarship, and was eminent for his piety. I allude to this era of classical study as an exhibition of Mr. Choate's literary influence

Mr. Choate had great respect and love for his Alma Mater, and contributed from his early professional income toward her support, as well as to influence her advancing curriculum; but was greatly disquieted, and even vexed, when declared rank in scholarship was abolished. He believed in laudable ambition and honorable competition. The old Puritan school-house system of rising from the foot to the head of the class stirred the little scholar with an ambition which grew with his years, and which he thought should not be ignored or repudiated in higher fields of study. He held that a great principle of human action was invaded by neglecting to rank scholarship; that life is largely made up of struggles for superiority in mental and physical efforts; that its rewards are won by merit; that the diligent, exact scholar should receive his merited honors; and that the idle or stupid should not be protected from the exposure of misspent time and opportunity. His own life was spent in incessant, honorable competition and legitimate reward.

For several years from 1826 I practiced law in Essex County at the same courts with Mr. Choate;

and from 1838 for a few years I lived in Boston, kept up my acquaintance with him, and knew quite well his habits. He died daily, retiring to bed exhausted, under great nervous prostration, with headache. Yet he would rise early, often long before daylight, and take a literary breakfast before his family or business claimed his attention. His clients, the courts, and classics compelled long days and short nights. I called upon him once in the afternoon, and asked him how early the next morning I could confer with him upon a matter I wished to investigate during the evening. " As early as you please, sir; I shall be up." " Do you mean before breakfast, Mr. Choate ? " " Before light if you wish." I called at the earliest dawn, and found him at his standing table, with a shade over his eyes, under a brilliant light, pressing forward some treatise upon Greek literature, which he said he hoped to live long enough to give to the public. The night had restored his wearied powers; he was elastic, as cheery and brilliant as the stars I had left shining above us.

Seeing and hearing Mr. Choate in the trial of causes was a perpetual surprise and pleasure. It seemed to make little difference with him whether his cause was of great or small importance; he tried to win it if possible, and ceased not to contest it until every consideration favorable to his own side and every one inimical to his adversary had been presented.

It has already been mentioned that Mr. Choate was offered a seat upon the bench of the Supreme Court of Massachusetts, but declined. It may be proper for me to add that in view of his health, and the arduous nature of his professional exertions, I pressed him to seek the higher honor of a seat upon the bench of the United States Supreme Court, and so escape the waste of his powers in the excitements of the advocate, and attain the more quiet and dignified life of the bench. Judge Woodbury's seat was at the time vacant, and I believed he could secure the appointment. He was then fifty years of age, and in the highest sense eligible. "But," said he, "I am too poor. I must remain as I am, live or die. I know my power and reputation in my profession, and I love it, but I do not know what the change would bring upon me, or whether I should like it. I cannot leave my profession." He survived only eight years.

He spent his money well for his family and his library, gave freely to the necessitous, and gave liberally of his well-earned fees when full payment might have embarrassed his client. On one occasion, I was in his office when a client asked for his bill for a written opinion upon a question of importance. Said Mr. Choate, " Hand me one hundred dollars, and I will give you a receipt in full; if you go to my partner in the other room, who keeps the books, he will make you pay one hundred and fifty, sure."

Mr. Choate, like Webster and Everett, was an old Whig politically, and " to the manner born ; " but toward the close of his life party lines underwent rapid changes, and men were very unceremoniously laid upon the shelf who were not thought to keep up with the " march of improvement." Mr. Webster lost the nomination for the presidency, and soon after died at Marshfield; and, although the nation honored his obsequies with every token of mourning, Mr. Choate could not smother his indignation toward the rising elements of power. The great expounder and statesman had been rejected through unworthy combinations. His chief, worthy of all homage and confidence, leader of the Whig party, and the supporter of its glory for twenty years, had been slaughtered in the house of his friends.

Mr. Choate's horror of new combinations and platforms drove him to Buchanan. " I can go nowhere else," said he to me, when I had a long interview with him in regard to his purpose. " But, Mr. Choate, what becomes of your long cherished

Whig principles?" "Whig principles! I go to
the Democrats to find them. They have assumed
our principles, one after another, till there is little
différence between us." Here he traced them one
after another as they had found adoption. "And
what becomes of your Whig anti-slavery opinions?" "I have settled that matter," said he, "I
am bound to seek the greatest amount of moral
good for the human race. I am to take things as
I find them, and work according to my best judgment for the greatest good of the greatest number, and I do not believe it is the greatest good
to the *slave* or the *free* that four million of slaves
should be turned loose in all their ignorance, poverty, and degradation, to trust to luck for a home
and a living." He amplified somewhat this statement, but the above represents fairly the conclusions of his argument. Mr. Choate's problem,
how to accomplish the greatest good for the greatest number, has been worked out on a different
plan from that which he wished to see adopted.
The war, the death lists, pollution of morals, destruction of prosperity, national debt, present condition and future destiny of the colored race, and
sectional discords are present elements in the
scales testing Mr. Choate's sagacity. Happy for
us if we can find advantages to counterbalance
them. Yours truly,

NATHAN CROSBY.

LETTER FROM HON. HENRY K. OLIVER.

THE Hon. Henry K. Oliver, a student at Dartmouth College when young Choate was there, writes as follows : —

MAYOR'S OFFICE, CITY OF SALEM, MASS.,
August 24, 1877.

DEAR SIR, — Your favor of the 26th of July brings vividly to my mind's eye

The face, the form, the man so true, — .

of my beloved college friend, the late Rufus Choate. Your note so quickened my mind's eye that it again sees his manly and attractive figure and strangely winning face ; — and my mind's ear that it again hears his deeply-resonant, sweet-toned, and impressive voice, wakening in me many a reminiscence of his gentleness of temper and disposition, his warm sympathies, his innate sense of right, his refined courtesy, his love of all that was beautiful in life, his attractiveness of person and manner, his memory, his thoroughness as a scholar, and his excellence in all that makes a good and great man.

My first acquaintance with him dates from the month of August, 1816, when, he then beginning his Sophomore year, I joined the Junior class at Dartmouth College. I had passed my first two years at Harvard, entering in 1814, a youngling not quite fourteen years of age; when my father, a Calvinist of the severer type, becoming uneasy at the alleged tendency of Harvard toward Unitarianism, and probably feeling the pressure of the greater expense thereat, transferred me to Hanover. I relinquished my old associations at Harvard with deepest regret, but the transplanted roots after a while found genial soil, and began to feed from the new earth. A few weeks domiciled me among my new associates, while the excitement attending the existence at Hanover, at one and the same time, of a " Dartmouth College " with its corps of teachers and some one hundred and forty students, and a " Dartmouth University " with its duet of teachers and its corporal's guard of students, helped me to think less of home and more of surroundings and duty, and I gradually settled down to my work.

Of those whose active kindness helped to lift me out of my slough of despond, I recall none with more earnest gratitude than him of whom I write, at whose room, in the house of Professor Ebenezer Adams, I was a frequent visitor.

23

He was about a year older than myself, but of
an almost incredible maturity of mind. Being
from my own State and county, he encouraged
me by considerate and timely sympathy, and stimulated me, as he did all of us, by his pertinac-
ity in study and success in his work. Yet such
was the simplicity of his character, his freedom of
intercourse with us all, his genial outflow in companionship,—"medicines that he gave us to make
us love him,"—that each of us, delighted with
him as a man, and charmed by him as a scholar,
was at all times ready to exclaim, like the shep-
herd in Virgil's Eclogue,—

"Non equidem invideo, miror magis!"

A passage describing Cicero has often come
to my mind when I have thought of Choate,—
" *Quum eas artes disceret, quibus ætas puerilis so-
let ad humanitatem informari, ingenium ejus ita il-
luxit, ut eum æquales e scholâ redeuntes, medium,
tanquam regem circumstantes, domum deducerent;
imo, eorum parentes pueri fama commoti in ludum
litterarium ventitabant ut eum viserent.*" We looked
upon him as *facile princeps*, no man in any of
the classes being even named with him in point
of scholarship. In fact we did not count him at
all in rating scholarship, but set him apart and
above us all, " himself his only parallel."

His method of study seemed to the rest of us to

have crystallized into an abiding habit, definite in manner and determinate in purpose. I have often seen him in the act of delving at his books. His large and well-shaped head usually rested upon his hands, his elbows upon the table, his fingers running through the profuse growth of his dark, curly hair. His eyes also were dark, with a mild yet penetrating look, always suggestive of sadness, as were the features of his expressive face, which enchained one's attention by its very pensiveness, in marked contrast, not seldom, with many a playful utterance, which flashed out with no effervescence of laughter, or uproar of boisterous merriment.

There was a custom, in our day, of assigning, on each alternate Wednesday, subjects to two or three members of the Senior and Junior classes, the essays on which were to be read in chapel on the next Wednesday fortnight. These readings were open to the public, and ordinarily there was plenty of room. But when it was Choate's turn to read, the chapel was crowded, the gentlemen, ladies, and even the youth of the village flocking to hear the brilliant essayist, led thither by his grasp of the subject, his eloquent diction, and his beautiful imagery. At times, and always at the appropriate time, his sense of humor, unconsciously operative, perhaps, lighted up his features with an infectious smile as he set forth some absurdity in a manner so luminous and palpable that the air of the chapel would undulate with the soft murmuring of restrained merriment. And yet no man was more tender in feeling, or had in him less of the spirit of ridicule, or more of charity and good-will to all mankind. If the phrase be permissible, his humor was characterized by a stately dignity, which, while fitting the occasion, most felicitously illustrated his intent, and had nothing in it of harshness. It lacerated no one's feelings, provoked no fretful retort. He was wholly free from any self-complacent consciousness of superiority in talent or acquirement over his college mates, — so free that I doubt whether he himself thought any such superiority existed, manifest though it was to all the rest of us. But neither in college nor in after-life, so far as I know, did he give token of any such cognition. To us, his companionship was a constant benediction, and we sought his society as we would seek a haven of repose and comfort.

His influence, both personal and as a scholar, was operative with every member of the seven classes that enjoyed college life with him, — an influence that, feeble in his earlier college life, assumed, before the end of the first year, a power and a reach far beyond that of any other mem-

ber of the college. His preparation had been a
little imperfect, and he did not, therefore, give us
at first the real impress of what he was. But having once taken root, and feeling the power and
strength of the wider instruction, he grew with
marvelous rapidity. His facility at concentrating
his mind upon any given subject, and acquiring
all that was to be learned about it, was without
parallel, and in every department of study rapidly put him far in advance of his fellows. The
general standard of scholarship among us received
from him a positive and most noticeable elevation.
This influence was felt among officials and under-
graduates, and it began to be realized that the
old rule of the arithmetics, that " more required
more," was making men work harder and with
more will, and that a decidedly new departure
had been taken, never to be retraced. And yet
the hindrances that in our time impeded both
teachers and taught were most perplexing and
discouraging. President Wheelock and the board
of trustees had got by the ears, the issue of the
contest bringing him to grief and to deposition
from office. A new president, Rev. Francis Brown,
was elected, and time was required for him to get
well into harness, and to make the college feel the
healthful influence which he afterwards so admirably and efficiently exerted. Never was college

official more beloved and revered. The rival institution, created by the State legislature, had been duly inaugurated, had been put into possession of the college seal, and the college library was its only building and chapel. We lads had looked out for the two libraries of the college societies, — the "Fraternity" and the "Social Friends," — and had safely removed them from the college buildings to private quarters; so that when Professors Dean and Carter of the university, with a horde of village roughs, knowing nothing of such removal, broke into the library room of the "Social Friends," the members of the "Fraternity," then in session, hearing the crash of axes and crowbars, rushed to the rescue, and made prisoners of the whole crowd, sending home the *ignobile vulgus*, but imprisoning Dean and Carter until they pledged their honor that they would "never do so again." They were then escorted to their homes, each by a trio of collegians. Neither name of these professors, nor that of Allen, president of the new university, will be found in the "Triennial Government Catalogue of Dartmouth," they being unrecognized interlopers. In fact, the whole creation of the university was a political fraud, "a thing of shreds and patches," which, at the bidding of the Supreme Court of the United States, after Webster's great argument, like an " insubstantial pageant faded," leaving " not a wrack behind." But it was a disturbing element for a time, and could not but occupy our thoughts and conversation, and unfavorably affect our study.

I remember well the poverty of our illustrative apparatus, and the ingenious devices to which Professor Adams was compelled to resort to supplement it. Not seldom was he constrained to leave to our imagination the practical demonstration of some principle in natural philosophy. So, too, were we without the college library, which, though then small, had, nevertheless, many valuable books of reference that would greatly have helped us through many a difficult passage in our classics. As for recitation-rooms and a chapel, we got them in the village wherever we could. The whole situation was a tangle of embarrassments; and if there ever was an actual " pursuit of knowledge under difficulties," it was at Dartmouth College, — 1815–1818, — when Choate was an undergraduate.

But the extraordinary state of affairs itself, the sympathy of the college instructors with the struggling and loyal students, and the sympathy of the students with the faithful and self-sacrificing teachers generated a spirit of earnest and successful industry; and I have always believed that the good order, the thoughtful fidelity to work, and the unbroken friendship between the teachers and the taught, supplemented by the strong religious influence which then pervaded the institution, were all ministrations which helped to turn evil into good for us all. Our successors at the college can never realize the weight of the troubles that embarrassed us, or the joy we felt when those troubles passed away. May they, in her prosperity, be as faithful to her as were we in her deep adversity.

But to return: I graduated in 1818, leaving Choate behind me. He graduated in 1819, with the valedictory, — an address which exhibited to the full his eminent scholarship, his profound thought, the breadth and extent of his reading, his comprehensive grasp of fact and power of statement, and the magnetism of his oratory.

He served afterward a single year as tutor, and then commenced a course of study at the Law School at Cambridge, continuing it in the office, at Washington, of Mr. Wirt, Attorney-General of the United States. His fidelity in study, and his purity of life, when an undergraduate, character-ized him while preparing for his profession. I lost sight of him mainly during these years, hav-ing myself entered upon the work of a teacher in the public Latin School of this city. He, however, reappeared in our neighborhood, opening his office in Danvers, that portion of the town now called Peabody, practically a suburb of Salem. Here he laid the foundation of his future success, by a faithfulness in small things which proved his fitness to be intrusted with the conduct of greater. I met him but occasionally, yet always received from him the same genial recognition that had so often made me happy in college; and I have always considered it, and shall continue to consider it, as one of the highest happinesses of a not short life, that I was permitted for so many years to enjoy the friendship of so good, so pure, so noble a man as Rufus Choate.

Very truly yours,

HENRY K. OLIVER.

LETTER FROM WILLIAM W. STORY, LL. D.

I AM indebted to William W. Story, LL. D., jurist, author, and now sculptor at Rome, for the following letter: —

MY DEAR SIR, — I beg you to accept my thanks for the two volumes, one containing the orations and addresses of Mr. Choate, and the other his life by Mr. Brown. These, as well as the articles in the "Albany Law Journal," which you were so kind as to send me, I have read with great interest and pleasure.

I wish it were in my power, as it certainly is in my good will, to furnish you, as you request, with any reminiscences of Mr. Choate which could be of interest either to his family and friends or to the public. But, unfortunately, I was never brought into any intimate relation with him; and such was the difference of our ages and positions during the period that I had the pleasure of knowing him, that I had few opportunities of coming into close personal contact with him, and, for the most part, only surveyed him at a distance, as one darkly groping his way on the outskirts of the profession of the law looks up to a great and dazzling reputation already in its zenith, and drawing to it the eyes of all.

My first personal acquaintance with him was while I was studying law in the office of Mr. Charles Sumner and Mr. George Stillman Hillard. His office was in the same building, and occasionally he would come in either to consult upon some professional question, or, what was more frequent, to relax his mind in wide excursions with them in the varied fields of literature, to wander into classic regions, to discuss critical questions, to dissect characters, persons, or authors, and, in a word, to talk *" de omnibus rebus et quibusdam aliis."* At these interviews I played the part of a listener, and better talk it would have been difficult to hear. His conversation, stimulated, as it was, by such companions as Hillard and Sumner, who were always ready to turn aside from the arid paths of the law into any " primrose path of dalliance," and who were both capable and willing to explore with him the wide regions of universal literature, was eminently interesting, and, *haud passibus æquis*, I followed as they led, drawn by a special charm. His conversation was sometimes grave and critical, with many an allusion and quotation from classic authors; sometimes philosophical, with discussions of theories and doctrines of politics, life, and thought; sometimes grimly humorous, with trenchant strokes of characterization and finesse of anatomizing. His humor was very peculiar, and often consisted of a new, original, and quite unexpected epithet; as, for instance, when he spoke of a likeness as being " flagrant; " or of a sly, sudden, and complete reversal of what he had previously seemed gravely to assert. As an instance of this latter peculiarity, I remember that once, when the conversation happened to turn upon a person whose manners and bearing were peculiarly distasteful, he gravely said, as if in deprecation of the criticism of others, " He is a person whom I myself should have no objection to meet " — and then, after a slight pause, added — " in a procession."

His love of epithets was remarkable, and the richness of his vocabulary so great that often it might be said of him, as it was of Shakespeare, that he needed somewhat to be restrained. But many as were the adjectives that he habitually used, they were never idly strung together without definiteness and distinction of meaning. As he added one to another, each seemed a new and calculated stroke to the characterization, and, as it were, a compressed sentence in itself. He had carefully studied the English language in its best authors, and was a master of its finer distinctions of expression; and overwhelming at times as were his adjectives, they were never hurriedly snatched at to fill a gap, but, on the contrary, were carefully selected, and with a purpose to strengthen, enlarge, or make precise his full meaning, culminating often in one of peculiar significance. On public occasions, as he uttered them, one after another, slowly and distinctly, and weighing on each, he lifted himself higher and higher, rising on tiptoe, his voice also rising with ever stronger and higher emphasis, until he came to the last word, and then he suddenly settled down upon his heels with a downward sway of the body, and, dropping his voice to a low inflection, flung it, as it were, almost carelessly down. It was like a wave that gathers and accumulates and heaves upward to its fullness of height and then bursts and falls exhausted on the beach.

In illustration of his highly, alliterative style and fondness for piling epithets one upon another, may be instanced the question he addressed to the jury in his well-known defense of Albert Tirrell against the charge of murder. If not absolutely true in fact, it is at least eminently characteristic of his manner — " What," he cried out, " must at such a moment have been the feelings of this fond, foolish, fickle-fated, and infatuated Albert, when," etc. Possibly this sentence was, to some extent, invented or enlarged afterwards; but it was evidently founded on fact. Nothing could be more characteristic than that, after the first word " fond," he should immediately have added " foolish," as if he remembered the old meaning of the word, and translated it into modern English. Each word is intensified beyond its predecessor, and each illustrates the view of Tirrell's mind which he desired to impress upon the jury.

In this connection may be told the *mot* of Mr. Justice Wilde, which, as far as I know, has not been recorded in print. This acute and able judge was somewhat dry and precise in his style and manner, and, in most respects, the complete opposite of Mr. Choate. On one occasion, just before the opening of the court, when Mr. Choate was to argue a case, a member of the bar asked the Judge if he had heard that Mr. Worcester had just published a new edition of his dictionary, with a great number of additional words. " No," he answered, " I have not heard of it. But for God's sake don't tell Choate."

No one would have relished this joke more than Mr. Choate himself, and I think he would have admitted that Judge Wilde had made a good point, where he was vulnerable. But, after all, it was not in the mind of the learned Judge, or of any other person, to desire to retrench that wonderful richness of language which the great advocate used with such masterly ability and eloquence. It was the fullness of his mind, the fineness of his fastidiousness, the extent of his culture that begot the peculiarities of his utterance. In his speeches, as in his writings, this double desire of limitation and exposition, combined with his large range of active and imaginative thought, led him often to overflow his banks with a prodigal stream which disdained the boundaries of simple periods. His sentences refuse to come to a conclusion. A new illustration or variation or development, limitation or side light strikes him before he can come to a pause, and carries him away with it; and, with parenthetical involvements, excursions beyond the direct line, inclusions of suspected objections which he is eager to anticipate, or imaginative illustrations and memories that will not be refused, he sweeps an undulating train of lengthening clauses along, anaconda-like in its movement, yet strong of grasp as are the anaconda's folds, until his sentence has grown into a paragraph. But, despite this singular involvement of style, there is no want of clearness either of thought or of expression; each part is knotted to the rest by vertebral articulation. They are all portions of one whole living thing.

His wonderful power over a jury was not the result of his eloquence, impetuous and often overwhelming as it was, so much as of his subtlety of logic, his acuteness of analysis, his eminent faculty of marshalling facts and incidents in a new and unexpected sequence and relation, so as to cast a doubt on what seemed clear before, or to throw a new light on what was previously obscure, his finesse at forcing, so to speak, his view, his imaginative elucidations by hypothetical suppositions and ingenious explanations of apparently simple events, and his penetration of character which enabled him to seize the weak points of witnesses and parties, and to draw into his confidence the jury.

He was in the habit of treating the jury with assumed deference and politeness, and often selected one among them to appeal to significantly, as if he were the sagacious person who really saw and appreciated the point he was enforcing. At times he would stop in full career, and say something to this effect, " But it is useless to urge this further. I see by the intelligent eye of the foreman that he has thoroughly comprehended the extreme force of this view." Then, again, he had great readiness of parry as well as of assault, and never was surprised so as to lose his guard or attack, or to be unready for a *réplique.* He was also wary and acute in the examination of witnesses, and so bland in his manner as to hide the point of his question. He never lost his temper, was uniformly courteous and urbane to his opponents and to the Bench, though he often concealed beneath this urbanity the keenest irony of criticism and argument. While submitting to the ruling of the Bench, he had the art to elude its consequences and diminish its importance. He was never headstrong, single-viewed, or obstinate to one absolute course. If he could not make a breach on one side, he changed his tactics and made an assault on another. But, besides and beyond all this, he entered into the facts of a case in an imaginative spirit, creating new possibilities of explanation, new theories of action, throwing subordinate incidents into strong light and color, giving positive value to what was negative, and casting prominent incidents into shade, treading with sure and balanced step along a line of attack or defense as narrow as " the unsteadfast footing of a spear."

His extraordinary defense of Tirrell will, I think, fully justify, in itself, all that I have said of him as an advocate before a jury.

In his arguments of law to the Court, where the arts he used in jury cases were of little avail, he showed himself to be a master of close logical

24

reasoning, of acute powers of comparison and discrimination, as well as of clear and persuasive argument. His guard was close, his rapidity and subtlety of fence remarkable, his points keen and well directed.

His personal appearance was remarkable. I think no one could come into his presence without being impressed by it. His broad, massive forehead was crowned with a dark mass of richly curling, fine, and almost turbulent hair, through which he constantly passed his hand, and beneath his overhanging brow were dark, deeply-sunken, and somewhat weary eyes of serious intent and expression, framed in dark circles. His nose was rather large, his upper lip short; and his under lip, projecting somewhat beyond, he constantly thrust out as if to grasp and hold it firm; while a strong jaw closed and locked up, as it were, the whole face with purpose and power. His cheeks were gaunt and hollow, as if worn by study. Indeed, the whole face was that of a thinker and student, which long hours of labor by day and night had made haggard. There was seriousness, gravity, and a certain pathos of character and sadness of experience in its repose. In its lighter moods, it was illumined by genial gleams of humor and the summer lightning of feeling, and in moments of excitement it glowed and radiated with inward fire like a forge when the bellows are in blast. His frame was large, well knit, and nervous. His ordinary gait in walking, as I remember him, was inclined to be slouching, as of a person engaged in introverted thought; and, in sitting, it was sunken and overweighed, as it were, into itself. When speaking in public, he was full of action and nervous gesticulation. He swayed backward and forward, advancing and retreating, emphasized by coming sharply down on his heels, now bending down, and now lifting himself to his full and commanding height, and enforcing his utterance with a sharp, impulsive, upward gesture.

I had a great admiration for him, not only on account of his power as an advocate, of his eminence as a public man, of his genial nature, humor, sensibility, and accomplishment in letters, but, beyond all this, for a certain somewhat, mysterious and poetic, which always seemed to me to haunt him, and which lay below all his outer show of character. There was something in his silent eyes, in his often abstracted and involved bearing, in the gloom and wan expression of his face, which seemed to hide an inner life, fed from secret springs, and given to far aspirations and longings outside the public and ordinary routine of the life he seemed to lead. This may have been all vision-

ary on my part, but I cannot refrain from stating this singular impression which he gave me.
What he had missed, what he wanted, I cannot
say ; nor can I say that he had missed or wanted
anything, except as we all miss and want something which is denied us, indefinite, unexplained,
perhaps, but not the less desired. Still, it always
seemed to me, from what I saw of him nearly,
that he had another life, behind and beneath this
that we knew, " of purer ether, of diviner air,"
perhaps of disappointment around which a mystery hovered. I give my impression for what it is
worth. It is quite possible that it is but a mere
unsubstantial fabric built by my own imagination
in dreamland.

But to return to facts. He brought scholarship
into his profession, and this gave a certain grace,
refinement, and happiness to all intercourse with
him. Sternly as he trod the dusty and thorny
path of the law, he snatched many an interval to
wander into the fields of Arcadia and there make
friends with the spirits of old, and drink of the
ancient springs of philosophy, poetry, history, and
ethics, as well as of the more modern " wells of
English undefiled." The fine edge of his intellect
was sharpened by constant attrition with the great
minds of the past, and the secret sources of feeling
kept fresh by their poetic and enlarging influ-

ences. His conversation was enriched with allusion and quotation from many an author; and many a flower, gathered in their gardens, gave fragrance and color to dry legal argument. You knew where he had been by the odor which ever clung to his commonest daily life. He was not a mere lawyer, nor did he deem it necessary to confine himself exclusively to the tread-mill of professional business. He was capable of severe and prolonged work, and few men have ever labored with more earnest zeal. The Law is a jealous mistress, and makes heavy demands on all who would win her prizes as he did. But she is apt to suck the blood of her too assiduous devotees, and leave them at last dry, rigid, and sapless. Earnest as Mr. Choate was in his duty to her, he did not forget that there are other fields of study beyond hers, to which she did not deny him entrance, and from which he brought back many a fragrant flower to wreathe about her careworn brow and enliven her dusty courts.

But it is time for me to stop. I did not mean to write an essay on Mr. Choate's genius, and you see that I can add little to what has already been said by others, and nothing that is worthy of publication. I regret extremely that I can find in my memory only these vague general impressions, and these few straws and chips of personal reminiscence, which are of no value save as a record of my admiration for one of the greatest advocates that ever adorned our own or any other country.   I have the honor to be,

Yours most faithfully,

W. W. STORY.

Honorable Chief Justice Neilson.

LETTER FROM HON. GEORGE P. MARSH.

Hon. George P. Marsh, the distingished philologist, author of works upon the English language, and for many years United States Minister to Italy, had the courtesy to send me the following. It was mailed·at Rome a few weeks before his death.

My dear Sir, — The advent of the usual crowd of strangers and the business demands of the commencement of another year have occupied me so constantly that I have not found time to thank you for your very interesting letter and for Mr. Brown's life of Choate, which I had, indeed, seen but had never had an opportunity of perusing.

I first knew Mr. Choate as a member of the Sophomore class at Dartmouth College in the autumn of 1816, when he already towered far above all our co-disciples, and held the same preëminence over those who came in contact with him which he retained through the changes of his after life. At that time scholarship, not power or influence, was his aim, and it was not until some years later that he thought of the bar as a desirable career. He was then engaged in reading Cicero's works, which, with such editions and such critical helps (*e. g.* the dictionaries of Schrevelius and Ainsworth) as most American scholars could then command, was a Herculean task, and I think the study of Cicero's orations taught him the value of amplification, or of abundant collateral illustrations, in oratory. This was a feature of his eloquence in which he excelled all other men, though I think his picturesque allusions were oftener poetic reminiscences than fruits of the actual observation of nature. As I was then fresh from the woods, where my boyish hours were chiefly spent, I observed his want of sympathy with trees and shrubs and rivers and rocks and mountains and plains, as *quasi* living and sentient beings, and this was the only defect I could discover in his mental organization. Having been born and bred in the interior of what was then popularly called *The New State*, I had enjoyed but a single momentary glimpse of the sea, and I did not at first perceive that the ocean occupied with Choate the place which the solid earth, with its thousand forms and myriad products, organic and inorganic, held with me; but with Mr. Dana, the distinguished author of " Two Years before the Mast," he was more expansive on this subject, and, as I learn from that gentleman, showed the greatest interest in nautical matters and in naval history. When I was in Congress (1843–49), I often talked with him about these things, but I found little response to my enthusiasm for Nature, and little interest in her material laws.

Choate habitually spoke freely of his professional allies and opponents, but his criticisms on them were generally favorable. Of Mr. Webster, whose method was in some respects the opposite of his own, he always spoke with the profoundest admiration, and I remember to have heard him mention Webster's astonishing power of concentrating his argument on a single point, to the support of which the many points which would have been taken by other lawyers were made subservient and auxiliary, not independent. He had a very exalted opinion of Jeremiah Mason, whose manner was equally opposite to his own, but in quite another direction, and he more than once said to me that he did not believe that any man ever *practiced* the English law more ably than Mason. Speaking of a celebrated lawyer who was censured for the excessive severity of his cross-examination, Choate said, " He defends himself by saying that he is never hard upon a witness unless he believes the witness to be lying. I think," added Choate, "*that* is true; but he has a way of *making* the witness lie by his very manner of examining him." Webster often consulted Choate in the preparation of his Congressional speeches, and particularly with reference to the quotations which he wished to introduce into them; and Mr. Choate sometimes did me the honor to confer with me on these points. On one occasion, I remember he asked me if I could furnish him with the original source of an expression which in a later age became proverbial: *Spartam quam habes hanc orna.* Being myself at a loss, I referred him to Mr. John Pennington of Philadelphia, who helped us out.

I was much interested in your remarks on Choate's vocabulary. His study of the English language was unceasing, and I think he spoke no other, sacrificing foreign languages to his mother tongue, although he read some Continental languages with sufficient facility for ordinary literary purposes. I should, from general recollection, have estimated his wealth of words higher than you find it. It interested me particularly from some shallow and ignorant criticisms on my lectures on the English language by a speaker who said he had made a careful estimate of his own habitual vocabulary, and found it to reach 30,000 words; and yet the critic did not know the philological meaning of the term *word* and confounded derivations from a *root* with inflections of a *stem*. I never met any other man with such a knowledge and command of all the resources of English as had Mr. Choate, and he had the rare gift of using words so that each made those with which it was connected bring out the best, or at least some special, meaning. He told me that he habitually *read* the dictionary, and, speaking of his translation of a part of Thucydides and other classics, he said he undertook the work for the sake of the English, not for Greek. Though Mr. Choate read Greek and Latin with facility and pleasure, and had a fair acquaintance with the literature of more than one Continental nation, yet he did not share in the fashionable American craze about the pursuit of foreign languages, and held that for an English-speaking person the English tongue was worth all others. I remember that he once found me reading Scarron, and inquired sharply how I found time for reading such trash. I answered that I had only a very indifferent French dictionary, and that I was studying Scarron for the sake of the vocabulary. " You may find old words enough," he replied, " in French authors fit to be read."

The critical adage, " Manner is matter," was never more forcibly exemplified than by Choate,

who would give wonderful effect both to the
grave and the gay, by mere manner. He would
use, sparingly indeed, but most effectively, popular cant words and phrases. For example, in a
conversation on the subject of New York politics,
he spoke of a conspicuous editor as having *squa-
boshed;* and of another, who had absconded, as
having *swartwouted.* The first of these occurs in
a letter printed by Mr. Brown. Such words, however, he seldom used except in jocular conversation. On the contrary, in his public addresses to
popular audiences he was very choice in his language, and often even stunned the jury by words
of "learned length and thundering sound." In
defending an action for *crim. con.,* referring to
some testimony of a character very damaging to
his clients, he said, "Well, suppose they did indulge in some innocent toying, by way of miti-
gating the asperities of hay-making!" This was
said in a tone of perfect seriousness, and did not
startle, but rather confounded, the jury he was addressing. Webster said of this rhetorical movement, "Choate is the only man in the world who
could have thus said *that.*" He sometimes took
great liberties with the jury. On one occasion,
observing by the manner of a juryman that he
was hostile to his client, he caught the man's eye,
and, pointing directly towards him, said, "I will

make this point plain — I will make it plain even to *you*, sir." The juryman quailed, and finally agreed to the verdict desired by Mr. Choate. I once heard him say to a lady, in introducing her to a new member of Congress, " He is the most learned man in the House — I mean of his age — I am two years older." This was not much to say, but the manner was altogether irresistible.

Mr. Choate was from boyhood a serious thinker, and a believer in the truth of Christianity, though I do not know that he ever became a member of any particular church. But the extreme sensitiveness, so characteristic of him, often led him to parry playfully any attempt on the part of the over-zealous to draw him into conversation on religious subjects. A prominent Christian gentleman was once making an earnest effort in that way, and he prefaced his remarks by referring to a recent instance of gross depravity, adding, " Ah ! Mr. Choate, this is a very sinful world ! " " Yes, it is," replied Mr. Choate, " and they say it will all burn up some day — what do you think ? " accompanying his answer with an irresistibly ludicrous expression of countenance ; the conversation ending with a hearty laugh on both sides.

I should say that one of Choate's most remarkable traits of character was his unresting, unflagging industry, coupled with a readiness to make

any and every sacrifice of his own likings or enjoyment to the one great object of securing the
highest position in his profession. This was with
him no vulgar ambition, but simply a love of, and
a desire for, perfection. I am not able to add
more at this time.

I am, my dear sir, very truly yours,

GEO. P. MARSH.

To CH. J. NEILSON.

LETTER FROM HON. JOHN WINSLOW.

————•————

"IT is a mistake to suppose that the man of genius is ever a fountain of self-generating energy; whosoever expends much in productive activity must take in much by appropriation; — whence comes what of truth is in the observation that genius is a genius for industry." — MAUDSLEY.

MY opportunities for observing Rufus Choate were chiefly when residing, in early life, in the vicinity of Boston. I saw and heard him on various public occasions in my youth, early manhood, and when a student at Cambridge Law School.

So much has been well said in estimation of Choate's genius and attainments that I do not feel like adding a word in that direction, except to say that his efforts on political and forensic occasions profoundly impressed me with a sense of his masterly attainments, his extraordinary powers, and wonderful genius. To speak of his genius as wonderful may, to one who never saw the man, appear extravagant; but it always seemed to me that his genius, as seen through his public efforts, was wonderful in a very special sense. Besides his liberal attainments as a scholar and a lawyer, and his great natural abilities, he seemed to have an added quality which few have, which stimulated his faculties to most vigorous and effective action. Sometimes this stimulating quality is called electricity, which, in our day of scientific progress, is a word implying, more than ever, large force, and, in a measure, unrevealed power and possibilities. In referring to Choate, one writer says, " When addressing a jury, his whole frame was charged with electricity, and literally quivered with emotion." Another speaks of " his electric bursts of humor."

A cool-headed lawyer, who heard Choate's famous address before the New England Society of New York, in 1843, says, " It came upon the audience like a series of electric shocks." Another well-known writer speaks of Choate's "magnetic individuality." We thus find Choate reminding observers of electricity, electric bursts, electric shocks, and magnetic batteries generally.

We are beginning to feel that it is not easy to limit what may be done with electricity. When Franklin drew it from the sky on a kite-string, it was thought marvelous. Since that day we have seen it guided in the storm, used in medicine, and become the obedient servant of man, who sends his message by means of it aroumd the world.

In later time it comes as a means of brilliant light, and has been proposed, though not successfully, as a means, through nice adjustments, to relieve, as was hoped, an afflicted nation, by informing it of the *locus* of the dreaded bullet in the body of our late beloved President. Edison and kindred spirits are at work developing the capacities of the telephone by the phonograph; and an Electrical Congress was lately in session in Paris, where, among many wonders, was exhibited an electric railway and a microtasimeter, which is so delicate that it will measure the calorific rays emitted by the fixed stars. What will come of these things who can tell?

We hear accounts of the late discovery by M. Faure, who has invented an accumulator of electricity, a sort of storage arrangement, the possible uses of which may not be limited to medicine and to the arts, but may touch some new and important problems.

So, in the case of Mr. Choate, I feel like insisting that in some mysterious way he anticipated M. Faure, and was, in fact, an accumulator and storehouse of that subtile force or source of energy we call electricity, which surcharged his brain and every nerve to an extraordinary degree, and so helped him, with striking effect, to display his masterly genius.

Some have claimed that the "eager and nipping air" of New England, especially in the region of Boston, has unusual vitalizing power in stimulating nerve and brain. However this may be, or to what extent the sensitive temperament of Choate may have been affected by it, must be left to conjecture.

To see Choate in one of his imaginative flights, or when making an impassioned appeal in his best strength for client or party, was a privilege to be long and gratefully remembered.

When referring to criticisms by lawyers and others of Choate's elocution and style, Mr. Webster said, "There is no man in the world besides Choate who could succeed with that style. It is his own. It is peculiar to him. It is as natural to him as any constitutional trait about him. Nobody can imitate him. He imitates nobody, and his style is most effective."

Choate was a diligent student. Great and brilliant as were his talents, his success was largely due to his profound and constant studies. Some one has said his genius was mainly "science in disguise." If by this is meant that his culture was large, unremitting, and generous, from which he drew effectively in his forensic and other public performances, it is true.

My first remembrance of Choate in politics was

in the memorable campaign of 1840, when the prevailing cry was "Tippecanoe and Tyler too." The canvass was very spirited, and, as the result showed, quite one-sided. A notable Whig meeting, showing the temper and spirit of the campaign, was held at Bunker Hill, in September. The gathering of people was tremendous, and their enthusiasm immense. There was a procession four miles long, in which were large delegations from various States, with many banners. I remember one delegation of several hundred men from Louisiana. This delegation, on its march in the afternoon back to Boston, encountered a drenching rain-storm, and one of the men, perhaps a printer, extemporized a banner to suit the occasion, upon which were quickly printed the words, "Any rain but the reign of Matty Van Buren." There were on the rostrum at Bunker Hill many leading men, and Webster, who was the principal orator, spoke in ponderous majesty. Choate spoke in the evening in Boston, and was received with great favor and applause. He was all aglow, full of fire and action such as no other man did or could exhibit. Catching the spirit of the occasion, as he stood there addressing the people with a mind freighted with serious thought, and occasionally making some apt reference to Bunker Hill and its patriotic associations, it was evident that Choate was then and there the favorite orator, at least of New England, if not of the whole country.

Referring to another political occasion, I remember to have heard Choate at Concord, in 1844, on the fourth day of July, when there was a large gathering brought together to espouse the election of Henry Clay. Webster and Berrien and Winthrop and Greeley and Lawrence were there. Choate was in good condition, and hopeful of victory. He referred to South Carolina, with tremulous gesture, as the " Palmetto State," and, with regretful feeling, alluded to her career as a nullifier of the tariff laws in Jackson's term. He advocated a protective tariff, and wanted to know, in his effective manner, whether the Free Traders would carry their doctrine so far as to make us dependent upon foreign nations for the gunpowder we might have to use in our defense against foreign aggression. Among other speakers, Horace Greeley followed Choate, under the big tent. I remember Greeley's white pants, somewhat colored by green grass, also his peculiar voice and intonation, and manner generally. He commenced and continued in a quiet, thoughtful way, but as one who had something worth saying to the people. He was listened to attentively, as he deserved to be.

Probably no two speakers could be more unlike in style, manner, and action, than Horace Greeley and Rufus Choate.

I heard Choate again on an occasion not political. It was when he delivered his famous lecture on the Sea, before a literary association in a large hall. He seemed full of his wild subject, and swayed the audience with eloquence, as the storm sways the sea. The impression left upon me by this performance is as if I had listened to a breezy, reverent poem, descriptive of the mighty power of the sea, and what may be encountered there in calm or in storm. His manner was very impressive. The tone of the discourse was in the main serious, and in the spirit of Bryant, who says, —

> " The sea is mighty, but a mightier sways
> His restless billows."

All regret that the manuscript of this thrilling lecture was lost.

I heard Choate again on a winter evening in 1851, on a very quiet and undemonstrative occasion. The place was the Massachusetts Senate Chamber, and his audience a Senate committee and a few others. The special topic was a proposed separation of West Roxbury from Roxbury, which would create a new town government. Choate was retained to support the measure, and, small in number as was the audience, he found in his topic enough to arouse his enthusiasm. He made an eloquent plea for towns and town governments, and the usefulness and glory thereof. He insisted that they are important factors in educational growth, especially in what pertains to state and national interests, and that their continuance was essential to the welfare of the country. In this argument, Choate, as was his habit, treated his subject as thoroughly and eloquently as if addressing a large audience.

In the year 1847, when the breach was more apparent than before in Massachusetts between the Conscience and the Cotton Whigs, the former had hopes that both Choate and Webster would soon become identified with them. In this chapter of political history, there was a memorable day in Faneuil Hall, in September, when I was present as a spectator, and which may properly be referred to here, as illustrative of the political atmosphere of the period. The Whig State Convention was in session, and many leading men of both sides were there. The contest was, as to the platform, whether it should be conservative or of an anti-slavery type. Before it was reported, Sumner made a speech of great power and eloquence in favor of aggressive action against the usurpation of the slave power. In his speech he made a graceful and forcible appeal to Mr. Webster, and said, " Dedicate, sir, the golden years of experience which are yet in store for you to removing from your country its greatest evil. In this cause you shall find inspirations to eloquence higher than any you have yet confessed." Winthrop was then called out, and made an able reply. There were two reports on the platform, as was expected. Speeches were made by Stevenson, Stephen C. Phillips, Linus Child, Charles Francis Adams, and Charles Allen. The debate was able, attended by much excitement, and lasted until night. The conservatives became alarmed, and decided to send for Webster. Abbott Lawrence, who was a member of the convention, soon appeared, with Webster upon his arm, amid tremendous applause. Both Conscience and Cotton joined in manifestations of respect. As Webster reached the rostrum, the applause was renewed with great vigor, and the whole scene was grand and inspiring. Webster took his seat, and listened to Charles Allen, one of the ablest of the Conscience men, who resumed and finished a stern and inflexible speech. Webster then arose, the convention rising with him, and in a short address made a plea of great power for harmony. A friend tells me that Sumner said he knew, when he saw " Black Dan " coming, it was all up with his side that year. It was in this speech that

Webster's famous words were uttered which have been so widely quoted. He had been speaking of his warm attachment to the Whig party, and how he loved to inhale its "odor of liberty." Then followed the memorable words spoken in his grandest and most impressive manner. "Others," he said, "rely on other foundations and other hopes for the welfare of the country; but, for my part, in the dark and troubled night that is on us, I see no star above the horizon promising light to guide us, but the intelligent, patriotic, united Whig party of the United States." At this moment every look and gesture of the orator were in harmony with his thought. He seemed to speak as if standing in a dark background, his lustrous eyes looking above the horizon for the star that should give the promised light to guide the convention and the people. The power of the speech and the spectacle was seen and felt in the fact that a convention of turbulent men, at once subdued, were ready for adjournment without further strife.

I heard Choate on several political occasions in Faneuil Hall, some of which are memorable. It will be remembered that Webster delivered his famous, and, according to his opponents of that day, infamous, 7th of March speech in the Senate, in 1850, the tone of which was compromise with

the South for the sake of peace and the Union.
Choate was in full sympathy with Webster, as
may be seen in his political speeches of that period. In April, 1851, Webster, who was on a short
visit to Marshfield, was invited by many citizens
of Boston to a public reception in Faneuil Hall.
Mr. Choate was to address him for the citizens.
Great indignation was aroused by the refusal of
the mayor and aldermen to allow the use of the
hall for the proposed meeting. The reason given
was that Wendell Phillips and the Abolitionists
having been refused the use of the hall for fear
of a riot, they could not consistently grant the
hall to any one else. Webster and his friends,
particularly Choate, were very indignant. A good
many things were said and done to set the matter
right. Choate was very active, and wished Mr.
Webster to know that the action of the city authorities did not represent the citizens or the best
sentiment of Boston. Choate sent friends to
Marshfield to so assure Mr. Webster, among whom
were Peter Harvey and Fletcher Webster, the latter taking a letter from Choate. Webster said
sadly to Harvey, " Fletcher came down and merely told me the bald fact that the city government
had refused the hall, and brought me a note from
Choate which I could not read. By the way, tell
Mr. Choate to write better; his handwriting is

barbarous. I could not read a single word. There is the letter; just look at it; tell Choate to go to a writing-school, and take a quarter's lessons." Webster finally wrote a letter, which was much admired by his friends, to the committee who invited him, in which he said, " I shall defer my visit to Faneuil Hall, the cradle of American liberty, until its doors shall fly open on golden hinges to lovers of UNION as well as lovers of LIBERTY."

In the next year, on a spring afternoon, " When the May sun sheds an amber light," Webster appeared in Faneuil Hall at a kindly reception tendered him by citizens of both parties. This was soon after his carriage accident. He was quite unwell, and much affected by the exhibition of general kindness and respect. How well I remember his appearance when he thundered, " This is Faneuil Hall — Open."

In the year 1850, and soon after, many large union meetings, so-called, were held in various parts of the country in support of the compromise measures of 1850. There were several held in Faneuil Hall, where such men as Webster, Choate, Curtis, Winthrop, and Ashman addressed the people. I was present at one in November of 1851, I think, when Hon. B. R. Curtis, then an eminent member of the Boston bar, and afterwards

Judge of the United States Supreme Court, and Choate spoke. The hall was closely packed by intelligent men standing, and there was much excitement. Curtis, who presided, led off in a calm, logical speech, and Choate followed. I shall attempt no statement of what he said. It was a fervent appeal to the country, especially to the North, to stand by the Union in the spirit of sacrifice and concession. In the course of his argument, the views of men like Charles Francis Adams, Henry Wilson, and Charles Sumner, who were then at the front of the anti-slavery hosts, got some hard knocks. I was sitting very near Choate, on the side of the famous rostrum, and shall not forget one of his gestures. He had reached in high heat the climax of his speech, when, under great excitement, almost frenzy, upon emphasizing his final point, he quickly bent forward and downward so that his curling hair nearly touched the floor. In an instant he was erect again, his whole appearance intensely nervous and magnetic, and drew from the vast audience round after round of applause, and cheers.

The Duke of Argyll, in his treatise on "The Reign of Law," presents a view which may in some measure explain Mr. Choate in action as an orator : —

"When, through the motor nerves, the will

orders the muscles into action, that order is enforced by a discharge of the electric force, and upon this discharge, the contractile force is set free to act, and does accordingly produce the contraction which is desired. Such is, at least, one suggestion as to the means employed to place human action under the control of the human will, in that material frame which is so wonderfully and fearfully made. And whether this hypothesis be accurate or not, it is certain that some such adjustment of Force to Mechanism is involved in every bodily movement which is subject to the will." Whether all or any of this is applicable to, or accounts for, the appearance of Mr. Choate in action, in court, or on the rostrum, is the question submitted.

If "every bodily movement" of the great orator, "subject to the will," can thus be explained, he at least was probably innocent of all knowledge of the law that "through the motor nerves the will orders the muscles into action," "by a discharge of the electric force," in the manner stated.

In July of 1851, Choate delivered an oration before the Story Association of Cambridge Law School, of whose graduating class I was a member. A procession was formed, which marched to the church where the address was delivered. My place in the procession happened to be next to the orator. As showing of what flimsy stuff history is sometimes made, I may in this connection give an incident. There was more or less vague hinting that the great orator was occasionally addicted to the use of opium. Some were inclined to explain his nervous action and great excitement, when speaking, by the opium theory. As the procession was waiting for its march, Choate took from his vest pocket some small particle and put it into his mouth. " Do you see that," whispered a bystander, " Choate is getting ready for his speech; he has just taken some opium." As a matter of fact, the remark of the wiseacre would have been as just if made of the Rev. Obadiah Smith, or some other solemn personage who by chance might have attracted attention in a similar way. Rather than encourage the opium scandal, I preferred to rest my theory upon electricity, or Boston east wind, as the motive power that inspired the great orator as no other man of the time was inspired.

The topic of the oration in the church was obedience and respect for law as essential for the maintenance of the Union, which is to be preferred beyond and above all things else as a means of political salvation for the country. He made an elaborate and eloquent appeal to the young men of the Law School to throw their personal and political influence for the conservative side of the great conflict which he seemed to feel, almost as a prophet, was imminent. His appeal, like Webster's, was " to lovers of Union as well as to lovers of Liberty."

It was my good fortune to see Choate in court engaged in trials on various occasions. It is not worth while, perhaps, to state in detail what I saw and heard on such occasions. In every case he seemed to be absorbed for his client's cause. There was no case in his hands, especially before a jury, that he did not make a thing of life, and of profound interest.

Many anecdotes and incidents of Choate as a lawyer in the courts have been given, some of which, I trust, will find a place in this book. I happened in court one Saturday, in Boston, when Choate had charge of a case that involved some improvement in the handling of cotton. In the course of a very spirited argument to the jury, he took occasion to discuss our agricultural and manufacturing resources as coöperative in developing the country and promoting general prosperity. He made a masterly and interesting statement of his view, which was in itself broad statesmanship.

When he brought forward somnambulism as a defense in part for his client, Tirrell, who was indicted for murder, there were many good women and children, not to speak of " the rest of mankind," who thought the defense very absurd, if not very wicked. The jury, however, thought otherwise.

I am indebted to a prominent citizen of Brooklyn, a native of Salem, where Choate studied law, for the following. Leverett Saltonstall, who was an able and noted Massachusetts Federalist, was not an admirer of the irrepressible Caleb Cushing, then a rising man in his region. Cushing, though a younger man than Saltonstall, was considered his rival, and rumor was afloat to the effect that Cushing's wife had written and published in a newspaper a very eulogistic article about her husband, which rumor Saltonstall was willing to believe. Choate at this time was a young lawyer in Saltonstall's office in Salem. One morning while at his desk, S. rushed in excitedly and exclaimed, " Cushing is dead and buried, — dead and buried." " Dead ! " said Choate — " and buried ! When ? where ? " " Dead and buried ! " cried Saltonstall. " Well," said Choate, " you don't tell me when he died or where he is buried ; but I 'll venture he is not buried so deep but what he 'll sprout."

I am also indebted to a gentleman, now of Brooklyn, formerly of Boston, who was a client of Choate's, for the following : The client had been

consulting Choate in litigations concerning some
vessels about to arrive at New York. One day
the client said, "Mr. Choate, the vessels will soon
arrive in New York, and I am going there to re-
side. Now, what lawyer do you think of that you
would advise me to consult in this matter?"
"Let me see," said Choate. Then turning to his
partner, he said, "Crowninshield, what is the
name of that young lawyer in New York, who did
so well in defending Monroe Edwards, and had a
counterfeit $1,000 bill put on him for his fee?"
"His name is Evarts," said Crowninshield. "Yes,"
said Choate, "Evarts, he is the man for you. Employ him."

Is not this an instance, *in re* Evarts, of coming
events casting their shadows before? Choate
must have felt the coming greatness of New
York's distinguished lawyer.

A few days previous to Choate's oration before
the Story Association at Cambridge, to which
I have referred, Choate was under discussion at
the Law Library among a group of a dozen students. The conversation turned chiefly upon the
comparative merits of Choate and Brougham, as
lawyers and orators. I remember how ardently
one of the students, of rather mature years,
from the Southwest; insisted that Choate was
the greater lawyer and orator, and referred to

cases and occasions in the career of each to prove his position. There was a disposition to acquiesce in the view that Choate was the superior. While this circumstance is not decisive, it is useful as showing how deep an impression Choate was then making upon appreciative minds.

The late Mr. Somerby was a distinguished member of the Boston bar, and was frequently associated with Choate in the trial of causes. He was an enthusiastic admirer of Choate, and one day, while riding with a friend through Mount Auburn Cemetery, took off his hat at a certain spot with so reverent an air that his companion asked him the reason. Mr. Somerby pointed to a grave near by, and said, " There is the grave of Rufus Choate. The man who goes by that grave without taking off his hat is not fit to live on earth."

In his intercourse with the bar, Mr. Choate, though resolute, was disposed to be kind and courteous. One day I saw him engaged in court, in Boston, in a jury trial involving some question of patent right in a rifle. One of his adversaries was a well-known lawyer of the New York bar, who seemed to be very earnest and pronounced in his ways and methods. He was quite an expert in his knowledge of fire-arms, and handled the rifle as if familiar with its use. He would hold and aim it as if about to fire in the court-room. Choate did not shine in that way. In the course of the trial, his New York adversary made some abrupt and impolite remark to Choate as to the admissibility of certain evidence. In reply, Choate, who was evidently not pleased with the remark, noticed it by referring, in a sombre way, to the learned counsel from New York, whom he could *not* call his brother.

A Plymouth friend sends me the following: A gentleman was in his study one day, and Mr. Choate, who had a closet in which he kept bottles and glasses and ice-water, had taken out his decanter, and was enjoying a social glass (a thing, by the way, which he did very rarely, and with great moderation), when he heard some one coming up the stairs, and, expecting the Rev. Dr. Adams, he suddenly and hastily gathered all the implements, thrust them into the closet, and shut it, when his library door opened, and, instead of Dr. Adams, there appeared before him his friend, Mr. Peter Harvey. "Why, Harvey! is that you? I thought it was a Presbyterian foot-fall." And he immediately replaced the paraphernalia so suddenly hidden from sight.

A Boston gentleman says, "On one evening, when Mr. Brough and others gave a concert in Boston, my informant was one of the last comers of a crowded audience, and consequently had to take his seat near the door, and as far as the dimensions of the hall would permit from the singers' platform. He was happy to find himself seated next to Mr. Choate. At a late period of the performance, Mr. Brough came upon the stage, and comported himself so oddly that my friend said to Mr. Choate, 'I think the man must be drunk.' 'I smelled his breath the moment he came upon the stage,' replied Choate."

He once passed the night at the once famous inn of Mrs. Nicholson, in Plymouth,— a somewhat rambling house, in which the only room not necessarily used as a passage-way to other rooms was occupied by Justice Wilde of the Supreme Court. Most of the members of the Plymouth bar, inmates of the house, including Eddy, Coffin, Baylies, Packard, and Young, were playing cards until a late hour. At breakfast, Justice Wilde, whose Puritanical manner was not unmixed with humor, knowing well the situation of things, said, " Well, Mr. Choate, I suppose you slept well?" " Admirably, your Honor, except that I slept in the highway," replied Mr. Choate.

I remember hearing Mr. Choate defend the master of the schooner Sally Ann, tried in the United States Court, in Boston, on a charge of casting away his vessel, in defraud of the underwriters, on the coast of St. Domingo. The jury had disagreed in a former trial, conducted by District Attorney Robert Rantoul, Jr. George Lunt, appointed his successor, had secured additional testimony, with, as he thought, a certainty of conviction. The testimony on both sides was closed; and, during a short recess taken before the arguments, Mr. Choate, in passing through the entry, accidentally overheard the colored cook of the vessel, who had been called as a government witness, but not used, speak of the captain's crying when he left his vessel and took to his boat. Choate hurried into court, and, with great impressiveness, asked permission to put in an important piece of testimony, which had only at that moment come to his knowledge. With the permission of the judge, the cook was called; and, in reply to the question of Mr. Choate as to the deportment of the master on leaving his vessel, said, " He cried like a child." " That is all," said Mr. Choate; and, with this single straw of sentiment to save his case, his appeals to the jury were so pathetic that a verdict of acquittal followed, wrung out of the chords in the human heart, which he knew so well how to touch, and which resented the idea that a man could cry over the loss of his dear Sally Ann if he were guilty of her destruction.

I am indebted to a venerable and learned member of the Boston bar for the following: —

One day, at the close of the testimony in an important trial in a civil action, in which Mr. Choate was engaged before the Supreme Court, at Dedham, Judge Shaw said he did not think there was any question of fact to submit to the jury, and the better course would be to take a verdict *pro forma,* and reserve the law questions for the full bench. Then, turning to Mr. Choate, the judge said, " Mr. Choate, upon the view suggested, if agreeable to you, I will order a verdict against your client." Choate stepped forward, and, bowing in his fine manner, gravely replied: " If your Honor please, as to whether the course you propose will be agreeable to me, I desire to say that I do not remember any case ever in my charge wherein I would not have found it agreeable to have a verdict in favor of my client." The reply and Choate's inimitable manner caused much merriment among the lawyers and spectators.

The late Vice-President Wilson — a name likely to grow in importance in American political history — was, I think, a warm admirer of the genius and eloquence of Rufus Choate, though not of his entire political course. I remember meeting Mr. Wilson (whom I knew as a life-long friend) soon

after the Whig National Convention that nomi-
nated General Scott, in 1852, at Baltimore.
Choate was there, strenuously advocating the
nomination of Mr. Webster. In speaking of the
convention, Wilson said that Choate made an
ingenious and brilliant speech for Webster, upon
the basis of accepting the compromise measure
of 1850 as a finality, and that there was no
orator in the convention that equaled Choate.

In his work entitled "Rise and Fall of the Slave
Power in America," Mr. Wilson, in referring to
the resolutions introduced by Mr. Ashman, which
were believed to be in harmony with Mr. Webster's views, speaks of "the impassioned and brilliant speech which Mr. Choate made on their reception and in their behalf." Again, he states
in the same work, that, "In answer to vociferous
calls, Mr. Choate addressed the convention in a
speech of great forensic brilliancy and force, in
which, however, was far more apparent the special pleading of the advocate than the calm consideration of the statesman."

In the same work, the author refers, in a kindly
way, to the part taken by Mr. Choate as counsel
for the Commonwealth, in 1836, when the Supreme
Court decided, in the case of the slave child Med,
brought to that State by its owner, "that an
owner of a slave in another State where slavery is

warranted by law, voluntarily bringing such slave
into this State, has no authority to retain him
against his will, or carry him out of the State
against his consent, for the purpose of being held
in slavery." This important opinion, which was so
much quoted in subsequent controversies, was delivered by Chief Justice Shaw. Again, on the 9th
of August, 1842, the Ashburton Treaty was signed
at Washington. It was largely aimed at the
suppression of the slave trade, and required the
United States to coöperate with an armed force
on the coast of Africa. The treaty was bitterly
assailed in the Senate by Mr. Benton of Missouri,
Mr. Buchanan, Mr. Conrad of Louisiana, and others. The latter said, "If ratified, Great Britain
will unfurl the banner of abolition still more conspicuously before your slaves. She will accustom
them to consider her as their benefactor, the cham-
pion of their rights, the avenger of their wrongs."
Referring to the hot debate in the Senate, and
characterizing the motives of the men and news-
papers that opposed the treaty (which was ratified), Mr. Wilson, in his work, says that "Many
saw their true spirit, but none more fitly described
them than Rufus Choate, then in the Senate, who
spoke of them as 'restless, selfish, reckless, the
cankers of a calm world and a long peace, pining
with thirst of notoriety, slaves to their hatred of

England, to whom the treaty is distasteful, to whom any treaty and all things but the glare and clamor, the vain pomp and hollow circumstance, the toil and agony and inadequate results of war, — all but those would be distasteful and dreary.' "

Again, in the same work, Mr. Wilson refers to Mr. Choate's opposition to the joint resolution for the annexation of Texas in 1844, and says, " Rufus Choate, of Massachusetts, made a brilliant and eloquent speech in opposition, both on the ground of power and expediency. ' We could not,' he contended, ' admit Texas by the joint resolution of the House, if it would insure a thousand years of liberty to the Union. If, like the fabled garden of old, its rivers should run pearls, and its trees bear imperial fruit of gold, — yet even we could not admit her, because it would be a sin against the Constitution.' "

In their earlier private and public life, Sumner and Choate were warm friends, though differing widely on political questions in later years. Mr. Pierce, author of Memoirs, etc., of Sumner, mentions several incidents that show this. As early as 1834, Sumner was brought into personal relations with Choate when he was in Washington, a member of the House, and Sumner was there on a professional errand.

In 1834, and for several years after, No. 4

Court Street, Boston, must have been an attractive place. There were gathered there, at this period, several lawyers, since well known, some of whom have achieved permanent fame. On the same floor with Sumner and Hillard were Theophilus Parsons, Rufus Choate, the two Chandlers, and John A. Andrew, afterwards governor. On a floor above was Horace Mann, who in after years displayed great ability as a member of Congress, and when in charge of important educational interests. Here also were Edward G. Loring and Luther S. Cushing. When Hillard left the building in 1856, he wrote in verse a graceful "Farewell to Number Four," which called forth some happy rejoinders. Judge Story, Greenleaf, Felton, Park Benjamin, and George Bancroft were frequent callers at No. 4, which was thus closely identified with the daily life of Mr. Choate. Hillard, writing to Sumner from New York, in 1836, recalls, in contrast with the law offices of that city, " our cool and pleasant office, and the quiet and cultivated friends who drop in."

In 1834–35 we find Sumner and Choate with Edward Everett, Hillard, and others, announced in a course of lectures before the Boston Lyceum at Boylston Hall. In a letter to Longfellow in August, 1837, Sumner refers to Choate in terms of mutual friendship. Mr. Pierce says that Sum-

ner " much enjoyed his friendly relations with
Rufus Choate, whose office was at No. 4 Court
Street. They talked of politics and literature,
particularly of Burke, for whom Mr. Choate had
an extravagant admiration. When the latter was
in the United States Senate, 1841–42, they treated
of the same themes in correspondence. Later
they were associated professionally in the boun-
dary dispute between Massachusetts and Rhode
Island." In June, 1841, Sumner wrote Dr. Lieber, " Choate will be glad to renew his acquaintance with you ; his speech on McLeod's case is
masterly." In 1842, Sumner wrote two articles
maintaining the qualified right of search, which
attracted much attention. Choate, while in the
Senate, worked with Sumner, approving the position taken. In February, 1842, in a letter to
Dr. Lieber, Sumner wrote, " I am glad you like
Choate so well. His position here is very firm.
He is the leader of our bar, with an overwhelming superfluity of business, with a strong taste for
books and learned men, with great amiableness of
character, with uncommon eloquence and untiring industry." Again, in a letter to Lord Morpeth, September 6, 1842, touching the Ashburton
Treaty, Sumner refers to what Choate thinks influenced the British authorities in the matter. In
a letter to Dr. Lieber, September, 1843, Sumner

writes, " Choate is entirely uncommitted on the subject of international copyright. He has never looked at it; and, if he sees his way clear to be its advocate, he will enter into it. He asked me to state to him in a few words the argument on both sides. I thought of Madame de Staël and Fichte, — " ' Donnez moi vos idées en dix mots.' I did it, and he muses still."

In 1844, Perkins edited the American edition of " Brown's Chancery Reports," and dedicated it to Mr. Choate. Sumner wrote to Perkins, " Your dedication cannot fail to give great pleasure to Mr. Choate. It is a beautiful, and, I think, a well deserved, tribute from a former pupil. It is with hesitation that I venture to touch rudely what is chiseled so carefully. But, as a general rule, it seems to me that one cannot be too abstemious of adjectives in an inscription which should be close and lapidary in its character." While Sumner's view is doubtless correct, it may be that " adjectives," even in an inscription, did not worry Choate, who knew how to marshal them in long array ; as, for instance, the following, when he spoke of a harness as " a safe, sound, substantial, suitable, second-rate, second-hand harness," or spoke of the Greek mind as " subtle, mysterious, plastic, apprehensive, comprehensive, available."

Mr. Choate felt a proper reverence for the

things that belong to religion. Whether he believed in a creed, in a technical, Calvinistic sense,
is doubtful. But that he had a deep religious
nature, which found expression in various ways,
there can be no doubt.

My cousin, the late Rev. Hubbard Winslow,
who for several years was pastor of the Bowdoin
Street Church, in Boston, was an admiring and
warm friend of both Webster and Choate, and
received from them many tokens of reciprocal
regard. I visited Marshfield, in 1862, with Dr.
Winslow, at the Webster mansion, when I saw, in
the kind welcome extended to him, and expressions of friendship at dinner, ample evidence of
mutual respect and esteem. Dr. Winslow once
gave me a touching account of his baptism of
one of Mr. Choate's children, — Caroline, the
youngest, and deeply beloved, who was sick, and
near death. Having received a note from Mr.
Choate, requesting his kind offices in the baptism
of his child, Dr. Winslow went to the residence,
and there met the family in great affliction. In
his account of what occurred, and his description
of the scene, with Mr. Choate as a central figure,
and heart-stricken father, Dr. Winslow left a clear
impression upon my mind that he thought Choate
a sincere and profound believer. I will not here
repeat the story of the baptism scene, as related

to me by the minister; it was an experience which brought out impressively, in the presence of death, the affectionate and reverent side of Mr. Choate's character.

Hon. E. L. Pierce and the late Professor Longfellow were appointed literary executors by Sumner's will. I am permitted, by the kindness of Mr. Pierce, to subjoin several interesting letters of Choate's to his friend Sumner, which further illustrate his views and character.

In closing this contribution thus made in compliance with the polite request of Judge Neilson, my regret is that I did not see and know more of the patriotic, scholarly lawyer, of whom it may be justly said he was *primus inter pares.*

Burke, whom Choate admired so much, said of Lord Chatham, "A great and celebrated name; a name that keeps the name of this country respectable in every other on the globe." So, for his own country, the name of Rufus Choate, as an accomplished jurist, shall fulfill a like office.

JOHN WINSLOW.

LETTERS BY CHOATE TO SUMNER.

WASHINGTON, Saturday, *May 29*, 1841.

MY DEAR SIR, — I found the inclosed, addressed to me here, and have great pleasure in giving it a chance to pass under your critical, and yet benevolent, eye. I have hardly done more than wash off the " variation of each " dust accumulated, all the way from Boston, on my pen, ink, and paper, — more commonly in this country, and more conveniently, called stationery, since it included wafers, wax candles, penknives, and the like, — and settle myself in an airy third-story. Yet I see and feel — in green peas, ripe cherries, mown grass, roses, and a thermometer at 80° — the new climate I have come to.

The President is in high spirits — making a good impression. He will stand by *Mr. Webster*, and the talk of an unfriendly conservative action is *true*, but not *terrifying*. Cushing will not be Speaker, and White, I should think, will, — of Kentucky, — a Clay nomination. But, I forget the worthlessness of this gossip, — and leave you to your studies, business, ladies, and claret

Very truly yours,

R. CHOATE.

WASHINGTON.

MY DEAR SUMNER, — I have just received the memorandum, and will turn it *nocturna et diurna manu*, — to quote obscure and unusual Latin words. I hope it will do your friend's business, and the Pope's, and England's, and the lone Imperial mother's, — as you say.

Mr. Webster is so much excited (and confidentially gratified) with the *squaboshment* of the Whigs[1] that he will talk of nothing else. He thinks he can *Seal* better with Sir Robert Peel *et id genus*. Can he? Your acquaintance was made with so whiggish a set that I suppose you mourn as for the flight of liberty. But, mark you, how much more *peaceably, purely, intellectually*, did this roaring democracy of ours change its whole government and whole policy, last fall, than England has done it now.

Yes, Everett's is a good appointment. Ask me, when I get home, if we did not come near losing him in the Senate, from abolitionism, — *entre nous*, — if we do, the Union goes to pieces

---

[1] Lord Melbourne's Ministry.

like a potter's vessel. But as Ercles' vein is not lightly nor often to be indulged in — (*nec Deus inter sit nisi, et cet.*).

I give love to Hillard, salute you, and am

Very truly yours,

R. C.

We shall have a veto after all, *ut timeo.*

DEAR SUMNER, — I have this moment received the inclosed, with a civil note from our friend of Waterloo and the Encyclopedia. I hope you and he are plotting nothing against Christianity, though I doubt about you both grievously. He expects you to answer through me, and I beg you would. In a line to ——, yesterday, I adverted to the cases of Dr. Howe and Mrs. Bayard, *quod vide.* Neither goes as we would wish, alas for the wishes of friendship and the dreams of love.

We shall this morning, probably, — it is near 8 A. M., and our committee meets at 10, — report a more erect and self-sustaining and respected charter than Mr. Ewing's.

The debauched state of public opinion exceeds belief. *Pejor actus.* Write me a long letter.

Very truly yours,

R. CHOATE.

21 *June,* 1841.

(PRIVATE.)

September 12th, 1841.

My dear Sumner, — I am indignant at such indolent and careless discourtesy — but hang, shoot, and drown me if I can help it. I have spoken to him a hundred times — and although I do not think he takes strongly to the application — indeed — there is no vacancy — I did suppose he had written.

Just now, a real crisis — harassed — distract — arranging cabinets — etc., etc. — he is impenetrable to these duties of kindness, propriety — I read him your letter — in a voice loud enough for Faneuil Hall. He surely will *write*, at least.

(Private.)

We spent yesterday all day on Everett. Although I say, as I should not say it, I am innocent of the man's blood. After five hours, we found by sounding round the Chamber we should be 24 × 24 — so we adjourned, and I have great hopes we shall carry it to-morrow.

The session ends to-morrow, but I shall stay three or four days. " God bless you."

Very truly yours,

R. CHOATE.

27

WASHINGTON, *December* 9, 1841.

MY DEAR SIR, — I have just got yours, shall
have great pleasure in expressing myself in Mr.
T.'s behalf. The "all powerful words" are few,
nay, rather lost — but just and friendly ones all
may speak.

Yes, I ought to have composed that strife as I
ought to have done much other good — *Pulcher
et multa minans, vero nec recti nec suaviter.*

But not to diffuse myself in any more philosophy — all thrown away on young chaps,

I abruptly declare myself, truly yours,

R. CHOATE.

MY DEAR SIR, — I have received and trans-
mitted your papers for Lieber; and read the
D. A. with edification and assent. We are wrong.

Lieber sent me a strong paper on this same
subject. He is the most fertile, indomitable, un-
sleeping, combative, and propagandizing person of
his race. I have bought "Longfellow," and am
glad to hear of his run.

Politics are unpromising — but better than last
session. The *juste milieu* will vindicate itself.

With much love to G. S. H.,

Yours faithfully,

R. CHOATE.

7 *January,* 1842.

C. SUMNER, ESQ.

WASHINGTON, *January 24th,* 1842.

MY DEAR SIR, — I cry your pardon in the matter of your letter. It was all just right, and showed me well enough that you were quite enough in earnest — but was an uncommon document for Boards of Commissioners. However, I sent it, with high praise of you and the Doctor.

You are clearly right in the Search question. I never was more gratified than to have been asked — by a spoon, though — if I did not write it.

Discuss the Creole — as quick — and as well as you possibly can.

Lord Morpeth is just come, and pleases universally. He attends our atrocious spectacles in H. H., with professional relish.

Most truly yours,

R. C.

MY DEAR SUMNER, — I hoped to write before now to tell you what can be done for the elegant and tuneful Professor.

No *certain* thing do I get yet, but I trust soon to have. It is the age of patronage of genius you see. *Regnat Apollo,* as one may say. . . .

That was a most rich speech of Hillard's, as is all his speáking, whether to listening crowds or to appreciating circles of you and me. We hear that one Mrs. Dickens called on him and Mrs.

Hillard with a significant and expressive civility and respect. In his heart, I have no doubt the Secretary of State agrees with you. But think of this: Shall we not give E. a right by treaty to search for enough to find the American character, — on condition that by treaty she agrees to assist our slave ships in distress in the W. I.? To get such treaties, must we not begin by denying all her claims to search? How cheerful, genial, and fragrant, as it were, are our politics! What serried files of armed men, shoulder to shoulder, keeping time to the music of duty and glory, animated by a single soul, are the Whigs! But this delicious winter bears us swiftly through it all, and the sun of to-day lights up the Potomac; and burns with the flush and glory of June. Dexter says this city reminds one of *Rome.* I suppose he meant in its spaces — solitudes, quiet, vices, and so forth — though the surrounding country is undoubtedly beautiful. Love to Hillard. Lieber writes in Latin. I mean to answer him in any tongue whatever he chooses to speak, and for that purpose must break off and go at him.

Truly yours,

R. CHOATE.

19 *February,* 1842.

WASHINGTON, 10 P. M.

DEAR SUMNER AND HILLARD, — I have addressed myself with tears of entreaty to the Secretary; and, if no hidden snag or planter lies under the muddy flood, we shall scull the Doctor into port. There, as Dr. Watts says, he may

> " Sit and sing himself away,"

or exclaim, —

> " Spes et fortuna, valete — inveni nunc portum,
> Lusistis me satis — ludite nunc alios " —

which is from the Greek, you know, in Dalzell's " Græe. Majora," vol. 2d, — and closes some editions of Gil Blas !

The voting on the Ashburton Treaty at nine at' night — seats full — lights lighted, — hall as still as death — was not without *grandness*. But why speak of this to the *procurantes* of that denationalized Boston and Massachusetts ?

Yours truly,

R. CHOATE.

MY DEAR SIR, — I did not get your letter till 10 o'clock P. M., yesterday, Saturday, and it comes unaccompanied by that more sober and more business-like memorandum to which it refers. Where is that ? I had previously written letters for a Mr. Beal and a Mr. Kittredge — and sent them by the ears to the Board. Your letter is so full of rhetoric, poetry and a certain fashionable un-concernedness that I dare not send that. Dr. Sewall has received nothing. This is Sunday, and I think to-night I shall get the other papers, and to-morrow the Board shall have them.

I hope the race will not be so far to the swift that we shall catch and outrun these mortal men. I have a notion Kittredge is thorough and honest, but I suspect his price is high.

I will retain this letter till evening.

Sunday evening, 9 o'clock. I get nothing more from you, so that all I have is your note. In this predicament, I think I will address a note to the Board, stating that the Doctor will apply, and suggesting, generally, the ground of his equity.

Very truly yours,

R. CHOATE.

17 *January*, 1842.

MY DEAR SIR, — I mourn that I cannot get you yet a copy of the opinions, otherwise called *Old Fields*. I am in collusion with Tims; and if man can do it, Tims is he. I have never got one for myself, or I would send that. I send you my speech, so that if you do not get Anne Page, you, however, have the great lubberly boy.

Never reading Buckingham,[1] I only guess, from

---

[1] Editor of Boston paper.

your kind hint, that he abuseth me. The tariff speech, I assure you, I sent him.

Lord Ashburton is a most interesting man, quick, cheerful, graceful-minded, keen, and prudent. The three young men are also clever; young rather; one a Whig, — all lovers of Lord Morpeth. Maine comes in with such exacting purposes, that, between us, I doubt.

R. CHOATE.

2 *June.*

MY DEAR SUMNER, — Ten thousand thanks for your seasonable kindness. I won't quit till I beat both those speeches out and out.

Read not a word of what is called my Oregon speech till I send one.

I shall return all the papers by W. F. Hillard, Esq. Doubtless originals should be kept at home safe. But nothing is lost or mutilated.

Most truly yours,

R. CHOATE.

25 *February,* 1844.

MY DEAR SUMNER, — I thank you for the documents. The case is assigned for the 20th, — and being, as Mr. Justice Catron expressly declared, a case of " Sovereign States," it has, before this tribunal of strict constructionists, a terrified and implicit precedence.

Great swelling words of prescription ought to be spoken. For the rest, I see no great fertility or *heights* in it.

Most hurriedly yours,

' R. CHOATE.

Saturday, 5 P. M.

Saturday, *February* 17, 1844.

MY DEAR SIR, — To my horror and annoyance, the court has just continued our cause to the next term.

The counsel of Rhode Island moved it yesterday, assigning for cause that the court was not full; that the Chief Justice could not sit, by reason of ill health; Mr. Justice Story did not sit, and there was a vacancy on the bench. The court was, therefore, reduced to six judges. We opposed the motion.

To-day, Mr. Justice McLean said that, on interchanging views, they *found that three of the six*, who would try it, have formerly, on the argument of the plea, come to an opinion in favor of Massachusetts, and that, therefore, they thought it not proper to proceed. If Rhode Island should fail, he suggested, she might have cause of dissatisfaction.

I regret this result, on all accounts, and especially that the constant preparatory labors of a month are, for the present, wholly lost. I had actually withdrawn from the Senate Chamber to make up this argument, which may now never be of any use to anybody. (Private.) Shall I ask you, as a confidential and special act of friendship, to make this matter known to the public through *any of our papers*, in such manner, *inter alia*, as to convey the fact that counsel of Massachusetts have somewhat engrossingly prepared briefs in the cause ?

It explains: Silence elsewhere is true and right and kind. The honest truth is, I have spent a full month, day and night, on the thing. Please, in this, state your general labors in procuring the local proofs.

There is one quite important piece of evidence to be at once looked up. We ran the line between us and Plymouth in 1664.

It is of great consequence to show that, in so doing, we asserted our present construction of the charter, and that the "Angle-tree" is far south of Balfry's Station. It is important to show that, in 1670 and 1671, we ran a line towards the west, from the "Angle-tree" south of the present line.

Mr. Mitchell will know in regard to the mode of proving these matters.

We ought to have our connections and relations, too, up to 1713, since her acquiescence is as high circumstantial evidence as Rhode Island's.

Excuse all this. Yours,

R. CHOATE.

MY DEAR SUMNER, — The book itself is come at last, looking as much as to say, "*Quos ego sed magnos pro est et componere fluctus.*" So has Mr. Packenham come, for did he not sit an hour last evening at the birth-night ball, with Mrs. Bayard? Henceforth no peace with England. Nay, her very ambassadors should be cast into wells. Truly yours,

R. CHOATE.

February 23, 1844.

May I ask you to assure Dr. Palfrey that his book is here, and to tell me how you denominate him, — *quo nomine quadit,* — *Dr. Esq.,* arma or toga?

These transitions play the devil with classifications.

February, 1844.

MY DEAR SUMNER, — All the papers came safe, except, as yet, the whole volume, which is to come by Harnden.

I shall print the useful, — keep all safely, with the entire file. Some of them are very good.

The continuance of the cause rendered it partially to be regretted that so much trouble was given. But it is better to close the printing at once.

Please thank Dr. Palfrey, and dry his and Mr. Felt's tears. I knew it would be like defending a city by holding up upon the walls, against darts and catapults, little children, images of gods, cats, dogs, onions, and all other Egyptian *theogonies*, — but better so than to be taken.

Yours truly,

R. CHOATE.

MY DEAR SUMNER, — I have written, by this mail, to Mr. Palfrey, Secretary of State, to send me instantly certain papers for Massachusetts *vs.* Rhode Island. May I entreat you to go, as soon as possible, to the State House, see my letter, and aid and urge its objects. You will know the what and where, and a *mail* saved is all one, — as it were, a kingdom for a horse.

I thank you for your views, — excellent and seasonable. I will speak them to the Court so they shall never know anything else again as long as they live. Please be most prompt.

Yours,

R. CHOATE.

15th February. The case is for the 20th ! !

DEAR SUMNER, — I have just had your letter read to me, on a half-sick bed, and got up, redolent of magnesia and roasted apples, to embrace you for your Burkeism generally, and for your extracts and references. It is odd that I have, on my last year's brief, a passage or two from him on that very topic which he appreciates so profoundly, but am most happy to add yours. By the way, I always admired that very letter in Prior, if it is the same.

I hope you review Burke in the "North American Review," though I have not got it, and you do not say so. Mind that he is the fourth Englishman, — Shakespeare, Bacon, Milton, Burke. I hope you take one hundred pages for the article. Compare, contrast with Cicero, — both knowing all things, — but God knows where to end on Burke. No Englishman, or countryman of ours has the least appreciation of Burke. The Whigs never forgave the last eight or ten years of that life of glory, and the Tories never forgave what preceded; and we, poor unidealized, Tom Pinified democrats, do not understand his marvelous English, universal wisdom, illuminated, omniscient mind, and are afraid of his principles. What coxcombical rascal is it that thinks Bolingbroke a better writer? Take, page by page, the illusions, the felicities, the immortalities of truth, variety, reason, height, depth, everything, Boling-broke is a voluble prater to Burke.

Amplify on his letter in reply to the Duke of Bedford. How mournful, melodious, Cassandra-like! Out of Burke might be cut 50 Mackin-toshes, 175 Macaulays, 40 Jeffreys, and 250 Sir Robert Peels, and leave him greater than Pitt and Fox together.

I seem to suppose your article is not written, as I hope it is. God bless you.

Yours truly,

R. CHOATE.

Mr. Gorden shall be shown all that we have, certainly.

BOSTON, *December* 21, 1851.

MY DEAR MR. SUMNER, — I thank you for the copy of your beautiful speech, and for the making of it. All men say it is a successful one, parlia-mentarily expressing it, and I am sure it is sound, safe, steering between cold-shoulderism and inhos-pitality, on the one side, and the splendid folly and wickedness of coöperation, on the other. Cover the Magyar with flowers, lave him with perfume, serenade him with eloquence, and let him go home alone if he will not live here. Such is all that is permitted to wise states aspiring to "true grandeur." I wish to Heaven you would

write me *de rebus congressus.* How does the
Senate strike you? The best place this day on
earth for reasoned, thoughtful, yet stimulant
public speech. Think of that.

Most truly yours, — in the union, —

RUFUS CHOATE.

APPENDIX.

APPENDIX.

———◆———

REMARKS BEFORE THE CIRCUIT COURT ON THE DEATH OF MR. WEBSTER.

[Mr. Webster died on Sunday morning, October 24, 1852. The members of the Suffolk Bar met on Monday morning, and appointed a committee to report a series of resolutions. These were read and adopted at an adjourned meeting, Thursday, October 28th, and immediately presented to the Circuit Court of the United States for the District of Massachusetts, — Curtis and Sprague, Justices, on the bench. They were read by the Hon. George S. Hillard, after which Mr. Choate made the following remarks.]

May it please your Honors, — I have been requested by the members of the Bar of this Court to add a few words to the resolutions just read, in which they have embodied, as they were able, their sorrow for the death of their beloved and illustrious member and countryman, Mr. Webster; their estimation of his character, life, and genius; their sense of the bereavement, — to the country as to his friends, — incapable of repair; the pride, the fondness, — the filial and the patriotic pride and fondness, — with which they cherish, and would consign to history to cherish, the memory of a great and good man.

28

And yet I could earnestly have desired to be excused from this duty. He must have known Mr. Webster less, and loved him less, than your Honors, or than I have known and loved him, who can quite yet, — quite yet, — before we can comprehend that we have lost him forever, — before the first paleness with which the news of his death overspread our cheeks has passed away, — before we have been down to lay him in the Pilgrim soil he loved so well, till the heavens be no more, — he must have known and loved him less than we have done who can come here quite yet, to recount the series of his service, to display with psychological exactness the traits of his nature and mind, to ponder and speculate on the secrets — on the marvelous secrets — and source of that vast power, which we shall see no more in action, nor aught in any degree resembling it, among men. These first moments should be given to grief. It may employ, it may promote a calmer mood, to construct a more elaborate and less unworthy memorial.

For the purposes of this moment and place, indeed, no more is needed. What is there for this Court or for this Bar to learn from me, here and now, of him? The year and the day of his birth; that birthplace on the frontier, yet bleak and waste; the well, of which his childhood drank, dug by that father of whom he has said, that "Through the fire and blood of seven years of revolutionary war he shrank from no danger, no toil, no sacrifice, to serve his country, and to raise his children to a condition better than his own;" the elm-tree that father planted, fallen now, as father and son have fallen; that training of the giant infancy on catechism and Bible, and Watts's version of the Psalms, and the traditions of Plymouth, and Fort William Henry, and the Revolution, and the age of Washington and Franklin, on the banks of the Merrimack, flowing sometimes in flood and anger from its secret springs in the crystal hills; the two district schoolmasters, Chase and Tappan; the village library; the dawning of the love and ambition of letters; the few months at Exeter and Boscawen; the life of college; the probationary season of school-teaching; the clerkship in the Fryeburg Registry of Deeds; his admission to the bar, presided over by judges like Smith, illustrated by practicers such as Mason, where, by the studies, in the contentions of nine years, he laid the foundation of the professional mind; his irresistible attraction to public life; the oration on commerce; the Rockingham resolutions; his first term of four years' service in Congress, when, by one bound, he sprang to his place by the side of the foremost of the rising American statesmen; his removal to this State; and then the double and parallel current in which his life, studies, thoughts, cares have since flowed, bearing him to the leadership of the bar by universal acclaim, bearing him to the leadership of public life, — last of that surpassing triumvirate, shall we say the greatest, the most widely known and admired? — all these things, to their minutest details, are known and rehearsed familiarly. Happier than the younger Pliny, happier than Cicero, he has found his historian, unsolicited, in his lifetime, and his countrymen have him all by heart!

There is, then, nothing to tell you, — nothing to bring to mind. And then, if I may borrow the language of one of his historians and friends, — one of those through whose beautiful pathos the common sorrow uttered itself yesterday, in Faneuil Hall, — " I dare not come here and dismiss in a few summary paragraphs the character of one who has filled such a space in the history, one who holds such a place in the heart, of his country. It would be a disrespectful familiarity to a man of his lofty spirit, his great soul, his rich endowments, his long and honorable life, to endeavor thus to weigh and estimate them," — a half-hour of words, a handful of earth, for fifty years of great deeds, on high places !

But, although the time does not require anything elaborated and adequate, — forbids it, rather, — some broken sentences of veneration and love may be indulged to the sorrow which oppresses us.

There presents itself, on the first and to any observation of Mr. Webster's life and character, a twofold eminence, — eminence of the very highest rank, — in a twofold field of intellectual and public display, — the profession of the law and the profession of statesmanship, — of which it would not be easy to recall any parallel in the biography of illustrious men.

Without seeking for parallels, and without asserting that they do not exist, consider that he was, by universal designation, the leader of the general American bar ; and that he was, also, by an equally universal designation, foremost of her statesmen living at his death ; inferior to not one who has lived and acted since the opening of his own public life. Look at these aspects of his greatness separately, and from opposite sides of the surpassing elevation. Consider that his single career at the bar may seem to have been enough to employ the largest faculties, without repose, for a lifetime; and that, if then and thus the "*infinitus forensium rerum labor*" should have conducted him to a mere professional reward, — a bench of chancery or law, the crown of the first of advocates, *jurisperitorum eloquentissimus*, — to the pure and mere honors of a great magistrate, — that that would be as much as is allotted to the ablest in the distribution of fame. Even that half, if I may say so, of his illustrious reputation, — how long the labor to win it, how worthy of all that labor! He was bred first in the severest school of the common law, in which its doctrines were expounded by Smith, and its administration shaped and directed by Mason, and its foundation principles, its historical sources and illustrations, its connection with the parallel series of statutory enactments, its modes of reasoning, and the evidence of its truths, he grasped easily and completely; and I have myself heard him say, that for many years, while still at the bar, he tried more causes, and argued more questions of fact to the jury than perhaps any other member of the profession anywhere. I have heard from others how, even then, he exemplified the same, direct, clear, and forcible exhibition of proofs, and the reasonings appropriate to proofs, as well as the same marvelous power of discerning instantly what we call the decisive points of the cause in law and fact, by which he was later more widely celebrated. This was the first epoch in his professional training.

With the commencement of his public life, or with his later removal to this State, began the second epoch of his professional training, conducting him through the gradation of the national tribunals to the study and practice of the more flexible, elegant, and scientific jurisprudence of commerce and of chancery, and to the grander and less fettered investigations of international, prize, and constitutional law, and giving him to breathe the air of a more famous forum, in a more public presence, with more variety of competition, although he never met abler men, as I have heard him say, than some of those who initiated him in the rugged discipline of the courts of New Hampshire; and thus, at length, by these studies, these labors, this contention, continued without repose, he came, now many years ago, to stand *omnium assensu* at the summit of the American bar.

It is common, and it is easy, in the case of all in such position, to point out other lawyers, here and there, as possessing some special qualification or attainment more remarkably, perhaps, because more exclusively, — to say of one that he has more cases in his recollection at any given moment, or that he was earlier grounded in equity, or has gathered more black letter or civil law, or knowledge of Spanish or of Western titles, — and these comparisons were sometimes made with him. But when you sought a counsel of the first rate for the great cause, who would most surely discern, and most powerfully expound, the exact law, required by the controversy, in season for use; who could most skillfully encounter the opposing law; under whose powers of analysis, persuasion, and display, the asserted right would assume the most probable aspect before the intelligence of the judge; who, if the inquiry became blended with or resolved into facts, could most completely develop and most irresistibly expose them; one " the law's whole thunder born to wield," — when you sought such a counsel, and could have the choice, I think the universal profession would have turned to him. And this would be so in nearly every description of cause, in any department. Some able men wield civil inquiries with a peculiar ability; some criminal. How lucidly and how deeply he elucidated a question of property, you all know. But then, with what address, feeling, pathos, and prudence he defended, with what dignity and crushing power, *accusatorio spiritu*, he prosecuted the accused of crime, whom he believed to have been guilty, few have seen; but none who have seen can ever forget it.

Some scenes there are, some Alpine eminences rising above the high table-land of such a professional life, to which, in the briefest tribute, we should love to follow him. We recall that day, for an instance, when he first announced, with decisive display, what manner of • man he was, to the Supreme Court of the nation. It was in 1818, and it was in the argument of the case of Dartmouth College. William Pinkney was recruiting his great faculties, and replenishing that reservoir of professional and elegant acquisition, in Europe. Samuel Dexter, " the honorable man, and the counselor, and the eloquent orator," was in his grave. The boundless old-school learning of Luther Martin ; the silver voice and infinite analytical ingenuity and resources of Jones; the fervid genius of Emmett pouring itself along *immenso ore;* the ripe and beautiful culture of Wirt and Hopkinson, — the steel point, unseen, not unfelt, beneath the foliage ; Harper himself, statesman as well as lawyer, — these, and such as these, were left of that noble bar. That day Mr. Webster opened the cause of Dartmouth College to a tribunal unsurpassed on earth in all that gives illustration to a bench of law, not one of whom any longer survives.

One would love to linger on the scene, when, after a masterly argument of the law, carrying, as we may now know, conviction to the general mind of the court, and vindicating and settling for his lifetime his place in that forum, he paused to enter, with an altered feeling, tone, and manner, with these words, on his peroration: "I have brought my *Alma Mater* to this presence, that, if she must fall, she may fall in her robes, and with dignity ; " and then broke forth in that strain of sublime and pathetic eloquence, of which we know not much more than that, in its progress, Marshall, — the intellectual, the self-controlled, the unemotional,— announced, visibly, the presence of ·the unaccustomed enchantment.

Other forensic triumphs crowd on us, in other competition, with other issues. But I must commit them to the historian of constitutional jurisprudence.

And now, if this transcendent professional reputation were all of Mr. Webster, it might be practicable, though not easy, to find its parallel elsewhere in our own, or in European or classical biography.

But, when you consider that, side by side with this, there was growing up that other reputation, — that of the first American statesman; that, for thirty-three years, and those embracing his most Herculean works at the bar, he was engaged as a member of either House, or in the highest of the executive departments, in the conduct of the largest national affairs, in the treatment of the largest national questions, in debate with the highest abilities of American public life, conducting diplomatic intercourse in delicate relations with all manner of foreign powers, investigating whole classes of truths, totally unlike the truths of the law, and resting on principles totally distinct, — and that here, too, he was wise, safe, controlling, trusted, the foremost man; that Europe had come to see in his life a guaranty for justice, for peace, for the best hopes of civilization, and America to feel surer of her glory and her safety as his great arm enfolded her, — you see how rare, how solitary, almost, was the actual greatness! Who, anywhere, has won, as he had, the double fame, and worn the double wreath of Murray and Chatham, of Dunning and Fox, of Erskine and Pitt, of William Pinkney and Rufus King, in one blended and transcendent superiority?

I cannot attempt to grasp and sum up the aggregate of the service of his public life at such a moment as this; and it is needless. That life comprised a term of more than thirty-three years. It produced a body of performance, of which I may say, generally, it was all which the first abilities of the country and time, employed with unexampled toil, stimulated by. the noblest patriotism, in the highest places of the state, in the fear of God, in the presence of nations, could possibly compass.

He came into Congress after the war of 1812 had begun ; and, though probably deeming it unnecessary, according to the highest standards of public necessity, in his private character, and objecting, in his public character, to some of the details of the policy by which it was prosecuted, and standing by party ties in general opposition to the administration, he never breathed a sentiment calculated to depress the tone of the public mind, to aid or comfort the enemy, to check or chill the stirrings of that new, passionate, unquenchable spirit of nationality, which then was revealed, or kindled to burn till we go down to the tombs of states.

With the peace of 1815 his more cherished public labors began ; and thenceforward he devoted himself — the ardor of his civil youth, the energies of his maturest manhood, the autumnal wisdom of the ripened year — to the offices of legislation and diplomacy; of preserving the peace, keeping the honor, establishing the boundaries, and vindicating the neutral rights of his country; restoring a sound currency, and laying its foundation sure and deep; in upholding public credit; in promoting foreign commerce and domestic industry; in developing our uncounted material resources, — giving the lake and the river to trade, — and vindicating and interpreting the Constitution and the law. On all these subjects, — on all measures practically in any degree affecting them, — he has inscribed his opinions and left the traces of his hand. Everywhere the philosophical and patriot statesman and thinker will find that he has been before him, lighting the way, sounding the abyss. His weighty language, his sagacious warnings, his great maxims of empire will be raised to view, and live to be deciphered when the final catastrophe shall lift the granite foundation in fragments from its bed.

In this connection, I cannot but remark to how extraordinary an extent had Mr. Webster, by his acts, words, thoughts, or the events of his life, associated himself forever in the memory of all of us with every historical incident, or, at least, with every historical epoch, with every policy, with every glory, with every great name and fundamental institution, and grand or beautiful image, which are peculiarly and properly American. Look backwards to the planting of Plymouth and Jamestown; to the various scenes of colonial life in peace and war; to the opening and march and close of the revolutionary drama; to the age of the Constitution; to Washington and Franklin and Adams and Jefferson; to the whole train of causes, from the Reformation downwards, which prepared us to be republicans; to that other train of causes which led us to be unionists, — look round on field, workshop, and deck, and hear the music of labor rewarded, fed, and protected; look on the bright sisterhood of the States, each singing as a seraph in her motion, yet blending in a common harmony, — and there is nothing which does not bring him by some tie to the memory of America. We seem to see his form and hear his deep, grave speech everywhere. By some felicity of his personal life; by some wise, deep, or beautiful word, spoken or written; by some service of his own, or some commemoration of the services of others, it has come to pass that "our granite hills, our inland seas, and prairies, and fresh, unbounded, magnificent wilderness," our encircling ocean, the Rock of the Pilgrims, our new-born sister of the Pacific, our popular assemblies, our free schools, all our cherished doctrines of education, and of the influence of religion, and material policy, and the law, and the Constitution, give us back his name. What American landscape will you look on, what subject of American interest will you study, what source of hope or of anxiety, as an American, will you acknowledge, that does not recall him?

I shall not venture, in this rapid and general recollection of Mr. Webster, to attempt to analyze that intellectual power which all admit to have been so extraordinary, or to compare or contrast it with the mental greatness of others, in variety or degree, of the living or the dead; or even to attempt to appreciate, exactly, and in reference to canons of art, his single attribute of eloquence. Consider, however, the remarkable phenomenon of excellence in three unkindred, one might have thought, incompatible forms of public speech, — that of the forum, with its double audience of bench and jury, of the halls of legislation, and of the most thronged and tumultuous assemblies of the people.

Consider, further, that this multiform eloquence, ex-

actly as his words fell, became at once so much accession to permanent literature, in the strictest sense,
solid, attractive, and rich, and ask how often in the
history of public life such a thing has been exemplified.
Recall what pervaded all these forms of display, and
every effort in every form, — that union of naked intellect, in its largest measure, which penetrates to the
exact truth of the matter in hand, by intuition or by
inference, and discerns everything which may make it
intelligible, probable, or credible to another, with an
emotional and moral nature profound, passionate, and
ready to kindle, and with an imagination enough to
supply a hundred-fold more of illustration and ag-
grandizement than his taste suffered him to accept;
that union of greatness of soul with depth of heart,
which made his speaking almost more an exhibition of
character than of mere genius; the style, not merely
pure, clear Saxon, but so constructed, so numerous as
far as becomes prose, so forcible, so abounding in un-
labored felicities; the words so choice; the epithet so
pictured; the matter absolute truth, or the most exact
and specious resemblance the human wit can devise;
the treatment of the subject, if you have regard to
the kind of truth he had to handle, — political, ethical,
legal, — as deep, as complete as Paley's, or Locke's,
or Butler's, or Alexander Hamilton's, of their subjects;
yet that depth and that completeness of sense, made
transparent as through crystal waters, all embodied in
harmonious or well-composed periods, raised on winged
language, vivified, fused, and poured along in a tide of
emotion, fervid, and incapable to be withstood; recall

the form, the eye, the brow, the tone of voice, the presence of the intellectual king of men, — recall him thus, and, in the language of Mr. Justice Story, commemorating Samuel Dexter, we may well " rejoice that we have lived in the same age, that we have listened to his eloquence, and been instructed by his wisdom."

I cannot leave the subject of his eloquence without returning to a thought I have advanced already. All that he has left, or the larger portion of all, is the record of spoken words. His works, as already collected, extend to many volumes, — a library of reason and eloquence, as Gibbon has said of Cicero's, — but they are volumes of speeches only, or mainly; and yet who does not rank him as a great American author? an author as truly expounding, and as characteristically exemplifying, in a pure, genuine, and harmonious English style, the mind, thought, point of view of objects, and essential nationality of his country as any other of our authors, professedly so denominated? Against the maxim of Mr. Fox, his speeches read well, and yet were good speeches — great speeches — in the delivery. For so grave were they, so thoughtful and true, so much the eloquence of reason at last, so strikingly always they contrived to link the immediate topic with other and broader principles, ascending easily to widest generalizations, so happy was the reconciliation of the qualities which engage the attention of hearers, yet reward the perusal of students, so critically did they keep the right side of the line which parts eloquence from rhetoric, and so far do they rise above the penury of mere debate, that the general reason of the country has enshrined them at once, and forever, among our classics.

It is a common belief that Mr. Webster was a various reader; and I think it is true, even to a greater degree than has been believed. In his profession of politics, nothing, I think, worthy of attention had escaped him; nothing of the ancient or modern prudence; nothing which Greek or Roman or European speculation in that walk had explored, or Greek or Roman or European or universal history or public biography exemplified. I shall not soon forget with what admiration he spoke, at an interview to which he admitted me, while in the Law School at Cambridge, of the politics and ethics of Aristotle, and of the mighty mind which, as he said, seemed to have "thought through" so many of the great problems which form the discipline of social man. American history and American political literature he had by heart, — the long series of influences which trained us for representative and free government; that other series of influences which moulded us into a united government; the colonial era; the age of controversy before the revolution; every scene and every person in that great tragic action; every question which has successively engaged our politics, and every name which has figured in them, — the whole stream of our time was open, clear, and present ever to his eye.

Beyond his profession of politics, so to call it, he had been a diligent and choice reader, as his extraordinary style in part reveals; and I think the love of reading would have gone with him to a later and riper age, if to such an age it had been the will of God to preserve him. This is no place or time to appreciate this branch of his acquisitions; but there is an interest inexpressible in knowing who were any of the chosen from among the great dead in the library of such a man. Others may correct me, but I should say of that interior and narrower circle were Cicero, Virgil, Shakespeare, — whom he knew as familiarly as the Constitution, — Bacon, Milton, Burke, Johnson, — to whom I hope it is not pedantic nor fanciful to say, I often thought his nature presented some resemblance; the same abundance of the general propositions, required for explaining a difficulty and refuting a sophism, copiously and promptly occurring to him; the same kindness of heart and wealth of sensibility, under a manner, of course, more courteous and gracious, yet more sovereign; the same sufficient, yet not predominant, imagination, stooping ever to truth, and giving affluence, vivacity, and attraction to a powerful, correct, and weighty style of prose.

I cannot leave this life and character without selecting and dwelling a moment on one or two of his traits, or virtues, or felicities, a little longer. There is a collective impression made by the whole of an eminent person's life, beyond and other than, and apart from, that which the mere general biographer would afford the means of explaining. There is an influence of a great man derived from things indescribable, almost, or incapable of enumeration, or singly insufficient to account for it, but through which his spirit transpires, and his individuality goes forth on the contemporary generation. And thus, I should say, one grand tendency of his life and character was to elevate the whole tone of the public mind. He did this, indeed, not merely by example. He did it by dealing, as he thought, truly and in manly fashion, with that public mind. He evinced his love of the people, not so much by honeyed phrases as by good counsels and useful service, *vera pro gratis*. He showed how he appreciated them by submitting sound arguments to their understandings, and right motives to their free will. He came before them, less with flattery than with instruction; less with a vocabulary larded with the words *humanity* and *philanthropy*, and *progress* and *brotherhood*, than with a scheme of politics, an educational, social, and governmental system, which would have made them prosperous, happy, and great.

What the greatest of the Greek historians said of Pericles, we all feel might be said of him, — "He did not so much follow as lead the people, because he framed not his words to please them, like one who is gaining power by unworthy means, but was able and dared, on the strength of his high character, even to brave their anger by contradicting their will."

I should indicate it, as another influence of his life, acts, and opinions, that it was, in an extraordinary degree, uniformly and liberally conservative. He saw with vision as of a prophet, that if our system of united government can be maintained till a nationality shall be generated, of due intensity and due comprehension, a glory indeed millennial, a progress without end, a triumph of humanity hitherto unseen, were ours; and, therefore, he addressed himself to maintain that united government.

Standing on the Rock of Plymouth, he bade distant generations hail, and saw them rising, "demanding life, impatient for the skies," from what then were "fresh, unbounded, magnificent wildernesses;" from the shore of the great, tranquil sea, not yet become ours. But observe to what he welcomes them; by what he would bless them. "It is to good government." It is to "treasures of science and delights of learning." It is to the "sweets of domestic life, the immeasurable good of rational existence, the immortal hopes of Christianity, the light of everlasting truth."

It will be happy, if the wisdom and temper of his administration of our foreign affairs shall preside in the time which is at hand. Sobered, instructed by the examples and warnings of all the past, he yet gathered, from the study and comparison of all the eras, that there is a silent progress of the race, — without pause, without haste, without return, — to which the counselings of history are to be accommodated by a wise philosophy. More than, or as much as, that of any of our public characters, his statesmanship was one which recognized a Europe, an old world, but yet grasped the capital idea of the American position, and deduced from it the whole fashion and color of its policy; which discerned that we are to play a high part in human affairs, but discerned, also, what part it is, — peculiar, distant, distinct, and grand as our hemisphere; an influence, not a contact, — the stage, the drama, the catastrophe, all but the audience, all our own, — and if ever he felt himself at a loss, he consulted, reverently, the genius of Washington.

In bringing these memories to a conclusion, — for I omit many things because I dare not trust myself to speak of them, — I shall not be misunderstood, or give offense, if I hope that one other trait in his public character, one doctrine, rather, of his political creed, may be remembered and be appreciated. It is one of the two fundamental precepts in which Plato, as expounded by the great master of Latin eloquence and reason and morals, comprehends the duty of those who share in the conduct of the State, — "*ut quæcunque agunt,* TOTUM *corpus reipublicæ curent, nedum partem aliquam tuentur, reliquas deserant ;* " that they comprise in their care the whole body of the Republic, nor keep one part and desert another. He gives the reason, — one reason, — of the precept, "*qui autem parti civium consulunt, partem negligunt, rem perniciosissimam in civitatem inducunt, seditionem atque discordiam.*" The patriotism which embraces less than the whole induces sedition and discord, the last evil of the state.

How profoundly he had comprehended this truth; with what persistency, with what passion, from the first hour he became a public man to the last beat of the great heart, he cherished it; how little he accounted the good, the praise, the blame of this locality or that, in comparison of the larger good and the general and thoughtful approval of his own, and our, whole America, — she this day feels and announces. Wheresoever a drop of her blood flows in the veins of men, this trait is felt and appreciated. The hunter beyond Superior; the fisherman on the deck of the nigh night-foundered skiff; the sailor on the uttermost sea, — will feel, as he hears these tidings, that the protection of a sleepless, all-embracing, parental care is withdrawn from him for a space, and that his pathway henceforward is more solitary and less safe than before.

But I cannot pursue these thoughts. Among the eulogists who have just uttered the eloquent sorrow of England at the death of the great Duke, one has employed an image and an idea which I venture to modify and appropriate.

" The Northmen's image of death is finer than that of other climes; no skeleton, but a gigantic figure that envelops men within the massive folds of its dark garment." Webster seems so enshrouded from us, as the last of the mighty three, themselves following a mighty series, — the greatest closing the procession. The robe draws round him, and the era is past.

Yet how much there is which that all-ample fold shall not hide, — the recorded wisdom, the great example, the assured immortality.

They speak of monuments!

> " Nothing can cover his high fame but heaven ;
> No pyramids set off his memories
> But the eternal substance of his greatness;
> To which I leave him."

INDEX.

460   *INDEX.*

№ 784621

CPSIA information can be obtained
at www.ICGtesting.com
Printed in the USA
BVHW04*2354081018
529297BV00038B/481/P